I0836951

GARNERED SHEAVES.

GARNERED SHEAVES:

THE

COMPLETE POETICAL WORKS

OF

J. G. HOLLAND.

NEW YORK:
SCRIBNER, ARMSTRONG & CO.
1873.

LANGE, LITTLE & HILLMAN,
PRINTERS, ELECTROTYPERS AND STEREOTYPERS,
108 to 114 Wooster Street, N. Y.

CONTENTS.

BITTER-SWEET.

KATHRINA.

MARBLE PROPHECY,

AND

OTHER POEMS.

LIST OF ILLUSTRATIONS.

BITTER-SWEET.

KATHRINA.

Bitter-Sweet.

PICTURE.

Winter's wild birthnight! In the fretful East
The uneasy wind moans with its sense of cold,
And sends its sighs through gloomy mountain gorge,
Along the valley, up the whitening hill,
To tease the sighing spirits of the pines,
And waste in dismal woods their chilly life.
The sky is dark, and on the huddled leaves—
The restless, rustling leaves—sifts down its sleet,
Till the sharp crystals pin them to the earth,
And they grow still beneath the rising storm.
The roofless bullock hugs the sheltering stack,
With cringing head and closely gathered feet,
And waits with dumb endurance for the morn.
Deep in a gusty cavern of the barn

The witless calf stands blatant at his chain;
While the brute mother, pent within her stall,
With the wild stress of instinct goes distraught,
And frets her horns, and bellows through the
night.
The stream runs black; and the far waterfall
That sang so sweetly through the summer eves,
And swelled and swayed to Zephyr's softest breath,
Leaps with a sullen roar the dark abyss,
And howls its hoarse responses to the wind.
The mill is still. The distant factory,
That swarmed yestreen with many fingered life
And bridged the river with a hundred bars
Of molten light, is dark, and lifts its bulk
With dim, uncertain angles, to the sky.

* * * * * *

Yet lower bows the storm. The leafless trees
Lash their lithe limbs, and, with majestic voice,
Call to each other through the deepening gloom;
And slender trunks that lean on burly bough,
Shriek with sharp abrasion; and the oak,
Mellowed in fibre by unnumbered frosts,

Yields to the shoulder of the Titan Blast.
Forsakes its poise, and, with a booming crash,
Sweeps a fierce passage to the smothered rocks,
And lies a shattered ruin.

* * * * * * *

Other scene :—

Across the swale, half up the pine-capped hill,
Stands the old farm-house with its clump of barns—
The old red farm-house—dim and dun to-night,
Save where the ruddy firelights from the hearth
Flap their bright wings against the window panes,—
A billowy swarm that beat their slender bars,
Or seek the night to leave their track of flame
Upon the sleet, or sit, with shifting feet
And restless plumes, among the poplar boughs—
The spectral poplars, standing at the gate.

And now a man, erect, and tall, and strong,
Whose thin white hair, and cheeks of furrowed bronze,

And ancient dress, betray the patriarch,
Stands at the window, listening to the storm,
And as the fire leaps with a wilder flame—
Moved by the wind—it wraps and glorifies
His stalwart frame, until it flares and glows
Like the old prophets, in transfigured guise,
That shape the sunset for cathedral aisles.
And now it passes, and a sweeter shape
Stands in its place. O blest maternity!
Hushed on her bosom in a light embrace,
Her baby sleeps, wrapped in its long white robe;
And as the flame, with soft, auroral sweeps,
Illuminates the pair, how like they seem,
O Virgin Mother! to thyself and thine!
Now Samuel comes with curls of burning gold
To hearken to the voice of God without:
"Speak, mighty One! Thy little servant hears!"
And Miriam, maiden, from her household cares
Comes to the window in her loosened robe,—
Comes with the blazing timbrels in her hand,—
And, as the noise of winds and waters swells,
It shapes the song of triumph to her lips:

"The horse and he who rode are overthrown!"
And now a man of noble port and brow,
And aspect of benignant majesty,
Assumes the vacant niche, while either side
Press the fair forms of children, and I hear:
"Suffer the little ones to come unto me!"

PERSONS.

HERE dwells the good old farmer, Israel,
In his ancestral home—a Puritan
Who reads his Bible daily, loves his God,
And lives serenely in the faith of Christ.
For three score years and ten his life has run
Through varied scenes of happiness and woe;
But, constant through the wide vicissitude,
He has confessed the giver of his joys,
And kissed the hand that took them; and whene'er
Bereavement has oppressed his soul with grief,
Or sharp misfortune stung his heart with pain,
He has bowed down in childlike faith, and said,
"Thy will, O God—thy will be done, not mine!"

HERE DWELLS THE GOOD OLD FARMER ISRAEL.

His gentle wife, a dozen summers since,
Passed from his faithful arms and went to heaven ;
And her best gift—a maiden sweetly named—
His daughter Ruth—orders the ancient house,
And fills her mother's place beside the board,
And cheers his life with songs and industry.
But who are these who crowd the house to-night—
A happy throng ? Wayfaring pilgrims, who,
Grateful for shelter, charm the golden hours
With the sweet jargon of a festival ?
Who are these fathers ? who these mothers ? who
These pleasant children, rude with health and joy ?

It is the Puritan's Thanksgiving Eve ;
And gathered home, from fresher homes around,
The old man's children keep the holiday—
In dear New England, since the fathers slept—
The sweetest holiday of all the year.
John comes with Prudence and her little girls,
And Peter, matched with Patience, brings his boys—
Fair boys and girls with good old Scripture names—

Joseph, Rebekah, Paul, and Samuel;
And Grace, young Ruth's companion in the house,
Till wrested from her last Thanksgiving Day
By the strong hand of Love, brings home her babe,
And the tall poet David, at whose side
She went away. And seated in the midst,
Mary, a foster-daughter of the house,
Of alien blood—self-aliened many a year—
Whose chastened face and melancholy eyes
Bring all the wondering children to her knee,
Weeps with the strange excess of happiness,
And sighs with joy.

What recks the driving storm
Of such a scene as this? And what reck these
Of such a storm? For every heavy gust
That smites the windows with its cloud of sleet,
And shakes the sashes with its ghostly hands,
And rocks the mansion till the chimney's throat
Through all its sooty caverns shrieks and howls,
They give full bursts of careless merriment,
Or songs that send it baffled on its way.

PRELUDE.

Doubt takes to wings on such a night as this ;
And while the traveller hugs his fluttering cloak,
And staggers o'er the weary waste alone,
Beneath a pitiless heaven, they flap his face,
And wheel above, or hunt his fainting soul,
As, with relentless greed, a vulture throng,
With their lank shadows mock the glazing eyes
Of the last camel of the caravan.
And Faith takes forms and wings on such a night.
Where love burns brightly at the household hearth,
And from the altar of each peaceful heart
Ascends the fragrant incense of its thanks,
And every pulse with sympathetic throb
Tells the true rhythm of trustfulest content,

They flutter in and out, and touch to smiles
The sleeping lips of infancy; and fan
The blush that lights the modest maiden's cheeks ;
And toss the locks of children at their play.

Silence is vocal if we listen well :
And Life and Being sing in dullest ears
From morn to night, from night to morn again,
With fine articulations ; but when God
Disturbs the soul with terror, or inspires
With a great joy, the words of Doubt and Faith
Sound quick and sharp like drops on forest leaves;
And we look up to where the pleasant sky
Kisses the thunder-claps, and drink the song.

A Song of Doubt.

The day is quenched, and the sun is fled;
  God has forgotten the world!
The moon is gone, and the stars are dead;
  God has forgotten the world!

Evil has won in the horrid feud
  Of ages with the Throne;

Evil stands on the neck of Good,
  And rules the world alone.

There is no good; there is no God;
  And Faith is a heartless cheat,
Who bares the back for the Devil's rod,
  And scatters thorns for the feet.

What are prayers in the lips of death,
  Filling and chilling with hail?
What are prayers but wasted breath,
  Beaten back by the gale?

The day is quenched, and the sun is fled;
  God has forgotten the world!
The moon is gone, and the stars are dead;
  God has forgotten the world!

A Song of Faith.

Day will return with a fresher boon;
  God will remember the world!
Night will come with a newer moon;
  God will remember the world!

Evil is only the slave of Good;
  Sorrow the servant of Joy;
And the soul is mad that refuses food
  Of the meanest in God's employ.

The fountain of joy is fed by tears,
  And love is lit by the breath of sighs;
The deepest griefs and the wildest fears
  Have holiest ministries.

Strong grows the oak in the sweeping storm;
  Safely the flower sleeps under the snow;
And the farmer's hearth is never warm
  Till the cold wind starts to blow.

Day will return with a fresher boon;
  God will remember the world!
Night will come with a newer moon;
  God will remember the world!

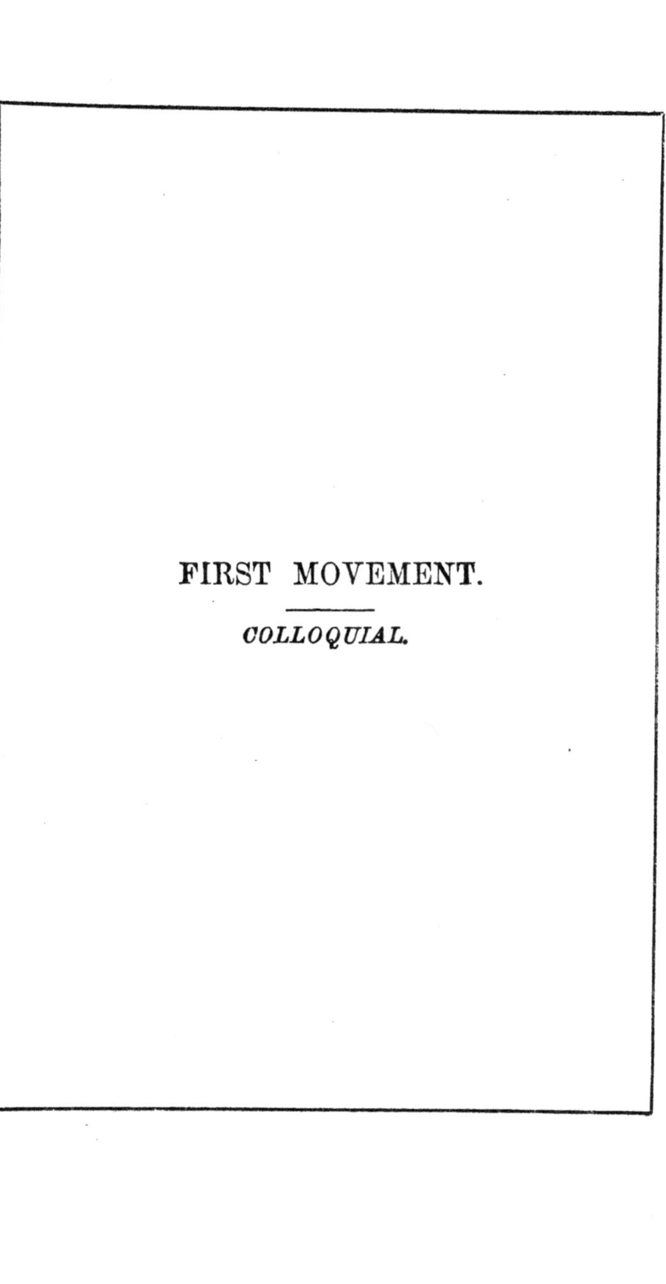

FIRST MOVEMENT.

COLLOQUIAL.

FIRST MOVEMENT.

LOCALITY—*The square room of a New England farm-house.*

PRESENT—ISRAEL, *head of the family;* JOHN, PETER, DAVID, PATIENCE, PRUDENCE, GRACE, MARY, RUTH *and* CHILDREN.

THE QUESTION STATED AND ARGUED.

ISRAEL.

RUTH, touch the cradle. Boys, you must be still!
The baby cannot sleep in such a noise.
Nay, Grace, stir not; she'll soothe him soon
enough,
And tell him more sweet stuff in half an hour
Than you can dream, in dreaming half a year.

RUTH.

[*Kneeling and rocking the cradle.*

What is the little one thinking about?
Very wonderful things, no doubt.
Unwritten history!
Unfathomed mystery!
Yet he laughs and cries, and eats and drinks,
And chuckles and crows, and nods and winks,
As if his head were as full of kinks
And curious riddles as any sphinx!
Warped by colic, and wet by tears,
Punctured by pins, and tortured by fears,
Our little nephew will lose two years;
And he'll never know
Where the summers go;—
He need not laugh for he'll find it so!

Who can tell what a baby thinks?
Who can follow the gossamer links

  By which the mannikin feels his way
Out from the shore of the great unknown,
Blind, and wailing, and alone,
  Into the light of day?—
Out from the shore of the unknown sea,
Tossing in pitiful agony,—
Of the unknown sea that reels and rolls,
Speckled with the barks of little souls—
Barks that were launched on the other side,
And slipped from Heaven on an ebbing tide!
  What does he think of his mother's eyes?
What does he think of his mother's hair?
  What of the cradle-roof that flies
Forward and backward through the air?
  What does he think of his mother's breast—
Bare and beautiful, smooth and white,
Seeking it ever with fresh delight—
  Cup of his life and couch of his rest?
What does he think when her quick embrace
Presses his hand and buries his face

Deep where the heart-throbs sink and swell
With a tenderness she can never tell,
  Though she murmur the words
  Of all the birds—
Words she has learned to murmur well?
  Now he thinks he'll go to sleep!
  I can see the shadow creep
  Over his eyes, in soft eclipse,
  Over his brow, and over his lips,
  Out to his little finger tips!
  Softly sinking, down he goes!
  Down he goes! Down he goes!

[Rising, and carefully retreating to her seat.

  See! He is hushed in sweet repose!

DAVID.

[Yawning.

Behold a miracle! Music transformed
To morphine, and the drowsy god invoked
By the poor prattle of a maiden's tongue!
A moment more, and we should all have gone

Down into dreamland with the babe! Ah, well!
There is no end of wonders.

RUTH.

None, indeed!
When lazy poets who have gorged themselves,
And cannot keep awake, make the attempt
To shift the burden of their drowsiness,
And charge a girl with what they owe to greed.

DAVID.

At your old tricks again! No sleep induced
By song of yours, or any other bird's,
Can linger long when you begin to talk.
Grace, box your sister's ears for me, and save
The trouble of my rising.

RUTH.

[Advancing, and kneeling by the side of Grace.

Sister mine,
Now give the proof of your obedience

To your imperious lord! Strike, if you dare!
I'll wake your baby if you lift your hand.
Ha! king; ha! poet; who is master now—
Baby or husband? Pr'ythee, tell me that.
Were I a man,—thank Heaven I am not!—
And had a wife who cared not for my will
More than your wife for yours, I'd hang myself,
Or wear an apron. See! she kisses me!

DAVID.

And answers to my will, though well she knows
I'll spare to her so terrible a task,
And take the awful burden on myself;
Which I will do, in future, if she please!

RUTH.

Now have you conquered! Look! I am your
slave.
Denounce me, scourge me, anything but kiss;
For life is sweet, and I alone am left
To comfort an old man.

ISRAEL.

Ruth, that will do!
Remember I'm a Justice of the Peace,
And bide no quarrels; and if you and David
Persist in strife, I'll place you under bonds
For good behavior, or condemn you both
To solitary durance for the night.

RUTH.

Father, you fail to understand the case,
And do me wrong. David has threatened me
With an assault that proves intent to kill;
And here's my sister Grace, his wedded wife,
Who'll take her oath, that just a year ago
He entered into bonds to keep the peace
Toward me and womankind.

DAVID.

I'm quite asleep.

ISRAEL.

We'll all agree, then, to pronounce it quits.

RUTH.

Till he awake again, of course. I trust
I have sufficient gallantry to grant
A nap between encounters, to a foe
With odds against him.

ISRAEL.

Peace, my daughter, peace!
You've had your full revenge, and we have had
Enough of laughter since the day began.
We must not squander all these precious hours
In jest and merriment; for when the sun
Shall rise to-morrow, we shall separate,
Not knowing we shall ever meet again.
Meetings like this are rare this side of Heaven,
And seem to me the best mementoes left
Of Eden's hours.

GRACE.

Most certainly the best,
And quite the rarest, but, unluckily,
The weakest, as we know; for sin and pain
And evils multiform, that swarm the earth,
And poison all our joys and all our hearts,
Remind us most of Eden's forfeit bliss.

DAVID.

Forfeit through woman.

GRACE.

Forfeit through her power;
A power not lost, as most men know, I think,
Beyond the knowledge of their trustful wives.

MARY.

[Rising and walking hurriedly to the window.

'Tis a wild night without.

RUTH.

And getting wild
Within. Now Grace, I—all of us—protest
Against a scene to-night. Look! You have driven
One to the window blushing, and your lord,
With lowering brow, is making stern essay
To stare the fire-dogs out of countenance.
These honest brothers, with their honest wives,
Grow glum and solemn, too, as if they feared
At the next gust to see the windows burst,
Or a riven poplar crashing through the roof.
And think of me!—a simple hearted maid
Who learned from Cowper only yesterday
(Or a schoolmaster, with a handsome face,
And a strange passion for the text), the fact,
That wedded bliss alone survives the fall.
I'm shocked; I'm frightened; and I'll never wed
Unless I—change my mind;

ISRAEL.

And I consent.

DAVID.

And the schoolmaster with the handsome face
Propose.

RUTH.

Your pardon, father, for the jest!
But I have never patience with the ills
That make intrusion on my happy hours.
I know the world is full of evil things,
And shudder with the consciousness. I know
That care has iron crowns for many brows;
That Calvaries are everywhere, whereon
Virtue is crucified, and nails and spears
Draw guiltless blood; that sorrow sits and drinks
At sweetest hearts, till all their life is dry;
That gentle spirits on the rack of pain

Grow faint or fierce, and pray and curse by
turns;
That Hell's temptations, clad in Heavenly guise,
And armed with might, lie evermore in wait
Along life's path, giving assault to all—
Fatal to most; that Death stalks through the
earth,
Choosing his victims, sparing none at last;
That in each shadow of a pleasant tree
A grief sits sadly sobbing to its leaves;
And that beside each fearful soul there walks
The dim, gaunt phantom of uncertainty,
Bidding it look before, where none may see,
And all must go: but I forget it all—
I thrust it from me always when I may;
Else I should faint with fear, or drown myself
In pity. God forgive me! but I've thought
A thousand times that if I had His power,
Or He my love, we'd have a different world
From this we live in.

ISRAEL.

Those are sinful thoughts,
My daughter, and too surely indicate
A wilful soul, unreconciled to God.

RUTH.

So you have told me often. You have said
That God is just, and I have looked around
To seek the proof in human lot, in vain.
The rain falls kindly on the just man's fields,
But on the unjust man's more kindly still;
And I have never known the winter's blast,
Or the quick lightning, or the pestilence,
Make nice discriminations when let slip
From God's right hand.

ISRAEL.

'Tis a great mystery;
Yet God is just, and,—blessed be His name!—

Is loving too. I know that I am weak,
And that the pathway of His Providence
Is on the hills where I may never climb.
Therefore my reason yields her hand to Faith,
And follows meekly where the angel leads.
I see the rich man have his portion here,
And Lazarus, in glorified repose,
Sleep like a jewel on the breast of Faith
In Heaven's broad light. I see that whom God loves
He chastens sorely, but I ask not why.
I only know that God is just and good:
All else is mystery. Why evil lives
Within His universe, I may not know.
I know it lives, and taints the vital air;
And that in ways inscrutable to me—
Yet compromising not his soundless love
And boundless power—it lives against His will.

I SEE THAT WHOM GOD LOVES HE CHASTENS SORELY.

RUTH.

I am not satisfied. If evil live
Against God's will, evil is king of all,
And they do well who worship Lucifer.
I am not satisfied. My reason spurns
Such prostitution to absurdities.
I know that you are happy; but I shrink
From your blind faith with loathing and with fear,
And feel that I must win it, if I win,
With the surrender, not of will alone,
But of the noblest faculty that God
Has crowned me with.

ISRAEL.

O blind and stubborn child!
My light, my joy, my burden and my grief!
How would I lead you to the wells of peace,
And see you dip your fevered palms and drink.
Gladly to purchase this would I lay down

The precious remnant of my life, and sleep,
Wrapped in the faith you spurn, till the archange
Sounds the last trump. But God's will be done!
I leave you with Him.

RUTH.

Father, talk not thus!
Oh, do not blame me! I would do it all,
If but to bless you with a single joy;
But I am helpless.

ISRAEL.

God will help you, Ruth.

RUTH.

To quench my reason? Can I ask the boon?
My lips would blister with the blasphemy.
I cannot take your faith; and that is why
I would forget that I am in a world

Where evil lives, and why I guard my joys
With such a jealous care.

DAVID.

There, Ruth, sit down!
'Tis the old question, with the old reply.
You fly along the path, with bleeding feet,
Where many feet have flown and bled before;
And he who seeks to guide you to the goal,
Has (let me say it, father,) stopped far short,
And taken refuge at a wayside inn,
Whose haunted halls and mazy passages
Receive no light, save through the riddled roof,
Pierced thick by pilgrim staves, that Faith may lie
Upon its back, and only gaze on heaven.
I would not banish evil if I could;
Nor would I be so deep in love with joy
As to seek for it in forgetfulness,
Through faith or fear.

RUTH.

Teach me the better way,
And every expiration from my lips
Shall be a grateful blessing on your head;
And in the coming world I'll seek the side
Of no more gracious angel than the man
Who gives me brotherhood by leading me
Home with himself to heaven.

ISRAEL.

My son,
Be careful of your words! 'Tis no light thing
To take the guidance of a straying soul.

DAVID.

I mark the burden well, and love it, too.
Because I love the girl and love her lord,
And seek to vindicate His love to her
And waken hers for Him. Be this my plea:

God is almighty—all-benevolent;
And naught exists save by His loving will.
Evil, or what we reckon such, exists,
And not against his will; else the Supreme
Is subject, and we have in place of God
A phantom nothing, with a phantom name.
Therefore I care not whether He ordain
That evil live, or whether He permit;
Therefore I ask not why, in either case,
As if He meant to curse me, but I ask
What He would have this evil do for me?
What is its mission? what its ministry?
What golden fruit lies hidden in its husk?
How shall it nurse my virtue, nerve my will,
Chasten my passions, purify my love,
And make me in some goodly sense like Him
Who bore the cross of evil while He lived,
Who hung and bled upon it when he died,
And now, in glory, wears the victor's crown?

ISRAEL.

If evil, then, have part and privilege
In the economy of holiness,
Why came the Christ to save us from its power
And bring us restoration of the bliss
Lost in the lapse of Eden?

DAVID.

And would you
Or Ruth have restoration of that bliss,
And welcome transplantation to the state
Associate with it?

RUTH.

Would I? Would I not?
Oh, I have dreamed of it a thousand times,
Sleeping and waking, since the torch of thought
Flashed into flame at Revelation's touch,
And filled my spirit with its quenchless fire.

Most envious dreams of innocence and joy
Have haunted me,—dreams that were born in sin,
Yet swathed in stainless snow. I've dreamed, and dreamed,
Of wondrous trees, crowned with perennial green,
Whose soft still shadows gleamed with golden lamps
Of pensile fruitage, or were flushed with life
Radiant and tuneful when broad flocks of birds
Swept in and out like sheets of living flame.
I've dreamed of aisles tufted with velvet grass,
And bordered with the strange intelligence
Of myriad loving eyes among the flowers,
That watched me with a curious, calm delight,
As rows of wayside cherubim may watch
A new soul walking into Paradise.
I've dreamed of sunsets when the sun supine
Lay rocking on the ocean like a god,
And threw his weary arms far up the sky,
And with vermilion-tinted fingers toyed

With the long tresses of the evening star.
I've dreamed of dreams more beautiful than all—
Dreams that were music, perfume, vision, bliss,—
Blent and sublimed, till I have stood enwrapped
In the quick essence of an atmosphere
That made me tremble to unclose my eyes
Lest I should look on God. And I have dreamed
Of sinless men and maids, mated in heaven,
Ere yet their souls had sought for beauteous forms
To give them human sense and residence,
Moving through all this realm of choice delights
For ever and for aye! with hands and hearts
Immaculate as light; without a thought
Of evil, and without a name for fear.
Oh, when I wake from happy dreams like these,
To the old consciousness that I must die,
To the old presence of a guilty heart,
To the old fear that haunts me night and day,
Why should I not deplore the graceless fall
That makes me what I am, and shuts me out

From a condition and society
As much above a sinful maiden's dreams
As Eden blest surpasses Eden curst ?

DAVID.

So you would be another Eve, and so—
Fall with the first temptation, like herself !
God seeks for virtue ; you for innocence.
You'll find it in the cradle—nowhere else—
Save in your dreams, among the grown up babes
That dwelt in Eden—powerless, pulpy souls
That showed a dimple for each touch of sin.
God seeks for virtue, and, that it may live,
It must resist, and that which it resists
Must live. Believe me, God has other thought
Than restoration of our fallen race
To its primeval innocence and bliss.
If Jesus Christ—as we are taught—was slain
From the foundation of the world, it was
Because our evil lived in essence then—

Coeval with the great, mysterious fact.
And He was slain that we might be transformed,—
Not into Adam's sweet similitude—
But the more glorious image of Himself,—
A resolution of our destiny
As high transcending Eden's life and lot
As He surpasses Eden's fallen lord.

RUTH.

You're very bold, my brother, very bold.
Did I not know you for an earnest man,
When sacred themes move you to utterance,
I'd chide you for those most irreverent words
Which make essential to the Christian scheme
That which the scheme was made to kill or cure.

DAVID.

Yet they do save some very awkward words,
That limp to make apology for God,
And, while they justify Him, half confess
The adverse verdict of appearances.

I am ashamed that in this Christian age
The pious throng still hug the fallacy
That this dear world of ours was not ordained
The theatre of evil ; for no law
Declared of God from all eternity
Can live a moment save by lease of pain.
Law cannot live, e'en in God's inmost thought,
Save by the side of evil. What were law
But a weak jest without its penalty ?
Never a law was born that did not fly
Forth from the bosom of Omnipotence
Matched, wing-and-wing, with evil and with good,
Avenger and rewarder—both of God.

RUTH.

I face your thought and give it audience ;
But I cannot embrace it till it come
With some of truth's credentials in its hands,—
The fruits of gracious ministries.

DAVID.

Does he
Who, driven to labor by the threat'ning weeds,
And forced to give his acres light and air
And traps for dew and reservoirs for rain,
Till, in the smoky light of harvest time,
The ragged husks reveal the golden corn,
Ask truth's credentials of the weeds? Does he
Who prunes the orchard boughs, or tills the field,
Or fells the forests, or pursues their prey,
Until the gnarly muscles of his limbs
And the free blood that thrills in all his veins
Betray the health that toil alone secures,
Ask truth's credentials at the hand of toil?
Do you ask truth's credentials of the storm,
Which, while we entertain communion here,
Makes better music for our huddling hearts
Than choirs of stars can sing in fairest nights?
Yet weeds are evils– evils toil and storm.

We may suspect the fair, smooth face of good;
But evil, that assails us undisguised,
Bears evermore God's warrant in its hands.

ISRAEL.

I fear these silver sophistries of yours.
If my poor judgment gives them honest weight,
Far less than thirty will betray your Lord.
You call that evil which is good, and good
That which is evil. You apologize
For that which God must hate, and justify
The life and perpetuity of that
Which sets itself against His holiness,
And sends its discords through the universe.

DAVID.

I sorrow if I shock you, for I seek
To comfort and inspire. I see around
A silent company of doubtful souls;
But I may challenge any one of them

To quote the meanest blessing of its life,
And prove that evil did not make the gift,
Or bear it from the giver to his hands.
The great salvation wrought by Jesus Christ—
That sank an Adam to reveal a God—
Had never come, but at the call of sin.
No risen Lord could eat the feast of love
Here on the earth, or yonder in the sky,
Had He not lain within the sepulchre.
'Tis not the lightly laden heart of man
That loves the best the hand that blesses all;
But that which, groaning with its weight of sin,
Meets with the mercy that forgiveth much.
God never fails in an experiment,
Nor tries experiment upon a race
But to educe its highest style of life,
And sublimate its issues. Thus to me
Evil is not a mystery, but a means
Selected from the infinite resource
To make the most of me.

RUTH.

Thank God for light!

These truths are slowly dawning on my soul,
And take position in the firmament
That spans my thought, like stars that know their
place.
Dear Lord! what visions crowd before my eyes—
Visions drawn forth from memory's mysteries
By the sweet shining of these holy lights!
I see a girl once lightest in the dance,
And maddest with the gayety of life,
Grow pale and pulseless, wasting day by day,
While death lies idly dreaming in her breast,
Blighting her breath, and poisoning her blood.
I see her frantic with a fearful thought
That haunts and horrifies her shrinking soul,
And bursts in sighs and sobs and feverish prayers;
And now, at last, the awful struggle ends.
A sweet smile sits upon her angel face,

And peace with downy bosom, nestles close
Where her worn heart throbs faintly ; closer still
As the death shadows gather ; closer still,
As on white wings, the outward-going soul
Flies to a home it never would have sought,
Had a great evil failed to point the way.
I see a youth whom God has crowned with power
And cursed with poverty. With bravest heart
He struggles with his lot, through toilsome years,—
Kept to his task by daily want of bread,
And kept to virtue by his daily task,—
Till, gaining manhood in the manly strife,—
The fire that fills him smitten from a flint—
The strength that arms him wrested from a fiend—
He stands, at last, a master of himself,
And, in that grace, a master of his kind.

DAVID.

Familiar visions these, but ever full

Of inspiration and significance.
Now that your eyes are opened and you see,
Your heart should take swift cognizance, and feel.
How do these visions move you?

RUTH.

Like the hand
Of a strong angel on my shoulder laid,
Touching the secret of the spirit's wings.
My heart grows brave. I'm ready now to work--
To work with God, and suffer with His Christ;
Adopt His measures, and abide His means.
If, in the law that spans the universe
(The law its maker may not disobey),
Virtue may only grow from innocence
Through a great struggle with opposing ill;
If I must win my way to perfectness
In the sad path of suffering, like Him
The overflowing river of whose life
Touches the flood-mark of humanity
On the white pillars of the heavenly throne,

Then welcome evil! Welcome sickness, toil
Sorrow and pain, the fear and fact of death!

ISRAEL.

And welcome sin?

RUTH.

Ah, David! welcome sin?

DAVID.

The fact of sin—so much;—it must needs be
Offences come; if woe to him by whom,
Then with good reason; but the fact of sin
Unlocked the door to highest destiny,
That Christ might enter in and lead the way.
God loves not sin, nor I; but in the throng
Of evils that assail us, there are none
That yield their strength to Virtue's struggling arm
With such munificent reward of power
As great temptations. We may win by toil

Endurance; saintly fortitude by pain;
By sickness, patience; faith and trust by fear;
But the great stimulus that spurs to life,
And crowds to generous development
Each chastened power and passion of the soul,
Is the temptation of the soul to sin,
Resisted, and re-conquered, evermore.

RUTH.

I am content; and now that I have caught
Bright glimpses of the outlines of your scheme
As of a landscape, graded to the sky,
And seen through trees while passing, I desire
No vision further till I make survey
In some good time when I may come alone,
And drink its beauty and its blessedness.
I've been forgetful in my earnestness,
And wearied every one with talk. These boys
Are restive grown, or nodding in their chairs,
And older heads are set, as if for sleep.

I beg their pardon for my theft of time,
And will offend no more.

DAVID.

Ruth, is it right
To leave a brother in such plight as this—
Either to imitate your courtesy,
Or by your act to be adjudged a boor?

RUTH.

Heaven grant you never note a sin of mine
Save of your own construction!

ISRAEL.

Let it pass!
I see the spell of thoughtfulness is gone,
Or going swiftly. I will not complain:
But ere these lads are fastened to their games,
And thoughts arise discordant with our theme,
Let us with gratitude approach the throne

And worship God. I wish once more to lead
Your hearts in prayer, and follow with my own
The leading of your song of thankfulness.
Then will I lease and leave you for the night
To such divertisement as suits the time,
And meets your humor;

[*They all arise and the old man prays.*

RUTH.

[*After a pause.*

David, let us see
Whether your memory prove as true as mine.
Do you recall the promise made by you
This night one year ago,—to write a hymn
For this occasion ?

DAVID.

I recall, and keep.
Here are the copies, written fairly out.
Here,—father, Mary, Ruth, and all the rest ;
There's one for each. Now what shall be the tune ?

ISRAEL.

The old One Hundredth—noblest tune of tunes!
Old tunes are precious to me as old paths
In which I wandered when a happy boy.
In truth they are the old paths of my soul,
Oft trod, well worn, familiar, up to God.

The Hymn.

[*In which all unite to sing.*

For Summer's bloom and Autumn's blight,
For bending wheat and blasted maize,
For health and sickness, Lord of light,
And Lord of darkness, hear our praise!

We trace to Thee our joys and woes,—
To Thee of causes still the cause,—
We thank Thee that Thy hand bestows;
We bless Thee that Thy love withdraws.

We bring no sorrows to Thy throne ;
  We come to Thee with no complaint.
In Providence Thy will is done,
  And that is sacred to the saint.

Here on this blest Thanksgiving Night,
  We raise to Thee our grateful voice ;
For what Thou doest, Lord, is right ;
  And thus believing, we rejoice.

GRACE.

A good old tune, indeed, and strongly sung ;
But, in my mind, the man who wrote the hymn
Had seemed more modest, had he paused awhile,
Ere by a trick he furnished other tongues
With words he only has the heart to sing.

DAVID.

Oh, Grace ! Dear Grace !

RUTH.

You may well cry for grace,
If that's the company you have to keep.

GRACE.

I thought you convert to his sophistry.
It makes no difference to him, you know,
Whether I plague or please.

RUTH.

It does to you.

ISRAEL.

There, children! No more bitter words like those!
I do not understand them; they awake
A sad uneasiness within my heart.
I found but Christian meaning in the hymn;
Aye, I could say *amen* to every line,
As to the breathings of my own poor prayer.
But let us talk no more. I'll to my bed.
Good night, my children! Happy thoughts be yours
Till sleep arrive—then happy dreams till dawn!

ALL.

Father, good night!

[ISRAEL *retires.*

RUTH.

There, little boys and girls—
Off to the kitchen! Now there's fun for you.
Play blind-man's-buff until you break your heads;
And then sit down beside the roaring fire,
And with wild stories scare yourselves to death.
We'll all be out there by-and-by. Meanwhile
I'll try the cellar; and if David, here,
Will promise good behavior, he shall be
My candle-bearer, basket-bearer, and—
But no! The pitcher I will bear myself.
I'll never trust a pitcher to a man
Under this house, and—seventy years of age.

[*The children rush out of the room with a shout, which wakes the baby.*

That noisy little youngster on the floor
Slept through the theology, but wakes with mirth—

Precocious little creature! He must go
Up to his chamber. Come, Grace, take him off,—
Basket and all. Mary will lend a hand,
And keep you company until he sleeps.

[GRACE *and* MARY *remove the cradle to the chamber, and* DAVID *and* RUTH *retire to the cellar.*

JOHN.

[*Rising and yawning.*

Isn't she the strangest girl you ever saw?

PRUDENCE.

Queer, rather, I should say. Grace, now, is strange.
I think she treats her husband shamefully.
I can't imagine what possesses her,
Thus to toss taunts at him with every word,
If in his doctrines there be truth enough,
He'll be a saint.

PATIENCE.

If he live long enough.

JOHN.

Well, now, I tell you such wild men as he,—
Men who have crazy crotchets in their heads,—
Can't make a woman happy. Don't you see?
He isn't settled. He has wandered off
From the old landmarks and has lost himself.
I may judge wrongly; but if truth were told
There'd be excuse for Grace, I warrant ye.
Grace is a right good girl, or was before
She married David.

PATIENCE.

Everybody says
He makes provision for his family,
Like a good husband.

PETER.

We can hardly tell.
When men get loose in their theology
The screws are started up in everything;

Of course, I don't apologize for Grace.
I think she might have done more prudently
Than introduce her troubles here to-night,
But, after all, we do not know the cause
That stirs her fretfulness.

Well, let it go!

What does the evening's talk amount to? Who
Is wiser for the wisdom of the hour?
The good old paths are good enough for me.
The fathers walked to heaven in them, and we,
By following meekly where they trod, may reach
The home they found. There will be mysteries:
Let those who like, bother their heads with them.
If Ruth and David seek to fathom all,
I wish them patience in their bootless quest.
For one, I'm glad the misty talk is done,
And we, alone.

PATIENCE.

And I.

JOHN.

I, too.

PRUDENCE.

And I.

FIRST EPISODE.

LOCALITY—*The Cellar Stairs and Cellar.*

PRESENT—DAVID *and* RUTH.

THE QUESTION ILLUSTRATED BY NATURE

RUTH.

LOOK where you step, or you'll stumble !
  Care for your coat, or you'll crock it ;
Down with your crown, man ! Be humble !
  Put your head into your pocket,
  Else something or other will knock it.
Don't hit that jar of cucumbers

Standing on the broad stair!
They have not waked from their slumbers
Since they stood there.

DAVID.

Yet they have lived in a constant jar!
What remarkable sleepers they are!

RUTH.

Turn to the left—shun the wall—
One step more– that is all!
Now we are on the ground
I will show you around.

Sixteen barrels of cider
Ripening all in a row!
Open the vent-channels wider!
See the froth drifted like snow,

Blown by the tempest below!
Those delectable juices
Flowed through the sinuous sluices
Of sweet springs under the orchard;
Climbed into fountains that chained them;
Dripped into cups that retained them,
And swelled till they dropped, and we gained them
Then they were gathered and tortured
By passage from hopper to vat,
And fell—every apple crushed flat.
Ah! how the bees gathered round them!
And how delicious they found them!
Oat-straw, as fragrant as clover,
Was platted, and smoothly turned over,
Weaving a neatly-ribbed basket;
And as they built up the casket,
In went the pulp by the scoop-full,
Till the juice flowed by the stoup-full,—
Filling the half of a puncheon
While the men swallowed their luncheon.

Pure grew the stream with the stress
  Of the lever and screw,
Till the last drops from the press
  Were as bright as the dew.
There were these juices spilled :
There were these barrels filled ;
Sixteen barrels of cider—
Ripening all in a row !
Open the vent-channels wider !
See the froth, drifted like snow,
Blown by the tempest below !

DAVID.

Hearts, like apples, are hard and sour,
Till crushed by Pain's resistless power ;
And yield their juices rich and bland
To none but Sorrow's heavy hand.
The purest streams of human love
  Flow naturally never,

But gush by pressure from above,
  With God's hand on the lever.
The first are turbidest and meanest;
The last are sweetest and serenest.

RUTH.

Sermon quite short for the text!
What shall we hit upon next?
Lift up the lid of that cask;
  See if the brine be abundant;
Easy for me were the task
  To make it redundant
With tears for my beautiful Zephyr—
  Pet of the pasture and stall—
Whitest and comeliest heifer,
  Gentlest of all!
  Oh it seemed cruel to slay her!
  But they insulted my prayer
  For her careless and innocent life,

And the creature was brought to the knife
With gratitude in her eye;
For they patted her back and chafed her head,
And coaxed her with softest words as they led
Her up to the ring to die.
Do you blame me for crying
When my Zephyr was dying?
I shut my room and my ears,
And opened my heart and my tears,
And wept for the half of a day;
And I could not go
To the rooms below
Till the butcher went away.

DAVID.

Life evermore is fed by death,
In earth and sea and sky;
And, that a rose may breathe its breath,
Something must die.

Earth is a sepulchre of flowers,
  Whose vitalizing mould
Through boundless transmutation towers,
        In green and gold.

The oak tree, struggling with the blast,
  Devours its father tree,
And sheds its leaves and drops its mast,
        That more may be.

The falcon preys upon the finch,
  The finch upon the fly,
And nought will loose the hunger-pinch
        But death's wild cry.

The milk-haired heifer's life must pass
  That it may fill your own,
As passed the sweet life of the grass
        She fed upon.

The power enslaved by yonder cask
  Shall many burdens bear;
Shall nerve the toiler at his task,
          The soul at prayer.

From lowly woe springs lordly joy;
  From humbler good diviner;
The greater life must aye destroy
          And drink the minor.

From hand to hand life's cup is passed
  Up Being's piled gradation,
Till men to angels yield at last
          The rich collation.

RUTH.

Well, we are done with the brute;
Now let us look at the fruit,—
Every barrel, I'm told,
From grafts half a dozen years old.

That is a barrel of russets;
But we can hardly discuss its
  Spheres of frost and flint,
Till, smitten by thoughts of Spring,
And the old tree blossoming,
Their bronze takes a yellower tint,
And the pulp grows mellower in't;
But oh! when they're sick with savors
  Of sweets that they dream of,
Sure, all the toothsomest flavors
  They hold the cream of!
You will be begging in May,
In your irresistible way,
For a peck of the apples in gray.

Those are the pearmains, I think,—
Bland and insipid as eggs;
They were too lazy to drink
  The light to its dregs,
And left them upon the rind—

A delicate film of blue—
Leave them alone ;—I can find
Better apples for you.

Those are the Rhode Island greenings ;
  Excellent apples for pies ;
There are no mystical meanings
  In fruit of that color and size.
They are too coarse and too juiceful ;
They are too large and too useful.

There are the Baldwins and Flyers,
Wrapped in their beautiful fires !
Color forks up from their stems
  As if painted by Flora,
Or as out from the pole stream the flames
  Of the Northern Aurora.

Here shall our quest have a close ;
Fill up your basket with those ;

Bite through their vesture of flame,
  And then you will gather
All that is meant by the name,
  "Seek-no-farther!"

DAVID.

The native orchard's fairest trees,
  Wild springing on the hill,
Bear no such precious fruits as these,
          And never will;

Till axe and saw and pruning knife
  Cut from them every bough,
And they receive a gentler life
          Than crowns them now.

And Nature's children, evermore,
  Though grown to stately stature,
Must bear the fruit their fathers bore—
          The fruit of nature;

Till every thrifty vice is made
  The shoulder for a cion,
Cut from the bending trees that shade
    The hills of Zion.

Sorrow must crop each passion-shoot,
  And pain each lust infernal,
Or human life can bear no fruit
    To life eternal.

For angels wait on Providence :
  And mark the sundered places,
To graft with gentlest instruments
    The heavenly graces.

RUTH.

Well, you're a curious creature !
You should have been a preacher.
  But look at that bin of potatoes—

Grown in all singular shapes—
Red and in clusters like grapes,
  Or more like tomatoes.
Those are Merinoes, I guess ;
  Very prolific and cheap ;
They make an excellent mess
  For a cow, or a sheep,
And are good for the table, they say,
When the winter has passed away.

Those are my beautiful Carters ;
Every one doomed to be martyrs
  To the eccentric desire
Of Christian people to skin them,—
  Brought to the trial of fire
For the good that is in them !
Ivory tubers—divide one !
  Ivory all the way through !
Never a hollow inside one ;
  Never a core, black or blue !

Ah, you should taste them when roasted!
  (Chestnuts are not half so good;)
And you would find that I've boasted
  Less than I should.
They make the meal for Sunday noon;
  And, if you ever eat one, let me beg
  You to manage it just as you do an egg.
Take a pat of butter, a silver spoon,
And wrap your napkin round the shell;
Have you seen a humming-bird probe the bell
Of a white-lipped morning-glory?
Well, that's the rest of the story!
But it's very singular, surely,
They should produce so poorly.
Father knows that I want them,
So he continues to plant them;
But, if I try to argue the question,
  He scoffs, as a thrifty farmer will:
And puts me down with the stale suggestion—
  "Small potatoes, and few in a hill."

DAVID.

Thus is it over all the earth !
  That which we call the fairest,
And prize for its surpassing worth,
          Is always rarest.

Iron is heaped in mountain piles,
  And gluts the laggard forges ;
But gold-flakes gleam in dim defiles,
          And lonely gorges.

The snowy marble flecks the land
  With heaped and rounded ledges,
But diamonds hide within the sand
          Their starry edges.

The finny armies clog the twine
  That sweeps the lazy river,
But pearls come singly from the brine,
          With the pale diver.

God gives no value unto men
  Unmatched by meed of labor;
And Cost of Worth has ever been
  The closest neighbor.

Wide is the gate and broad the way
  That open to perdition,
And countless multitudes are they
  Who seek admission.

But strait the gate, the path unkind,
  That lead to life immortal,
And few the careful feet that find
  The hidden portal.

All common good has common price;
  Exceeding good, exceeding;
Christ bought the keys of Paradise
  By cruel bleeding;

And every soul that wins a place
  Upon its hills of pleasure,

THE FINNY ARMIES CLOG THE TWINE THAT SWEEPS THE LAZY RIVER.

Must give its all, and beg for grace
To fill the measure.

Were every hill a precious mine,
And golden all the mountains;
Were all the rivers fed with wine
By tireless fountains;

Life would be ravished of its zest,
And shorn of its ambition,
And sink into the dreamless rest
Of inanition.

Up the broad stairs that Value rears
Stand motives beck'ning earthward,
To summon men to nobler spheres,
And lead them worthward.

RUTH.

I'm afraid to show you anything more;
For parsnips and art are so very long,

That the passage back to the cellar-door
  Would be through a mile of song.
But Truth owns me for an honest teller;
  And if the honest truth be told,
I am indebted to you and the cellar
  For a lesson and a cold.
And one or the other cheats my sight;
  (O silly girl! for shame!)
Barrels are hooped with rings of light,
  And stopped with tongues of flame.
Apples have conquered original sin,
  Manna is pickled in brine,
Philosophy fills the potato bin,
  And cider will soon be wine.
So crown the basket with mellow fruit,
  And brim the pitcher with pearls;
And we'll see how the old-time dainties suit
  The old-time boys and girls.

[They ascend the stairs

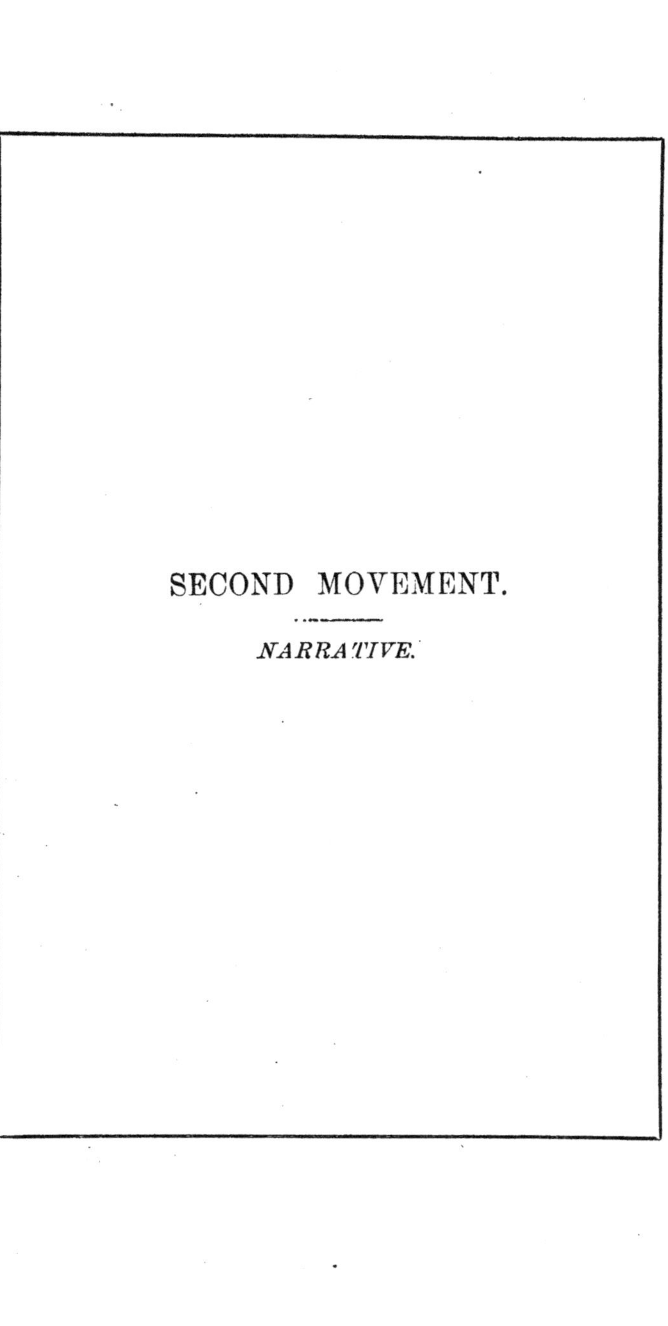

SECOND MOVEMENT.

NARRATIVE.

SECOND MOVEMENT.

LOCALITY—*A Chamber.*

PRESENT—GRACE, MARY, *and the* BABY.

THE QUESTION ILLUSTRATED BY EXPERIENCE.

GRACE.

[*Sings.*

Hither, Sleep! A mother wants thee!
  Come with velvet arms!
Fold the baby that she grants thee
  To thy own soft charms!

Bear him into Dreamland lightly!
  Give him sight of flowers!

Do not bring him back till brightly
  Break the morning hours!

Close his eyes with gentle fingers!
  Cross his hands of snow!
Tell the angels where he lingers
  They must whisper low!

I will guard thy spell unbroken
  If thou hear my call;
Come then, Sleep! I wait the token
  Of thy downy thrall.

Now I see his sweet lips moving;
  He is in thy keep;
Other milk the babe is proving
  At the breast of sleep!

MARY.

Sleep, babe, the honeyed sleep of innocence!
Sleep like a bud; for soon the sun of life

With ardors quick and passionate shall rise,
And, with hot kisses, part the fragrant lips—
The folded petals of thy soul! Alas!
What feverish winds shall tease and toss thee, then!
What pride and pain, ambition and despair,
Desire, satiety, and all that fill
With misery life's fretful enterprise,
Shall wrench and blanch thee, till thou fall at last,
Joy after joy down fluttering to the earth,
To be apportioned to the elements!
I marvel, baby, whether it were ill
That he who planted thee should pluck thee now,
And save thee from the blight that comes on all.
I marvel whether it would not be well
That the frail bud should burst in Paradise,
On the full throbbing of an angel's heart!

GRACE.

Oh, speak not thus! The thought is terrible.
He is my all; and yet, it sickens me

To think that he will grow to be a man.
If he were not a boy!

MARY.

Were not a boy?
That wakens other thoughts. Thank God for that!
To be a man, if aught, is privilege
Precious and peerless. While I bide content
The modest lot of woman, all my soul
Gives truest manhood humblest reverence.
It is a great and god-like thing to do!
'Tis a great thing, I think, to be a man.
Man fells the forests, ploughs and tills the fields,
And heaps the granaries that feed the world.
At his behest swift Commerce spreads her wings,
And tires the sinewy sea-birds as she flies,
Fanning the solitudes from clime to clime.
Smoke-crested cities rise beneath his hand,
And roar through ages with the din of trade.
Steam is the fleet-winged herald of his will,

MAN FELLS THE FORESTS, PLOUGHS AND TILLS THE FIELDS,
AND HEAPS THE GRANARIES THAT FEED THE WORLD.

Joining the angel of the Apocalypse
Mid sound and smoke and wond'rous circumstance,
And with one foot upon the conquered sea,
And one upon the subject land, proclaims
That space shall be no more. The lightnings veil
Their fiery forms to wait upon his thought,
And give it wing, as unseen spirits pause
To bear to God the burden of his prayer.
God crowns him with the gift of eloquence,
And puts a harp into his tuneful hands,
And makes him both His prophet and His Priest.
'Twas in his form the great Immanuel
Revealed Himself; the Apostolic Twelve,
Like those who since have ministered the Word,
Were men. 'Tis a great thing to be a man.

GRACE.

And fortunate to have an advocate
Across whose memory convenient clouds
Come floating at convenient intervals.

The harvest fields that man has honored most
Are those where human life is reaped like grain.
There never rose a mart, nor shone a sail,
Nor sprang a great invention into birth,
By other motive than man's love of gold.
It is for wrong that he is eloquent;
For lust that he indites his sweetest songs.
Christ was betrayed by treason of a man,
And scourged and hung upon a tree by men;
And the sad women who were at his cross,
And sought Him early at the sepulchre,
And since that day, in gentle multitudes
Have loved and followed him, have been man's
slaves,—
The victims of his power and his desire.

MARY.

And you, a wedded wife—well wedded, too—
Can say all this, and say it bitterly!

GRACE.

Perhaps because a wife ; perhaps because—

MARY.

Hush, Grace ! No more ! I beg you say no more.
Nay ! I will leave you at another word ;
For I could listen to a blasphemy,
Falling from bestial lips, with lighter chill
Than to the mad complainings of a soul
Which God has favored as he favors few.
I dare not listen when a woman's voice,
Which blessings strive to smother, flings them off
In mad contempt. I dare not hear the words
Whose utterance all the gentle loves dissuade
By kisses which are reasons, while a throng
Of friendships, comforts, and sweet charities—
The almoners of the All-bountiful—
With folded wings stand sadly looking on.
Believe me, Grace, the pioneer of judgment—

Ordained, commissioned—is ingratitude;
For where it moves, good withers; blessings die;
Till a clean path is left for Providence,
Who never sows a good the second time
Till the torn bosom of the graceless soil
Is ready for the seed.

GRACE.

Oh, could you know
The anguish of my heart, you would not chide!
If I repine, it is because my lot
Is not the blessed thing it seems to you.
O Mary! Could you know! Could you but know!

MARY.

Then why not tell me all? You know me, love,
And know that secrets make their graves with me;
So, tell me all; for I do promise you
Such sympathy as God through suffering
Has given me power to grant to such as you.

I bought it dearly, and its largess waits
The opening of your heart.

GRACE.

I am ashamed,—
In truth I am ashamed—to tell you all.
You will not laugh at me?

MARY.

I laugh at you?

GRACE.

Forgive me, Mary, for my heart is weak;
Distrustful of itself and all the world.
Ah, well! To what strange issues leads our life!
It seems but yesterday that you were brought
To this old house an orphaned little girl,
Whose large shy eyes, pale cheeks, and shrinking
ways
Filled all our hearts with wonder, as we stood

And stared at you until your heart o'erfilled
With the oppressive strangeness, and you wept.
Yes, I remember how I pitied you—
I who hade never wept, nor even sighed,
Save on the bosom of my gentle mother;
For my quick heart caught all your history
When with a hurried step you sought the sun,
And pressed your eyes against the window-pane
That God's sweet light might dry them. Well I
knew,
Though all untaught, that you were motherless.
And I remember how I followed you,—
Embraced and kissed you—kissed your tears
away—
Tears that came faster, till they bathed the lips
That would have sealed their flooded fountain-
heads;
And then we wound our arms around each other,
And passed out—out under the pleasant sky,
And stood among the lilies at the door.

I gave no formal comfort ; you, no thanks ;
For tears had been your language, kisses mine,
And we were friends. We talked about our dolls,
And all the pretty playthings we possessed.
Then we revealed, with childish vanity,
Our little stores of knowledge. I was full
Of a sweet marvel when you pointed out
The yellow thighs of bees that, half asleep,
Plundered the secrets of the lily-bells,
And called the golden pigment honey-comb.
And your black eyes were opened very wide
When I related how, one sunny day,
I found a well, half-covered, down the lane,
That was so deep and clear that I could see
Straight through the world, into another sky!

MARY.

Do you remember how the Guinea hens
Set up a scream upon the garden wall,
That frightened me to running, when you screamed
With laughter quite as loud ?

GRACE.

Ay, very well;
But better still the scene that followed all.
Oh, that has lingered in my memory
Like the divinest dream of Raphael—
The Dresden virgin prisoned in a print—
That watched with me in sickness through long
weeks,
And from its frame upon the chamber wall
Breathed constant benedictions, till I learned
To love the presence like a Roman saint.

My mother called us in; and at her knee,
Embracing still, we stood, and felt her smile
Shine on our upturned faces like the light
Of the soft summer moon. And then she stooped;
And when she kissed us, I could see the tears
Brimming her eyes. O sweet experiment!
To try if love of Jesus and of me
Could make our kisses equal to her lips!
Then straight my prescient heart set up a song,

And fluttered in my bosom like a bird.
I knew a blessing was about to fall,
As robins know the coming of the rain,
And bruit the joyous secret, ere its steps
Are heard upon the mountain tops. I knew
You were to be my sister ; and my heart
Was almost bursting with its love and pride.
I could not wait to hear the kindly words
Our mother spoke—her counsels and commands—
For you were mine—my sister ! So I tore
Your clinging hand from hers with rude constraint,
And took you to my chamber, where I played
With you, in selfish sense of property,
The whole bright afternoon.

And here again,
Within this same old chamber we are met.
We told our secrets to each other then ;
Thus let us tell them now ; and you shall be
To my grief-burdened soul what you have said,
So many times that I have been to yours.

MARY.

Alas! I never meant to tell my tale
To other ear than God's; but you have claims
Upon my confidence,—claims just rehearsed,
And other claims which you have never known.

GRACE.

And other claims which I have never known!
You speak in riddles, love. I only know
You grew to womanhood, were beautiful,
Were loved and wooed, were married and were blest;—
That after passage of mysterious years
We heard sad stories of your misery,
And rumors of desertion; but your pen
Revealed no secrets of your altered life.
Enough for me that you are here to-night,
And have an ear for sorrow, and a heart
Which disappointment has inhabited.
My history you know. A twelvemonth since

This fearful, festive night, and in this house,
I gave my hand to one whom I believed
To be the noblest man God ever made;—
A man who seemed to my infatuate heart
Heaven's chosen genius, through whose tuneful soul
The choicest harmonies of life should flow,
Growing articulate upon his lips
In numbers to enchant a willing world.
I cannot tell you of the pride that filled
My bosom, as I marked his manly form,
And read his soul through his effulgent eyes,
And heard the wondrous music of his voice,
That swept the chords of feeling in all hearts
With such divine persuasion as might grow
Under the transit of an angel's hand.
And, then, to think that I, a farmer's child,
Should be the woman culled from all the world
To be that man's companion,—to abide
The nearest soul to such a soul—to sit

Close by the fountain of his peerless life—
The welling centre of his loving thoughts—
And drink myself, the sweetest and the best,—
To lay my head upon his breast, and feel
That of all precious burdens it had borne
That was most precious—Oh ! my heart was wild
With the delirium of happiness—
But, Mary, you are weeping !

MARY.

Mark it not.

Your words wake memories which you may guess,
And thoughts which you may sometime know—
not now.

GRACE.

Well, we were married, as I said ; and I
Was not unthankful utterly, I think ;
Though, if the awful question had come then,
And stood before me with a brow severe
And steady finger, bidding me decide

Which of the two I loved the more, the God
Who gave my husband to me, or His gift,
I know I should have groaned, and shut my eyes.

We passed a honeymoon whose atmosphere,
Flooded with inspiration, and embraced
By a wide sky set full of starry thoughts,
And constellated visions of delight,
Still wraps me in my dreams—itself a dream.
The full moon waned at last, and in my sky,
With horn inverted, gave its sign of tears,
And then, when wasted to a skeleton,
It sank into a heavy sea of tears
That caught its tumult from my sighing soul.
My husband, who had spent whole months with me,
Till he was wedded to my every thought,
Left me through dreary hours,—nay, days,—alone!
He pleaded business—business day and night ;
Leaving me with a formal kiss at morn,
And meeting me with strange reserve at eve ;

And I could mark the sea of tenderness
Upon whose beach I had sat down for life,
Hoping to feel for ever as at first,
The love breeze from its billows, and to clasp
With open arms the silver surf that ran
To wreck itself upon my bosom, ebb,
Day after day receding, till the sand
Grew dry and hot, and the old hulls appeared
Of hopes sent out upon that faithless main
Since woman loved, and he she loved was false.
Night after night I sat the evening out,
And heard the clock tick on the mantel-tree
Till it grew irksome to me, and I grudged
The careless pleasures of the kitchen maids
Whose distant laughter shocked the lapsing hours.

MARY.

But did your husband never tell the cause
Of this neglect?

GRACE.

Never an honest word.
He told me he was writing; and, at home,
Sat down with heart absorbed and absent look.
I was offended, and upbraided him.
I knew he had a secret, and that from
The centre of its closely coiling folds
A cunning serpent's head, with forked tongue,
Swayed with a double story—one for me,
And one for whom I knew not—whom he knew.
His words, which wandered first as carelessly
As the free footsteps of a boy, were trained
To the stern paces of a sentinel
Guarding a prison door, and never tripped
With a suggestion.

I despaired at last
Of winning what I sought by wiles and prayers;
So, through long nights of sleeplessness I lay,
And held my ear beside his silent lips—

An eager cup—ready to catch the gush
Of the pent waters, if a dream-swung rod
Should smite his bosom. It was all in vain.
And thus months passed away, and all the while
Another heart was beating under mine.
May Heaven forgive me! but I grieved the charms
The unborn thing was stealing, for I felt
That in my insufficiency of power
I had no charm to lose.

MARY.

And did he not,
In this most tender trial of your heart,
Turn in relenting?—give you sympathy?

GRACE.

No—yes! Perhaps he pitied me, and that
Indeed was very pitiful; for what
Has love to do with pity? When a wife
Has sunk so hopelessly in the regard

Of him she loves that he can pity her,—
Has sunk so low that she may only share
The tribute which a mute humanity
Bestows on those whom Providence has struck
With helpless poverty, or foul disease ;
She may be pitied, both by earth and heaven,
Because he pities her. A pitied child
That begs its bread from door to door is blest;
A wife who begs for love and confidence,
And gets but alms from pity, is accurst.

Well, time passed on ; and rumor came at last
To tell the story of my husband's shame
And my dishonor. He was seen at night,
Walking in lonely streets with one whose eyes
Were blacker than the night,—whose little hand
Was clinging to his arm. Both were absorbed
In the half-whispered converse of the time ;
And both, as if accustomed to the path,
Turned down an alley, climbed a flight of steps

Entered a door, and closed it after them—
A door of adamant 'twixt hope and me.
I had my secret; and I kept it, too.
I knew his haunt, and it was watched for me,
Till doubt and prayers for doubt,—pale flowers
I nourished with my tears—were crushed
By the relentless hand of Certainty.

Oh, Mary! Mary! Those were fearful days.
My wrongs and all their shameful history
Were opened to me daily, leaf by leaf,
Though he had only shown their title-page;
That page was his; the rest were in my heart.
I knew that he had left my home for hers;
I knew his nightly labor was to feed
Other than me;—that he was loaded down
With cares that were the price of sinful love.

MARY.

Grace, in your heart do you believe all this?
I fear—I know—you do your husband wrong.

He is not competent for treachery.
He is too good, too noble, to desert
The woman whom he only loves too well.
You love him not!

GRACE.

I love him not? Alas!
I am more angry with myself than him
That, spite his falsehood to his marriage vows,
And spite my hate, I love the traitor still.
I love him not? Why am I here to-night—
Here where my girlhood's withered hopes are strewn
Through every room for him to trample on—
But in my pride to show him to you all,
With the dear child that publishes a love
That blessed me once, e'en if it curse me now?
You know I do my husband wrong! You think,
Because he can talk smoothly, and befool
A simple ear with pious sophistries,

He must be e'en the saintly man he seems.
We heard him talk to-night ; it was done well.
I saw the triumph of his argument,
And I was proud, though full of spite the while.
His stuff was meant for me ; and, with intent,
For selfish purpose, or in irony,
He tossed me bitterness, and called it sweet.
My heart rebelled, and now you know the cause
Of my harsh words to him.

MARY.

'Tis very sad !
Oh very—very sad ! Pray you go on !
Who is this woman ?

GRACE.

I have never learned.
I only know she stole my husband's heart,
And made me very wretched. I suppose
That at the time my little babe was born,

She went away! for David was at home
For many days. That pain was bliss to me—
I need no argument to teach me that—
Which caused neglect of her, and gave offence.
Since then, he has not where to go from me;
And, loving well his child, he stays at home.

So he lugs round his secret, and I mine.
I call him, husband; and he calls me, wife;
And I, who once was like an April day,
That finds quick tears in every cloud, have steeled
My heart against my fate, and now am calm.
I will live on; and though these simple folk
Who call me sister understand me not,
It matters little. There is one who does;
And he shall have no liberty of love
By any word of mine. 'Tis woman's lot,
And man's most weak and wicked wantonness.
Mine is like other husbands, I suppose;
No worse—no better.

MARY.

Ask you sympathy
Of such as I? I cannot give it you,
For you have shut me from the privilege.

GRACE.

I asked it once; you gave me unbelief.
I had no choice but to grow hard again.
'Tis my misfortune and my misery
That every hand whose friendly ministry
My poor heart craves, is held—withheld—by him,
And I must freeze that I may stand alone.

MARY.

And so, because one man is false, or you
Imagine him to be, all men are false;
Do I speak rightly?

GRACE.

Have it your own way.
Men fit to love, and fitted to be loved,

Are prone to falsehood. I will not gainsay
The common virtue of the common herd.
I prize it as I do the goodish men
Who hold the goodish stuff, and know it not.
These serve to fill an easy-going world,
And that to clothe it with complacency.

MARY.

I had not thought misanthropy like this
Could lodge with you; so I must e'en confess
A tale which never passed my lips before,
Nor sent its flush to any cheek but mine.
In this, I'll prove my friendship, if I lose
The friendship which demands the sacrifice.

I have come back, a worse than widowed wife;
Yet I went out with dream as bright as yours,—
Nay, brighter,—for the birds were singing then,
And apple-blossoms drifted on the ground
Where snow-flakes fell and flew when you were wed.

The skies were soft; the roses budded full;
The meads and swelling uplands fresh and green;—
The very atmosphere was full of love.
It was no girlish carelessness of heart
That kept my eyes from tears, as I went forth
From this dear shelter of the orphan child.
I felt that God was smiling on my lot,
And made the airs his angels to convey
To every sense and sensibility
The message of his favor. Every sound
Was music to me; every sight was peace;
And breathing was the drinking of perfume.
I said, content, and full of gratitude,
"This is as God would have it; and he speaks
These pleasant languages to tell me so."

But I had no such honeymoon as yours.
A few brief days of happiness, and then
The dream was over. I had married one
Who was the sport of vagrant impulses.

We had not been a fortnight wed, when he
Came home to me with brandy in his brain—
A maudlin fool—for love like mine to hide
As if he were an unclean beast. O Grace!
I cannot paint the horrors of that night.
My heart, till then serene, and safely kept
In Trust's strong citadel, quaked all night long,
As tower and bastion fell before the rush
Of fierce convictions; and the tumbling walls
Boomed with dull throbs of ruin through my brain.
And there were palaces that leaned on this—
Castles of air, in long and glittering lines,
Which melted into air, and pierced the blue
That marks the star-strewn vault of heaven;—all fell
With a faint crash like that which scares the soul
When desolation shivers through a dream
Smitten by nightmare,—fell and faded all
To utter nothingness; and when the morn
Flamed up the East, and with its crimson wings
Brushed out the paling stars that all the night

In silent, slow procession, one by one,
Had gazed upon me through the open sash,
And passed along, it found me desolate.

The stupid dreamer at my side awoke,
And with such helpless anguish as they feel
Who know that they are weak as well as vile.
I saw, through all his forward promises,
Excuses, prayers, and pledges that were oaths,
(What he, poor boaster, thought I could not see,)
That he was shorn of will, and that his heart
Was as defenceless as a little child's ;—
That underneath his fair good fellowship
He was debauched, and dead in love with sin ;—
That love of me had made him what I loved,—
That I could only hold him till the wave
Of some o'erwhelming impulse should sweep in,
To lift his feet and bear him from my arms.
I felt that morn, when he went trembling forth,
With bloodshot eyes and forehead hot with woe,

That thenceforth strife would be 'twixt Hell and
me—
The odds against me—for my husband's soul.

GRACE.

Poor dove! Poor Mary! Have you suffered thus?
You had not even pride to keep you up.
Were he my husband, I had left him then—
The ingrate!

MARY.

Not if you had loved as I;
Yet what you know is but a bitter drop
Of the full cup of gall that I have drained.
Had he left me unstained,—had I rebelled
Against the influence by which he sought
To bring me to a compromise with him,—
To make my shrinking soul meet his half way,—
It had been better; but he had an art,
When appetite or passion moved in him,
That clothed his sins with fair apologies,

And smoothed the wrinkles of a haggard guilt
With the good-natured hand of charity.
He knew he was a fool, he said, and said again;
But human nature would be what it was,
And life had never zest enough to bear
Too much dilution; those who worked like slaves
Must have their days of frolic and of fun.
He doubted whether God would punish sin;
God was, in fact, too good to punish sin;
For sin itself was a compounded thing,
With weakness for its prime ingredient.
And thus he fooled a heart that loved him well;
And it went toward his heart by slow degrees,
Till Virtue seemed a frigid anchorite,
And Vice, a jolly fellow—bad enough,
But not so bad as Christian people think.

This was the cunning work of months—nay, years;
And, meantime, Edward sank from bad to worse.
But he had conquered. Wine was on his board,

—WINE WAS ON HIS BOARD
WITHOUT MY PROTEST—WITH A GLASS FOR ME!

Without my protest—with a glass for me!
His boon companions came and went, and made
My home their rendezvous with my consent.
The doughty oath that shocked my ears at first,
The doubtful jest that meant, or might not mean,
That which should set a woman's brow aflame,
Became at last (oh, shame of womanhood!)
A thing to frown at with a covert smile;
A thing to smile at with a decent frown;
A thing to steal a grace from, as I feigned
The innocence of deaf unconsciousness.
And I became a jester. I could jest
In a wild way on sacred things and themes;
And I have thought that in his better moods
My husband shrank with horror from the work
Which he had wrought in me.

I do not know
If, during all these downward-tending years,
Edward kept well his faith with me. I know

He used to tell me, in his boastful way,
How he had broke the hearts of pretty maids,
And that if he were single—well-a-day!
The time was past for thinking upon that!
And I had heart to toss the badinage
Back in his teeth, with pay of kindred coin;
And tell him lies to stir his bestial mirth;
And make my boast of conquests: and pretend
That the true heart I had bestowed on him
Had flown, and left him but an empty hand.

I had some days of pain and penitence.
I saw where all must end. I saw, too well,
Edward was growing idle,—that his form
Was gathering disgustful corpulence,—
That he was going down, and dragging me
To shame and ruin, beggary and death.
But judgment came and overshadowed us;
And one quick bolt, shot from the awful cloud,
Severed the tie that bound two worthless lives.

What God hath joined together, God may part:—
Grace, have you thought of that?

GRACE.

You scare me. Mary!
Nay! Do not turn on me with such a look!
Its dread suggestion gives my heart a pang
That stops its painful beating.

MARY.

Let it pass!
One morn we woke with the first flush of light,
Our windows jarring with the cannonade
That ushered in the nation's festal day.
The village streets were full of men and boys,
And resonant with rattling mimicry
Of the black-throated monsters on the hill,—
A crashing, crepitating war of fire,—
And as we listened to the fitful feud,
Dull detonations came from far away,

Pulsing along the fretted atmosphere,
To tell that in the ruder villages
The day had noisy greeting, as in ours.

I know not why it was, but then, and there,
I felt a sinking sadness, passing tears—
A dark foreboding I could not dissolve
Nor drive away. But when, next morn, I woke
In the sweet stillness of the Sabbath day,
And found myself alone, I knew that hearts
Which once have been God's temple, and in which
Something divine still lingers, feel the throb
Along the lines that bind them to The Throne
When judgment issues; and, though dumb and
blind,
Shudder and faint with prophecies of ill.
How—by what cause—calamity should come,
I could not guess; that it was imminent,
Seemed just as certain as the morning's dawn.

We were to have a gala day, indeed.

There were to be processions and parades,
A great oration in a mammoth tent,
With dinner following, and toast and speech
By all the wordy magnates of the town;
A grand balloon ascension afterwards;
And in the evening, fireworks on the hill.
I knew that drink would flow from morn till night
In a wild maelstrom, circling slow around
The village rim, in bright careering waves,
But growing turbulent, and changed to ink
Around the village centre, till, at last,
The whirling, gurgling vortex would engulf
A maddened multitude in drunkenness.

And this was in my thought (the while my heart
Was palpitating with its nameless fear),
As, wrapped in vaguest dreams, and purposeless,
I laced my shoe and gazed upon the sky.
Then strange determination stirred in me;
And, turning sharply on my chair, I said,
"Edward, where'er you go to-day, I go!"

If I had smitten him upon the face,
It had not tingled with a hotter flame.
He turned upon me with a look of hate—
A something worse than anger—and, with oaths
Raved like a fiend, and cursed me for a fool.
But I was firm ; he could not shake my will ;
So, through the morning, until afternoon,
He stayed at home, and drank and drank again,
Watching the clock, and pacing up and down,
Until, at length, he came and sat by me,
To try his hackneyed tricks of blandishment.
He had not meant, he said, to give offence ;
But women in a crowd were out of place.
He wished to see the aeronauts embark,
And meet some friends ; but there would be a throng
Of boys and drunken boors around the car,
And I should not enjoy it ; more than this,
The rise would be a finer spectacle
At home than on the ground. I gave assent,

And he went out. Of course, I followed him ;
For I had learned to read him, and I knew
There was some precious scheme of sin on foot.

The crowd was heavy, and his form was lost
Quick as it touched the mass ; but I pressed on,
Wild shouts and laughter punishing my ears,
Till I could see the bloated, breathing cone,
As if it were some monster of the sky
Caught by a net and fastened to the earth—
A butt for jeers to all the merry mob.
But I was distant still ; and if a man
In mad impatience tore a passage from
The crowd that pressed upon him, or a girl,
Frightened or fainting, was allowed escape,
I slid like water to the vacant space,
And thus, by deftly won advances, gained
The stand I coveted.

We waited long ;

And as the curious gazers stood and talked

About the diverse currents of the air,
And wondered where the daring voyagers
Would find a landing-place, a young man said,
In words intended for a spicy jest,
A man and woman living in the town
Had taken passage overland for hell!

Then at a distance rose a scattering shout
That fixed the vision of the multitude,
Standing on eager tiptoe, and afar
I saw the crowd give way, and make a path
For the pale heroes of the crazy hour.
Hats were tossed wildly as they struggled on,
And the gap closed behind them, till, at length,
They stood within the ring. Oh, damning sight!
The woman was a painted courtesan;
The man, my husband! I was dumb as death.
My teeth were clenched together like a vice,
And every heavy heart-throb was a chill.
But there I stood, and saw the shame go on.

They took their seats, the signal gun was fired ;
The cords were loosèd, and then the billowy bulk
Shot toward the zenith !

Never bent the sky
With more cloudless depth of blue than then ;
And, as they rose, I saw his faithless arm
Slide o'er her shoulder, and her dizzy head
Drop on his breast. Then I became insane.
I felt that I was struggling with a dream—
A horrid phantasm I could not shake off.
The hollow sky was swinging like a bell ;
The silken monster swinging like its tongue ;
And as it reeled from side to side, the roar
Of voices round me rang, and rang again,
Tolling the dreadful knell of my despair.

At the last moment I could trace his form,
Edward leaned over from his giddy seat,
And tossed out something on the air. I saw

The little missive fluttering slowly down,
And stretched my hand to catch it, for I knew,
Or thought I knew, that it would come to me.
And it did come to me—as if it slid
Upon the cord that bound my heart to his—
Strained to its utmost tension—snapped at last.
I marked it as it fell. It was a rose.
I grasped it madly as it struck my hand,
And buried all its thorns within my palm ;
But the fierce pain released my prisoned voice,
And with a shriek, I staggered, swooned, and fell.

That night was brushed from life. A passing friend
Directed those who bore me rudely off ;
And I was carried to my home, and laid
Entranced upon my bed. The Sabbath morn
That followed all this din and devilry
Swung noiseless wide its doors of yellow light,
And in the hallowed stillness I awoke.
My heart was still ; I could not stir a hand.

I thought that I was dying or was dead,—
That I had slipped through smooth unconsciousness
Into the everlasting silences.
I could not speak ; but winning strength at last,
I turned my eyes to seek for Edward's face,
And saw an unpressed pillow. He was gone !

I was oppressed with awful sense of loss ;
And as a mother, by a turbid sea
That has ingulfed her fairest child, sits down
And moans over the waters, and looks out
With curious despair upon the waves,
Until she marks a lock of floating hair,
And by its threads of gold draws slowly in,
And clasps and presses to her frenzied breast
The form it has no power to warm again,
So I, beside the sea of memory,
Lay feebly moaning, yearning for a clew
By which to reach my own extinguished life.
It came. A burning pain shot through my palm.

And thorns awoke what thorns had put to sleep.
It all came back to me—the roar, the rush,
The upturned faces, the insane hurrahs,
The skyward shooting spectacle, the shame—
And then I swooned again.

GRACE.

But was he killed?
Did his foolhardy adventure end in wreck?
Or did it end in something worse than wreck?
Surely, he came again!

MARY.

To me, no more.
He had his reasons, and I knew them soon;
But, first, the fire enkindled in my brain
Burnt through long weeks of fever—burnt my frame
Until it lay upon the sheet as white
As the pale ashes of a wasted coal.
Then, when strength came to me, and I could sit

Braced by the double pillows that were mine,
A kind friend took my hand and told me all.

The day that Edward left me was the last
He could have been my husband; for the next
Disclosed his infamy and my disgrace.
He was a thief, and had been one for years,—
Defrauding those whose gold he held in trust;
And he was ruined—ruined utterly.
The very bed I sat on was not his,
Nor mine, except by tender charity.
A guilty secret menacing behind,
A guilty passion burning in his heart,
And by his side, a guilty paramour,
He seized upon this reckless whim, and fled
From those he knew would curse him ere he slept

My cup was filled with wormwood; and it grew
Bitter and still more bitter, day by day,
Changing from shame and hate, to stern revenge
Life had no more for me. My home was lost;

My heart unfitted to return to this ;
And, reckless of the future, I went forth—
A woman stricken, maddened, desperate.
I sought the city with as sure a scent
As vultures track a carcass through the air.
I knew him there delivered up to sin,
And longed to taunt him with his infamy,—
To haunt his haunts ; to sting his perjured soul
With sharp reproaches ; and to scare his eyes
With visions of his work upon my face.

But God had other means than my revenge
To humble him, and other thought for me.
I saw him only once ; we did not meet ;
There was a street between us ; yet it seemed
Wide as the unbridged gulf that yawns between
The rich man and the beggar.

'Twas at dawn.

I had arisen from the sleepless bed

Which my scant means had purchased, and gone
forth
To taste the air, and cool my burning brow.
I wandered on, not knowing where I went,
Nor caring whither. There were few astir;
The market wagons lumbered slowly in,
Piled high with carcasses of slaughtered lambs,
Baskets of unhusked corn, and mint, and all
The fresh, green things that grow in country fields.
I read the signs—the long and curious names—
And wondered who invented them, and if
Their owners knew how very strange they were.
A corps of weary firemen met me once,
Late home from service, with their gaudy car,
And loud with careless curses. Then I stopped,
And chatted with a frowsy-headed girl
Who knelt among her draggled skirts, and scrubbed
The heel-worn door-steps of a faded house.
Then, as I left her, and resumed my walk,
I turned my eyes across the street, and saw

A sight which stopped my feet, my breath, my heart.
It was my husband. Oh, how sadly changed!
His bloodshot eyes stared from an anxious face;
His hat was battered, and his clothes were torn
And splashed with mud. His poisoned frame
Had shrunk away, until his garments hung
In folds about him. Then I knew it all;
His life had been a measureless debauch
Since his most shameless flight; and in his eye,
Eager and strained, and peering down the stairs
That tumbled to the ante-rooms of hell,
I saw the thirst which only death can quench.
He did not raise his eyes; I did not speak;
There was no work for me to do on him!
And when, at last, he tottered down the steps
Of a dark gin-shop, I was satisfied,
And half-relentingly retraced my way.

I cannot tell the story of the months
That followed this. I toiled and toiled for bread,

And for the shelter of one stingy room.
Temptation, which the hand of poverty
Bears oft seductively to woman's lips,
To me came not. I hated men like beasts;
Their flattering words, and wicked, wanton leers,
Sickened me with ineffable disgust.

At length there came a change. One warm Spring
eve,
As I sat idly dreaming of the past,
And questioning the future, my quick ear
Caught sound of feet upon the creaking stairs,
And a light rap delivered at my door.
I said, "Come in!" with half defiant voice,
Although I longed to see a human face,
And needed labor for my idle hands.
But when the door was opened, and there stood
A man before me, with an eye as pure
And brow as fair as any little child's,
Matched with a form and carriage which combined

All manly beauty, dignity, and grace,
A quick blush overwhelmed my pallid cheeks,
And, ere I knew, and by no act of will,
I rose and gave him gentle courtesy.

He took a seat, and spoke with pleasant voice
Of many pleasant things—the pleasant sky,
The stars, the opening foliage in the park;
And then he came to business. He would have
A piece of exquisite embroidery;
My hand was cunning if report were true;
Would it oblige him? It would do, I said,
That which it could to satisfy his wish;
And when he took the delicate pattern out,
And spread the dainty fabric on his knees,
I knew he had a wife.

He went away
With kind "Good night," and said that with my
leave,

AND ERE I KNEW, AND BY NO ACT OF WILL,
I ROSE AND GAVE HIM GENTLE COURTESY.

He'd call and watch the progress of the work.
I marked his careful steps adown the stairs,
And then, his brisk, firm tread upon the stones,
Till in the dull roar of the distant streets
It mingled and was lost. Then I was lost—
Lost in a wild, wide-ranging reverie—
From which I roused not till the midnight hush
Was broken by the toll from twenty towers.

This is a man, I said—a man in truth;
My room has known the presence of a man,
And it has gathered dignity from him.
I felt my being flooded with new life.
My heart was warm; my poor, sore-footed thoughts
Sprang up full fledged through ether; and I felt
Like the sick woman who had touched the hem
Of Jesus' garment, when through all her veins
Leaped the swift tides of youth.

He had a wife!
Why, to a wrecked, forsaken thing like me

Did that thought bring a pang? I did not know:
But truth to tell, it gave me stinging pain.
If he was noble, he was naught to me;
If he was great, it only made me less;
If he loved truly, I was not enriched.
So, in my selfishness, I almost cursed
The unknown woman, thought for whom had brought
Her loving husband to me. What was I
To him? Naught but a poor unfortunate,
Picking her bread up at a needle's point.
He'll come and criticise my handiwork,
I said, and when it is at last complete,
He'll draw his purse and give me so much gold;
And then, forgetting me for ever, go
And gather fragrant kisses for the boon,
From lips that do not know their privilege.
I could be nothing but the medium
Through which his love should pass to reach its shrine;

The glass through which the sun's electric beams
Kindles the rose's heart, and still remains
Chill and serene itself—without reward!
Then came to me the thought of my great wrong.
A man had spoiled my heart, degraded me;
A wanton woman had defrauded me;
I would get reparation how I could!
He must be something to me—I to him!
All men, however good, are weak, I thought:
And if I can arrest no beam of love
By right of nature or by leave of law,
I'll stain the glass! And the last words I said,
As I lay down upon my bed to dream,
Were those four words of sin: "I'll stain the glass!"

GRACE.

Mary, I cannot hear you more; your tale,
So bitter and so passing pitiful
I have forgotten tears, and feel my eyes
Burn dry and hot with looking at your face,
Now gathers blackness, and grows horrible.

MARY.

Nay, you must hear me out; I cannot pause;
And have no worse to say than I have said—
Thank God, and him who put away my toils!

He came, and came again; and every charm
God had bestowed on me, or art could frame,
I used with keenest ingenuities
To fascinate the sensuous element
O'er which, mistrusted, and but half asleep,
His conscience and propriety stood guard.
I told with tears the story of my woe;
He listened to me with a thoughtful face,
And sadly sighed; and thus I won his ruth.
And then I told him how my life was lost;—
How earth had nothing more for me but pain;
Not e'en a friend. At this, he took my hand,
And said out of his nobleness of heart,
That I should have an honest friend in him;
On which I bowed my head upon his arm.

And wept again, as if my heart would break
With the full pressure of its gratitude.
He put me gently off, and read my face :
I stood before him hopeless, helpless, his !
His swift soul gathered what I meant it should.
He sighed and trembled ; then he crossed the floor
And gazed with eye abstracted on the sky ;
Then came and looked at me ; then turned,
As if affrighted at his springing thoughts,
And, with abruptest movement, left the room.

This time he took with him the broidered thing
That I had wrought for him ; and when I oped
The little purse that he rewarded me,
I found full golden payment five times told.
Given from pity ? thought I,—that alone ?
Is manly pity so munificent ?
Pity has mixtures that it knows not of !

It was a cruel triumph, and I speak

Of it with utter penitence and shame.
I knew that he would come again; I knew
His feet would bring him, though his soul rebelled;
I knew that cheated heart of his would toy
With the seductive chains that gave it thrall,
And strive to reconcile its perjury
With its own conscience of the better way
By fabrication of apologies
It knew were false.

And he did come again;
Confessing a strange interest in me,
And doing for me many kindly deeds.
I knew the nature of the sympathy
That drew him to my side, better than he;
Though I could see that solemn change in him
Which every face will wear, when Heaven and Hell
Are struggling in the heart for mastery.
He was unhappy; every sudden sound
Startled his apprehensions; from his heart

Rose heavy suspirations, charged with prayer,
Desire, and deprecation, and remorse;—
Sighs like volcanic breathings—sighs that scorched
His parching lips and spread his face with ashes,—
Sighs born in such convulsions of the soul
That his strong frame quaked like Vesuvius,
Burdened with restless lava.

Day by day
I marked his dalliance with sinful thought,
Without a throb of pity in my heart.
I took his gifts, which brought immunity
From toil and care, as if they were my right.
Day after day I saw my power increase,
Until that noble spirit was a slave—
A craven, helpless, self-suspected slave.

But this was not to last—thank God and him!
One night he came, and there had been a change.
My hand was kindly taken, but not held

In the way wonted. He was self-possessed;
The powers of darkness and his Christian heart
Had had a struggle—his the victory;
And on his manly brow the benison
Of a majestic peace had been imposed.
Was I to lose the guerdon of my guile?
He was my all, and by the only means
Left to a helpless, reckless thing, like me.
My heart made pledge the strife should be renewed.
I took no notice of his altered mood,
But strove, by all the tricks of tenderness,
To fan to life again the drooping flame
Within his heart;—with what success, at last,
The sequel shall reveal.

Strange fire came down
Responsive to my call, and the quick flash
That shrivelled resolution, vanquished will,
And with a blood-red flame consumed the crown
Of peace upon his brow, taught him how weak—

How miserably imbecile—he had become,
Tampering with temptation. Such a groan,
Wrung from such agony, as then he breathed,
Pray Heaven my ears may never hear again!
He smote his forehead with his rigid palm,
And sank, as if the blow had stunned him, to his knees,
And there, with face pressed hard upon his hands,
Gave utterance to frenzied sobs and prayers—
The wild articulations of despair.
I was confounded. He—a man—thought I,
Blind with remorse by simple look at sin!
And I—a woman—in the devil's hands,
Luring him Hellward with no blush of shame!
The thought came swift from God, and pierced my heart
Like a barbed arrow; and it quivered there
Through whiles of tumult—quivered—and was fast.

Thus, while I stood and marked his kneeling form.

Still shocked by deep convulsions, such a light
Illumed my soul, and flooded all the room,
That, without thought, I said, "The Lord is here!"
Then straight my spirit heard these wondrous words:
"Tempted in all points like ourselves was He—
Tempted, but sinless." Oh, what majesty
Of meaning did those precious words convey!
'Twas through temptation, thought I, that the Lord—
The mediator between God and men—
Reached down the hand of sympathetic love
To meet the grasp of lost Humanity;
And this man, kneeling, has the Lord in him,
And comes to mediate 'twixt Christ and me,
"Tempted but sinless;"—one hand grasping mine,
The other Christ's.

Why had he suffered thus?
Why had his heart been led far down to mine,
To beat in sinful sympathy with mine,

"TEMPTED IN ALL POINTS LIKE OURSELVES WAS HE—
TEMPTED BUT SINLESS."

But that my heart should cling to his and him,
And follow his withdrawal to the heights
From whence he had descended? Then I learned
Why Christ was tempted; and, as broad and full,
The heart of the great secret was revealed,
And I perceived God's dealings with my soul,
I knelt beside the tortured man and wept,
And cried to Heaven for mercy. As I prayed,
My soul cast off its shameful enterprise;
And when it fell, I saw my godless self—
My own degraded, tainted, guilty heart,
Which it had hidden from me. Oh, the pang—
The poignant throe of uttermost despair—
That followed the discovery! I felt
That I was lost beyond the grace of God,
And my heart turned with instinct sure and swift
To the strong struggler, praying at my side,
And begged his succor and his prayers. I felt
That he must lead me up to where the hand
Of Jesus could lay hold on me, or I was doomed.

Temptation's spell was past. He took my hand,
And, as he prayed that we might be forgiven,
And pledged our future loyalty to God
And his white throne within our hearts, I gave
Responses to each promise; then I crowned
His closing utterance with such Amen
As weak hearts, conscious of their weakness, give
When, bowed to dust and clinging to the robes
Of outraged mercy, they devote themselves
Once and forever to the pitying Christ.

Then we arose and stood upon our feet.
He gave me no reproaches, but with voice
Attempered to his altered mood, confessed
His own blameworthiness, and pressed the prayer
That I would pardon him, as he believed
That God had pardoned; but my heart was full,-
So full of its sore sense of wrong to him,
Of the deep guilt of shameful purposes
And treachery to worthy womanhood,

That I could not repeat his Christian words,
Asking forbearance on my own behalf.

He sat before me for a golden hour;
And gave me counsel and encouragement,
Till, like broad gates, the possibilities
Of a serener and a higher life
Were thrown wide open to my eager feet,
And I resolved that I would enter in,
And, with God's gracious help, go no more out.

For weeks he watched me with stern carefulness,
Nourished my resolution, prayed with me,
And led me, step by step, to higher ground,
Till, gathering impulse in the upward walk,
And strength in purer air, and keener sight
In the sweet light that dawned upon my soul,
I grasped the arm of Jesus, and was safe.
And now, when I look back upon my life,
It seems as if that noble man were sent

To give me rescue from the pit of death.
But from his distant height he could not reach
And act upon my soul; so Heaven allowed
Temptation's ladder 'twixt his soul and mine,
That they might meet and yield his mission thrift.
I doubt not in my grateful soul to-night
That had he stayed within his higher world,
And tried to call me to him, I had spurned
Alike his mission and his ministry.
That he was tempted, was at once my sin
And my salvation. That he sinned in thought,
And fiercely wrestled with temptation, won
For his own spirit that humility
Which God had sought to clothe him with in vain,
By other measures, and that strength which springs
From a great conflict and a victory.
We talked of this; and on our bended knees
We blessed the Great Dispenser for the means
By which we both had learned our sinful selves
And found the way to a diviner life.

So, with my chastened heart and life, I come
Back to my home, to live—perhaps to die.
God's love has been in all this discipline ;
God's love has used those awful sins of mine
To make me good and happy. I can mourn
Over my husband ; I can pray for him,
Nay, I forgive him ; for I know the power
With which temptation comes to stronger men.
I know the power with which it came to me.

And now, dear Grace, my story is complete.
You have received it with dumb wonderment,
And it has been too long. Tell me what thought
Stirs in your face, and waits for utterance.

GRACE.

That I have suffered little—trusted less ;
That I have failed in charity, and been
Unjust to all men—specially to one.
I did not think there lived a man on earth

Who had such virtue as this friend of yours,—
Weak, and yet strong. 'Twere but humanity
To give him pity in his awful strife;
To stint the meed of reverence and praise
For his triumphant conquest of himself,
Were infamy. I love and honor him;
And if I knew my husband were as strong,
I could fall down before, and worship him;
I could fall down, and wet his feet with tears—
Tears penitential for the grievous wrong
That I have done him. But alas! alas!
The thought comes back again. O God in Heaven
Help me with patience to await the hour
When the great purpose of Thy discipline
Shall be revealed, and, like this chastened one,
I can behold it, and be satisfied.

MARY.

Hark! They are calling us below, I think.

We must go down. We'll talk of this again
When we have leisure. Kiss the little one,
And thank his weary brain it sleeps so well.

[*They descend.*

SECOND EPISODE.

LOCALITY—*The Kitchen.*

PRESENT—JOSEPH, SAMUEL, REBEKAH, *and other* CHILDREN.

THE QUESTION ILLUSTRATED BY STORY.

JOSEPH.

Have we not had "Button-Button" enough,
And "Forfeits," and all such silly stuff?

SAMUEL.

Well, we were playing "Blind-Man's-Buff"
Until you fell, and rose in a huff,

And declared the game was too rude and rough.
Poor boy! What a pity he isn't tough!

ALL.

Ha! ha! ha! what a pretty boy!
Papa's delight, and mamma's joy!
Wouldn't he like to go to bed,
And have a cabbage-leaf on his head?

JOSEPH.

Laugh, if you like to! Laugh till you're grey;
But I guess you'd laugh another way
If you'd hit your toe, and fallen like me,
And cut a bloody gash in your knee,
And bumped your nose and bruised your shin,
Tumbled over the rolling-pin
That rolled to the floor in the awful din
That followed the fall of the row of tin
That stood upon the dresser.

SAMUEL.

Guess again—dear little guesser!
You wouldn't catch this boy lopping his wing,
Or whining over anything.
So stir your stumps,
Forget your bumps,
Get out of your dumps,
And up and at it again;
For the clock is striking ten,
And Ruth will come pretty soon and say
"Go to your beds
You sleepy heads!"
So—quick! What shall we play?

REBEKAH.

I wouldn't play any more,
For Joseph is tired and sore
With his fall upon the floor.

ALL.

Then he shall tell a story.

JOSEPH.

About old Mother Morey?

ALL.

No! Tell us another.

JOSEPH.

About my brother?

REBEKAH.

Now, Joseph, you shall be good,
And do as you'd be done by;
We didn't mean to be rude
When you fell and began to cry;
We wanted to make you forget your pain;
But it frets you, and we'll not laugh again.

JOSEPH.

Well, if you'll all sit still,
And not be frisking about,
Nor utter a whisper till
You've heard my story out,
I'll tell you a tale as weird
As ever you heard in your lives,
Of a man with a long blue beard,
And the way he treated his wives.

ALL.

Oh, that will be nice!
We'll be still as mice.

JOSEPH.

[*Relates the old story of Blue Beard, and* DAVID *and* RUTH *enter from the cellar unperceived.*

Centuries since there flourished a man,
(A cruel old Tartar as rich as the Khan,)

Whose castle was built on a splendid plan,
  With gardens and groves and plantations ;
But his shaggy beard was as blue as the sky,
And he lived alone, for his neighbors were shy,
And had heard hard stories, by the by,
  About his domestic relations.

Just on the opposite side of the plain
A widow abode, with her daughters twain ;
And one of them—neither cross nor vain—
  Was a beautiful little treasure ;
So he sent them an invitation to tea,
And having a natural wish to see
His wonderful castle and gardens, all three
  Said they'd do themselves the pleasure.

As soon as there happened a pleasant day,
They dressed themselves in a sumptuous way,
And rode to the castle as proud and gay
  As silks and jewels could make them ;

And they were received in the finest style,
And saw everything that was worth their while,
In the halls of Blue Beard's grand old pile,
  Where he was so kind as to take them.

The ladies were all enchanted quite ;
For they found old Blue Beard so polite
That they did not suffer at all from fright,
  And frequently called thereafter ;
Then he offered to marry the younger one,
And as she was willing the thing was done,
And celebrated by all the ton
  With feasting and with laughter.

As kind a husband as ever was seen
Was Blue Beard then, for a month, I ween ;
And she was as proud as any queen,
  And as happy as she could be, too ;
But her husband called her to him one day,
And said, " My dear, I am going away ;

It will not be long that I shall stay ;
  There is business for me to see to.

"The keys of my castle I leave with you ;
But if you value my love, be true,
And forbear to enter the Chamber of Blue !
  Farewell, Fatima ! Remember !"
Fatima promised him ; then she ran
To visit the rooms with her sister Ann ;
But when she had finished the tour, she began
  To think about the Blue Chamber.

Well, the woman was curiously inclined,
So she left her sister and prudence behind,
(With a little excuse) and started to find
  The mystery forbidden.
She paused at the door ;—all was still as night !
She opened it ; then through the dim blue light
There blistered her vision the horrible sight
  That was in that chamber hidden.

The room was gloomy and damp and wide,
And the floor was red with the bloody tide
From headless women, laid side by side,
  The wives of her lord and master!
Frightened and fainting, she dropped the key,
But seized it and lifted it quickly; then she
Hurried as swiftly as she could flee
  From the scene of the disaster.

She tried to forget the terrible dead,
But shrieked when she saw that the key was red,
And sickened and shook with an awful dread
  When she heard Blue Beard was coming.
He did not appear to notice her pain;
But he took his keys, and seeing the stain,
He stopped in the middle of the refrain
  That he had been quietly humming.

"Mighty well, madam!" said he, "mighty well!
What does this little blood-stain tell?
You've broken your promise; prepare to dwell

With the wives I've had before you!
You've broken your promise, and you shall die."
Then Fatima, supposing her death was nigh,
Fell on her knees and began to cry,
"Have mercy, I implore you!"

"No!" shouted Blue Beard, drawing his sword;
"You shall die this very minute," he roared.
"Grant me time to prepare to meet my Lord,"
The terrified woman entreated.
"Only ten minutes," he roared again;
And holding his watch by its great gold chain,
He marked on the dial the fatal ten.
And retired till they were completed.

"Sister, oh sister, fly up to the tower!
Look for release from this murderer's power!
Our brothers should be here this very hour;
Speak! Does there come assistance!"
"No: I see nothing but sheep on the hill."
"Look again, sister!" "I'm looking still,

But naught can I see, whether good or ill,
Save a flurry of dust in the distance."

"Time's up!" shouted Blue Beard, out from his room;
"This moment shall witness your terrible doom,
And give you a dwelling within the room
Whose secrets you have invaded."
"Comes there no help for my terrible need?"
"There are horsemen twain riding hither with speed."
"Oh! tell them to ride very fast indeed,
Or I must meet death unaided."

"Time's fully up! Now have done with your prayer,"
Shouted Blue Beard, swinging his sword on the stair;
Then he entered, and grasped her beautiful hair,
Swung his glittering weapon around him;
But a loud knock rang at the castle gate,

And Fatima was saved from her horrible fate.
For shocked with surprise. he paused too late;
  And then the two soldiers found him.

They were her brothers, and quick as they knew
What the fiend was doing, their swords they drew,
And attacked him fiercely, and ran him through,
  So that soon he was mortally wounded.
With a wild remorse was his conscience filled
When he thought of the hapless wives he had killed;
But quickly the last of his blood was spilled,
  And his dying groan was sounded.

As soon as Fatima recovered from fright,
She embraced her brothers with great delight;
And they were as glad and as grateful quite
  As she was glad and grateful.
Then they all went out from that scene of pain,
And sought in quietude to regain
Their minds, which had come to be quite insane,
  In a place so horrid and hateful.

'Twas a private funeral Blue Beard had;
For the people knew he was very bad,
And, though they said nothing, they all were glad
  For the fall of the evil-doer;
But Fatima first ordered some graves to be made,
And there the unfortunate ladies were laid,
And after some painful months, with the aid
  Of her friends, her spirits came to her.

Then she cheered the hearts of the suffering poor,
And an acre of land around each door,
And a cow and a couple of sheep, or more,
  To her tenantry she granted.
So all of them had enough to eat,
And their love for her was so complete
They would kiss the dust from her little feet,
  Or do anything she wanted.

SAMUEL.

Capital! Capital! Wasn't it good!

I should like to have been her brother;
And if I had been, you may guess there would
Have been little work for the other.
I'd have run him right through the heart, just so!
And cut off his head at a single blow,
And killed him so quickly he'd never know
What it was that struck him, wouldn't I Joe?

JOSEPH.

You are very brave with your bragging tongue;
But if you had been there, you'd have sung
A very different tune.
Poor Blue Beard! He would have been afraid
Of a little boy with a penknife blado,
Or a tiny pewter spoon!

SAMUEL.

It makes no difference what you say
(Pretty little boy, afraid to play!)

But it served him rightly any way.
  And gave him just his due.
And wasn't it good that his little wife
Should live in his castle the rest of her life,
  And have all his money too ?

REBEKAH.

I'm thinking of the ladies who
Were lying in the Chamber Blue,
With all their small necks cut in two.

I see them lying, half a score,
In a long row upon the floor,
Their cold, white bosoms marked with gore

I know the sweet Fatima would
Have put their heads on if she could ;
And made them live—she was so good ;

And washed their faces at the sink;
But Blue Beard was not sane, I think;
I wonder if he did not drink!

For no man in his proper mind
Would be so cruelly inclined
As to kill ladies who were kind.

RUTH.

[*Stepping forward with* DAVID.

Story and comment alike are bad;
These little follows are raving mad
  With thinking what they should do,
Supposing their sunny-eyed sister had
Given her heart—and her head—to a lad
  Like the man with the Beard of Blue.
    Each little jacket
    Is now a packet
  Of murderous thoughts and fancies;
    Oh, the gentle trade
    By which fiends are made

With the ready aid
Of these bloody old romances!
And the little girl takes the woman's turn,
And thinks that the old curmudgeon
Who owned a castle, and rolled in gold
Over fields and gardens manifold,
And kept in his house a family tomb,
With his bowling course and his billiard-room,
Where he could preserve his precious dead,
Who took the kiss of the bridal bed
From one who straightway took their head,
And threw it away with the pair of gloves
In which he wedded his hapless loves,
Had some excuse for his dudgeon.

DAVID.

We learn by contrast to admire
The beauty that enchains us;
And know the object of desire
By that which pains us.

The roses blushing at the door,
The lapse of leafy June,
The singing birds, the sunny shore,
The summer moon :—

All these entrance the eye or ear
By innate grace and charm ;
But o'er them reaching through the year
Hangs Winter's arm,

To give to memory the sign,
The index of our bliss,
And show by contrast how divine
The summer is.

From chilling blasts and stormy skies.
Bare hills and icy streams,
Touched into fairest life arise
Our summer dreams.

And virtue never seems so fair
  As when we lift our gaze
From the red eyes and bloody hair
    That vice displays.

We are too low,—our eyes too dark
  Love's height to estimate,
Save as we note the sunken mark
    Of brutal Hate.

So this ensanguined tale shall move
  Aright each little dreamer,
And Blue Beard teach them how to love
    The sweet Fatima.

They hate his crimes, and it is well;
  They pity those who died;
Their sense of justice when he fell
    Was satisfied.

No fierce revenges are the fruit
Of their just indignation;
They sit in judgment on the brute,
And condemnation;

And turn to her, his rescued wife,
Her deeds so kind and human;
And love the beauty of her life,
And bless the woman.

RUTH.

That is the way I suppose you would twist it;
And now that the boys are disposed of,
And the moral so handsomely closed off,
What do you say of the girl? That she missed it
When she thought of old Blue Beard as some do of
Judas,
Who with this notion essay to delude us:
That when he relented,
And fiercely repented,

He was hardly so bad
As he commonly had
The fortune to be represented?

DAVID.

The noblest pity in the earth
Is that bestowed on sin.
The Great Salvation had its birth
That ruth within.

The girl is nearest God, in fact;
The boy gives crime its due;
She blames the author of the act,
And pities too.

Thus, from this strange excess of wrong,
Her tender heart has caught
The noblest truth, the sweetest song,
The Saviour taught.

So, more than measured homily,
Of sage, or priest, or preacher,
Is this wild tale of cruelty
Love's gentle teacher.

It tells of sin, its deep remorse,
Its fitting recompense,
And vindicates the tardy course
Of Providence.

These boyish bosoms are on fire
With chivalric possession,
And burn with just and manly ire
Against oppression.

The glory and the grace of life,
And love's surpassing sweetness,
Rise from the monster to the wife
In high completeness;

And thence look down with mercy's eye
  On sin's accurst abuses,
And seek to wrest from charity
    Some fair excuses.

RUTH.

  These greedy mouths are watering
For the fruit within the basket;
And although they will not ask it,
Their jack-knives all are burning
And their eager hands are yearning
  For the peeling and the quartering.
So let us have done with our talk;
For they are too tired to say their prayers,
And the time is come they should walk
From the story below to the story up stairs.

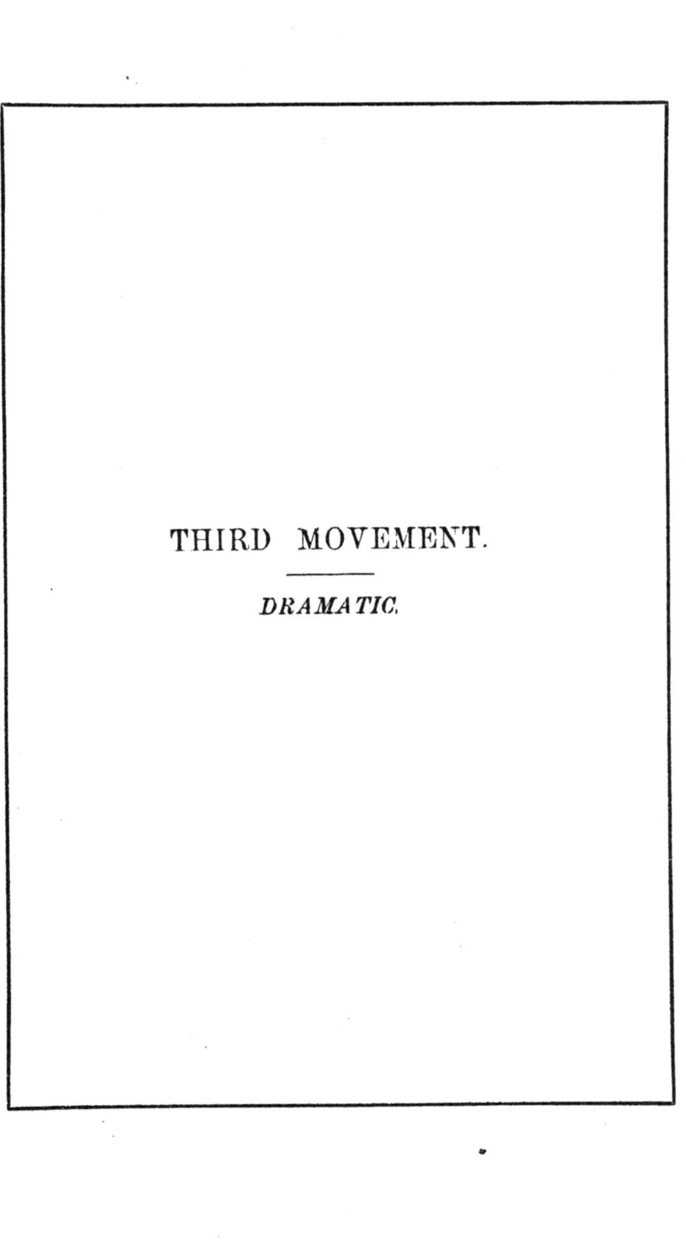

THIRD MOVEMENT.

DRAMATIC.

THE THIRD MOVEMENT.

LOCALITY—*The Kitchen.*

PRESENT—DAVID, RUTH, JOHN, PETER, PRUDENCE *and* PATIENCE.

THE QUESTION ILLUSTRATED BY THE DENOUEMENT.

JOHN.

Since the old gentleman retired to bed,
Things have gone strangely. David, here, and Ruth,
Have wasted thirty minutes underground
In explorations. One would think the house
Covered the entrance of the Mammoth Cave,
And they had lost themselves. Mary and Grace

Still hold their chamber and their conference,
And pour into each other's greedy ears
Their stream of talk, whose low, monotonous hum,
Would lull to slumber any storm but this.
The children are play-tired and gone to bed;
And one may know by looking round the room
Their place of sport was here. And we, plain folk,
Who have no gift of speech, especially
On themes which we and none may understand,
Have yawned and nodded in the great square room,
And wondered if the parted family
Would ever meet again.

RUTH.

John, do you see
The apples and the cider on the hearth?
If I remember rightly, you discuss
Such themes as these with noticeable zest
And pleasant tokens of intelligence;

Rather preferring scanty company
To the full circle. So, sir, take the lead,
And help yourself.

JOHN.

Aye! That I will, and give
Your welcome invitation currency,
In the old-fashioned way. Come! Help yourselves!

DAVID.

[*Looking out of the window.*

The ground is thick with sleet, and still it falls!
The atmosphere is plunging like the sea
Against the woods, and pouring on the night
The roar of breakers, while the blinding spray
O'erleaps the barrier, and comes drifting on
In lines as level as the window-bars.
What curious visions, in a night like this,
Will the eye conjure from the rocks and trees.
And zigzag fences! I was almost sure

I saw a man staggering along the road
A moment since; but instantly the shape
Dropped from my sight. Hark! Was not that a
call—
A human voice? There's a conspiracy
Between my eyes and ears to play me tricks,
Else wanders there abroad some hapless soul
Who needs assistance. There he stands again,
And with unsteady essay strives to breast
The tempest. Hush! Did you not hear that cry?
Quick, brothers! We must out, and give our aid.
None but a dying and despairing man
Ever gave utterance to a cry like that.
Nay, wait for nothing. Follow me!

RUTH.

Alas!
Who can he be, who on a night like this,
And on this night, of all nights in the year,
Holds to the highway, homeless?

PRUDENCE.

Probably
Some neighbor started from his home in quest
Of a physician ; or, more likely still,
Some poor inebriate, sadly overcome
By his sad keeping of the holiday.
I hope they'll give him quarters in the barn ;
If he sleep here, there'll be no sleep for me.

PATIENCE.

I'll not believe it was a man at all ;
David and Ruth are always seeing things
That no one else sees.

RUTH.

I see plainly now
What we shall all see plainly, soon enough.
The man is dead, and they are bearing him
As if he were a log. Quick ! Stir the fire,

And clear the settle! We must lay him there.
I will bring cordials, and flannel stuffs
With which to chafe him; open wide the door.

[*The men enter, bearing a body apparently lifeless, which they lay upon the settle.*

DAVID.

Now do my bidding, orderly and swift;
And we may save from death a fellow man.
Peter, relieve him of those frozen shoes,
And wrap his feet in flannel. This way, Ruth!
Administer that cordial yourself.
John, you are strong, and that rough hand of yours
Will chafe him well. Work with a will, I say!

* * * * * *

My hand is on his heart, and I can feel
Both warmth and motion. If we persevere,
He will be saved. Work with a will, I say!

* * * * * *

A groan? Ha! That is good. Another groan?
Better and better!

RUTH.

It is down at last !—
A spoonful of the cordial. His breath
Comes feebly, but is warm upon my hand.

DAVID.

Give him brisk treatment, and persistent, too ;
And we shall be rewarded presently,
For there is life in him.

* * * * * *

He moves his lips
And tries to speak.

* * * * * *

And now he opens his eyes.
What eyes ! How wandering and wild they are !

[*To the stranger.*

We are your friends. We found you overcome
By the cold storm without, and brought you in.
We are your friends, I say ; so be at ease,

And let us do according to your need.
What is your wish?

STRANGER.

My friends? O God in Heaven!
They've cheated me! I'm in the hospital.
Oh, it was cruel to deceive me thus!
No, you are not my friends. What bitter pain
Racks my poor body!

DAVID.

Poor man, how he raves!
Let us be silent while the warmth and wine
Provoke his sluggish blood to steady flow,
And each dead sense comes back to life again,
O'er the same path of torture which it trod
When it went out from him. He'll slumber soon,
And, when he wakens, we may talk with him.

PRUDENCE.

[*Sotto voce.*

Shall I not call the family? I think
Mary and Grace must both be very cold;
And they know nothing of this strange affair.
I'll wait them at the landing, and secure
Their silent entrance.

DAVID.

If it please you—well.

[PRUDENCE *retires, and returns with* GRACE *and* MARY.

MARY.

Why! We heard nothing of it—Grace and I:—
What a cadaverous hand! How blue and thin!

DAVID.

At his first wild awaking he bemoaned
His fancied durance in a hospital;

And since he spoke so strangely, I have thought
He may have fled a mad-house. Matters not!
We've done our duty, and preserved his life.

MARY.

Shall I disturb him if I look at him?
I'm strangely curious to see his face.

DAVID.

Go. Move you carefully, and bring us word
Whether he sleeps.

[MARY *rises, goes to the settle, and sinks back fainting.*

Why! What ails the girl?
I thought her nerves were iron. Dash her brow
And bathe her temples!

MARY.

There—there,—that will do.
'Tis over now.

DAVID.

The man is speaking. Hush !

STRANGER.

Oh, what a heavenly dream ! But it is past,
Like all my heavenly dreams, for never more
Shall dream entrance me. Death has never dreams,
But everlasting wakefulness. The eye
Of the quick spirit that has dropped the flesh
May close no more in slumber.

* * * * *

I must die !
This painless spell which binds my weary limbs—
This peace ineffable of soul and sense—
Is dissolution's herald, and gives note
That life is conquered and the struggle o'er.
But I had hoped to see her ere I died ;
To kneel for pardon, and implore one kiss,
Pledge to my soul that in the coming heaven
We should not meet as strangers, but rejoin

Our hearts and lives so madly sundered here,
Through fault and freak of mine. But it is well;
God's will be done!

* * * * * *

I dreamed that I had reached
The old red farm-house,—that I saw the light
Flaming as brightly as in other times
It flushed the kitchen windows; and that forms
Were sliding to and fro in joyous life,
Restless to give me welcome. Then I dreamed
Of the dear woman who went out with me
One sweet spring morning, in her own sweet spring,
To——wretchedness and ruin! Oh, forgive—
Dear, pitying Christ, forgive this cruel wrong,
And let me die! Oh, let me—let me die!
Mary! my Mary! Could you only know
How I have suffered since I fled from you,—
How I have sorrowed through long months of pain,
And prayed for pardon,—you would pardon me.

DAVID.

[Sotto voce.

Mary, what means this? Does he dream alone,
Or are we dreaming?

MARY.

Edward, I am here!
I am your Mary! Know you not my face?
My husband, speak to me! Oh, speak once more!
This is no dream, but kind reality.

EDWARD.

[Raising himself, and looking wildly around.

You, Mary? Is this heaven, and am I dead?
I did not know you died: when did you die?
And John and Peter, Grace and little Ruth
Grown to a woman; are they all with you?
'Tis very strange! O pity me, my friends!
For God has pitied me, and pardoned, too:

Else I should not be here. Nay, you seem cold,
And look on me with sad severity.
Have you no pardoning word—no smile for me?

MARY.

This is not Heaven's but Earth's reality;
This is the farm-house—these your wife and friends.
I hold your hand, and I forgive you all.
Pray you recline! You are not strong enough
To bear this yet.

EDWARD.

[Sinking back.

O toiling heart! O sick and sinking heart!
Give me one hour of service, ere I die!
This is no dream. This hand is precious flesh,
And I am here where I have prayed to be.
My God, I thank thee! Thou hast heard my prayer,
And, in its answer, given me a pledge
Of the acceptance of my penitence.

How have I yearned for this one priceless hour !
Cling to me, dearest, while my feet go down
Into the silent stream ; nor loose your hold,
Till angels clasp me on the other side.

MARY.

Edward, you are not dying—must not die ;
For only now are we prepared to live.
You must have quiet, and a night of rest.
Be silent, if you love me !

EDWARD.

If I love ?
Ah, Mary ! never till this blessed hour,
When power and passion, lust and pride are gone,
Have I perceived what wedded love may be ;—
Unutterable fondness, soul for soul ;
Profoundest tenderness between two hearts
Allied by nature, interlocked by life.

I know that I shall die ; but the low clouds
That closed my mental vision have retired,
And left a sky as clear and calm as Heaven.
I must talk now, or never more on earth :
So do not hinder me.

MARY.

[*Weeping.*

Have you a wish
That I can gratify ? Have you any words
To send to other friends ?

EDWARD.

I have no friends
But you and these, and only wish to leave
My worthless name and memory redeemed
Within your hearts to pitying respect.
I have no strength, and it becomes me not,
To tell the story of my life of sin.
I was a drunkard, thief, adulterer ;

And fled from shame, with shame, to find remorse
I had but few months of debauchery,
Pursued with mad intent to damp or drown
The flames of a consuming conscience, when
My body, poisoned, crippled by disease,
Refused the guilty service of my soul,
And at mid-day fell prone upon the street.
Thence I was carried to a hospital,
And there I woke to that delirium
Which none but drunkards this side of the pit
May even dream of.

But at last there came,
With abstinence and kindly medicines,
Release from pain, and peaceful sanity:
And then Christ found me, ready for His hand.
I was not ready for Him when He came
And asked me for my youth; and when He knocked
At my heart's door in manhood's early prime
With tenderest monitions, I debarred

His waiting feet with promise and excuse;
And when, in after years, absorbed in sin,
The gentle summons swelled to thunderings
That echoed through the chambers of my soul
With threats of vengeance, I shut up my ears;
And then He went away, and let me rush
Without arrest, or protest, toward the pit.
I made swift passage downward, till, at length,
I had become a miserable wreck—
Pleasure behind me; only pain before;
My life lived out; the fires of passion dead;
Without a friend; no pride, no power, no hope;
No motive in me, e'en to wish for life.
Then, as I said, Christ came, with stern and sad
Reminders of His mercy and my guilt,
And the door fell before Him.

I went out,
And trod the wildernesses of remorse
For many days. Then from their outer verge,

Tortured and blinded, I plunged madly down
Into the sullen bosom of despair;
But strength from Heaven was given me, and preserved
Breath in my bosom, till a light streamed up
Upon the other shore, and I struck out
On the cold waters, struggling for my life.
Fainting I reached the beach, and on my knees
Climbed up the thorny hill of penitence,
Till I could see, upon its distant brow,
The Saviour beck'ning. Then I ran—I flew—
And grasped his outstretched hand. It lifted me
High on the everlasting rock, and then
It folded me, with all my griefs and tears,
My sin-sick body and my guilt-stained soul,
To the great heart that throbs for all the world.

MARY.

Dear Lord, I bless thee! Thou hast heard my prayer,

And saved the wanderer! Hear it once again,
And lengthen out the life thou hast redeemed!

EDWARD.

Mary, my wife, forbear! I may not give
Response to such petition. I have prayed
That I may die. When first the love Divine
Received me on its bosom, and in mine
I felt the springing of another life,
I begged the Lord to grant me two requests—
The first that I might die, and in that world
Where passion sleeps, and only influence
From Him and those who cluster at His throne
Breathes on the soul, the germ of His great life,
Bursting within me, might be perfected.
The second, that your life, my love, and mine,
Might be once more united on the earth
In holy marriage, and that mine might be
Breathed out at last within your loving arms.

One prayer is granted, and the other waits
But a brief space for its accomplishment.

MARY.

But why this prayer to die ? Still loving me,—
With the great motive for desiring life,
And the deep secret of enjoyment won,—
Why pray for death ?

EDWARD.

Do you not know me, Mary ?
I am afraid to live, for I am weak.
I've found a treasure only life can steal ;
I've won a jewel only death will keep.
In such a heart as mine, the priceless pearl
Would not be safe. That which I would not take
When health was with me,—which I spurned away
So long as I had power to sin, I fear
Would be surrendered with that power's return,
And the temptation to its exercise.
For soul like mine, diseased in every part,

There is but one condition in which grace
May give it service. For my malady
The Great Physician draws the blood away
That only flows to feed its baleful fires;
For only thus the balsam and the balm
May touch the springs of healing.

So I pray
To be delivered from myself,—to be
Delivered from necessity of ill,—
To be secured from bringing harm to you.
Oh, what a boon is death to the sick soul!
I greet it with a joy that passes speech.
Were the whole world to come before me now,—
Wealth with its treasures; Pleasure with its cup;
Power robed in purple; Beauty in its pride,
And with Love's sweetest blossoms garlanded;
Fame with its bays, and Glory with its crown,
To tempt me lifeward, I would turn away,
And stretch my hands with utter eagerness

Toward the pale angel waiting for me now,
And give my hand to him, to be led out,
Serenely singing, to the land of shade.

MARY.

Edward, I yield you. I would not retain
One who has strayed so long from God and heaven,
When his weak feet have found the only path
Open for such as he.

EDWARD.

My strength recedes;
But ere it fail, tell me how fares your life.
You have seen sorrow ; but it comforts me
To hear the language of a chastened soul
From one perverted by my guilty hand.
You speak the dialect of the redeemed—
The Heaven-accepted. Tell me it is so,
And you are happy.

MARY.

With sweet hope and trust
I may reply, 'tis as you think and wish.
I have seen sorrow, surely, and the more
That I have seen what was far worse; but God
Sent his own servant to me to restore
My sadly straying feet to the sure path;
And in my soul I have the pledge of grace
Which shall suffice to keep them there.

EDWARD.

Ah, joy!
You found a friend; and my o'erflowing heart,
Welling with gratitude, pours out to him
For his kind ministry its fitting meed.
Oh, breathe his name to me, that my poor lips
May bind it to a benison, and that,
While dying, I may whisper it with those—
Jesus and Mary—which I love the best.
Name him, I pray you.

MARY

You would ask of me
To bear your thanks to him, and to rehearse
Your dying words?

GRACE.

He asks your good friend's name;
You do not understand him.

MARY.

It is hard
To give denial to a dying wish;
But, Edward, I've no right to speak his name.
He was a Christian man, and you may give
Of the full largess of your gratitude
All, without robbing God, you have to give,
And fail, e'en then, of worthy recompense.

EDWARD.

Your will is mine.

GRACE.

Nay, Mary, tell it him!
Where is he going he should bruit the name?
Remember where he lies, and that no ears
Save those of angels——

MARY.

There are others here
Who may not hear it.

RUTH.

We will all retire.
It is not proper we should linger here,
Barring the sacred confidence of hearts
Parting so sadly.

DAVID.

Mary, you must yield,
Nor keep the secret longer from your friends.

MARY.

David, you know not what you say.

DAVID.

I know;
So give the dying man no more delay.

MARY.

I will declare it under your command.
This stranger friend—stranger for many months—
This man, selectest instrument of Heaven,
Who gave me succor in my hour of need,
Snatched me from ruin, rescued me from want,
Counselled and cheered me, prayed with me, and then
Led me with careful hand into the light,
Was he now bending over you in tears—
David, my brother!

EDWARD.

Blessed be his name!
Brother by every law, above—below!

GRACE.

[*Pale and trembling.*

David? My husband? Did I hear aright?
You are not jesting! Sure you would not jest
At such a juncture! Speak, my husband, speak!
Is this a plot to cheat a dying man,
Or cheat a wife who, if it be no plot,
Is worthy death? What can you mean by this?

MARY.

Not more nor less than my true words convey.

GRACE.

Nay, David, tell me!

DAVID.

Mary's words are truth.

GRACE.

O mean and jealous heart, what hast thou done!
What wrong to honor, spite to Christian love,

Dear Husband ! David ! Look upon your wife !

And shame to self beyond self-pardoning !
How can I ever lift my faithless eyes
To those true eyes that I have counted false ;
Or meet those lips that I have charged with lies;
Or win the dear embraces I have spurned ?
O most unhappy, most unworthy wife !
No one but he who still has clung to thee,—
Proud, and imperious, and impenitent,—
No one but he who has in silence borne
Thy peevish criminations and complaints
Can now forgive thee, when in deepest shame
Thou bowest with confession of thy faults.
Dear husband ! David ! Look upon your wife !
Behold one kneeling never knelt to you !
I have abused you and your faithful love,
And in my great humiliation, pray
You will not trample me beneath your feet.
Pity my weakness, and remember, too,
That Love was jealous of thee, and not Hate—
That it was Love's own pride tormented me.

My husband, take me once more to your arms,
And kiss me in forgiveness ; say that you
Will be my counsellor, my friend, my love ;
And I will give myself to you again,
To be all yours—my reason, confidence,
My faith and trust all yours, my heart's best love,
My service and my prayers, all yours—all yours !

DAVID.

Rise, dearest, rise ! It gives me only pain
That such as you should kneel to such as I.
Your words inform me that you know how weak
I am whom you have only fancied weak.
Forgive you ? I forgive you everything :
And take the pardon which your prayer insures.
Let this embrace, this kiss, be evidence
Our jarring hearts catch common rhythm again,
And we are lovers.

RUTH.

Hush! You trouble him.
He understands this scene no more than we.
Mary, he speaks to you.

EDWARD.

Dear wife, farewell!
The room grows dim, and silently and soft
The veil is dropping 'twixt my eyes and yours,
Which soon will hide me from you—you from me.
Only one hand is warm; it rests in yours,
Whose full, sweet pulses throb along my arm,
So that I live upon them. Cling to me!
And thus your life, after my life is past,
Shall lay me gently in the arms of Death.
Thus shall you link your being with a soul
Gazing unveiled upon the Great White Throne.

Dear hearts of love surrounding me, farewell!
I cannot see you now; or, if I do,
You are transfigured. There are floating forms

That whisper over me like summer leaves ;
And now there comes, and spreads through all my
soul
Delicious influx of another life,
From out whose essence spring, like living flowers,
Angelic senses with quick ultimates,
That catch the rustle of ethereal robes,
And the thin chime of melting ministrelsy—
Rising and falling—answered far away—
As Echo, dreaming in the twilight woods,
Repeats the warble of her twilight birds.
And flowers that mock the Iris toss their cups
In the impulsive ether, and spill out
Sweet tides of perfume, fragrant deluges,
Flooding my spirit like an angel's breath.

* * * * * *

And still the throng increases ; still unfold
With broader span and more elusive sweep
The radiant vistas of a world divine.
But O my soul ! what vision rises now !

Far, far away, white blazing like the sun,
In deepest distance and on highest height,
Through walls diaphanous, and atmosphere
Flecked with unnumbered forms of missive power,
Out-going fleetly and returning slow,
A presence shines I may not penetrate ;
But on a throne, with smile ineffable,
I see a form my conscious spirit knows.
Jesus, my Saviour ! Jesus, Lamb of God !
Jesus who taketh from me all my sins,
And from the world ! Jesus, I come to Thee !
Come Thou to me ! O come, Lord, quickly ! Come!

DAVID.

Flown on the wings of rapture ! Is this death ?
His heart is still ; his beaded brow is cold ;
His wasted breast struggles for breath no more ;
And his pale features, hardened with the stress
Of Life's resistance, momently subside
Into a smile, calm as a twilight lake,

Sprent with the images of rising stars.
We have seen Evil in his countless forms
In these poor lives ; have met his armed hosts
In dread encounter and discomfiture ;
And languished in captivity to them,
Until we lost our courage and our faith ;
And here we see their Chieftain—Terror's King !
He cuts the knot that binds a weary soul
To faithless passions, sateless appetites,
And powers perverted, and it flies away
Singing toward Heaven. He turns and looks at us,
And finds us weeping with our gratitude —
Full of sweet sorrow,—sorrow sweeter far
Than the supremest ecstasy of joy.

And this is death ! Think you that raptured soul,
Now walking humbly in the golden streets,
Bearing the precious burden of a love
Too great for utterance, or with hushed heart
Drinking the music of the ransomed throng,

Counts death an evil?—evil, sickness, pain,
Calamity, or aught that God prescribed
To cure it of its sin, or bring it where
The healing hand of Christ might touch it? No!
He is a man to-night—a man in Christ.
This was his childhood, here; and as we give
A smile of wonder to the little woes
That drew the tears from out our own young eyes—
The kind corrections and severe constraints
Imposed by those who loved us—so he sees
A father's chastisement in all the ill
That filled his life with darkness; so he sees
In every evil a kind instrument
To chasten, elevate, correct, subdue,
And fit him for that heavenly estate—
Saintship in Christ—the Manhood Absolute!

L'ENVOY.

MIDNIGHT and silence! In the West unveiled,
The broad full moon is shining, with the stars.
On mount and valley, forest, roof, and rock,
On billowy hills smooth-stretching to the sky,
On rail and wall, on all things far and near,
Cling the bright crystals,—all the earth a floor
Of polished silver, pranked with bending forms
Uplifting to the light their precious weight
Of pearls and diamonds, set in palest gold.
The storm is dead; and when it rolled away
It took no star from heaven, but left to earth
Such legacy of beauty as the wind—
The light-robed shepherdess from Cuban groves-
Driving soft showers before her, and warm airs,
And her wide-scattered flocks of wet-winged birds,

Never bestowed upon the waiting Spring.
Pale, silent, smiling, cold, and beautiful!
Do storms die thus? And is it this to die?

Midnight and silence! In that hallowed room
God's full-orbed peace is shining, with the stars.
On head and hand, on brow, and lip, and eye,
On folded arms, on broad unmoving breast,
On the white-sanded floor, on everything,
Rests the pale radiance, while bending forms
Stand all around, loaded with precious weight
Of jewels such as holy angels wear.
The man is dead; and when he passed away
He blotted out no good, but left behind
Such wealth of faith, such store of love and trust,
As breath of joy, in-floating from the isles
Smiled on by ceaseless summer, and endued
With foliage and flowers perennial,
Never conveyed to the enchanted soul.
Do men die thus? And is it this to die?

Midnight and silence! At each waiting bed
Husband and wife, embracing, kneel in prayer;
And lips unused to such a benison
Breathe blessings upon evil, and give thanks
For knowledge of its sacred ministry.
An infant nestles on a mother's breast,
Whose head is pillowed where it has not lain
For months of wasted life—the tale all told,
And confidence and love for-aye secure.

The widow and the virgin; where are they?
The morn shall find them watching with the dead,
Like the two angels at the tomb of Christ,—
One at the head, the other at the foot,—
Guarding a sepulchre whose occupant
Has risen, and rolled the heavy stone away!

THE END.

KATHRINA.

KATHRINA.

A TRIBUTE.

More human, more divine than we—
  In truth all human, all divine—
Is woman, when good stars agree
  To temper with their beams benign
The hour of her nativity.

The fairest flower the green earth bears,
  Bright with the dew and light of heaven,
Is, of the double life she wears,
  The type, in grace and glory given
By soil and sun in equal shares.

True sister of the Son of Man:
  True sister of the Son of God:
What marvel that she leads the van
  Of those who in the path He trod,
Still bear the cross and wear the ban?

If God be in the sky and sea,
  And live in light and ride the storm,
Then God is God, although He be
  Enshrined within a woman's form,
And claims glad reverence from me.

So, as I worship Him in Christ,
  And in the Forms of Earth and Air,
I worship Him imparadised,
  And throned within her bosom fair
Whom vanity hath not enticed.

O! woman—mother! Woman—wife!—
  The sweetest names that language knows!
Thy breast, with holy motives rife,
  With holiest affection glows,
Thou queen, thou angel of my life!

Noble and fine in his degree
  Is the best man my heart receives ;
And this my heart's supremest plea
  For him : he feels, acts, lives, believes,
And seems, and is, the likest thee.

O men ! O brothers ! Well I know
  That with her nature in our souls
Is born the elemental woe—
  The brutal impulse that controls,
And drives, or drags, the godlike low.

Ambition, appetite and pride—
  These throng and thrall the hearts of men ;
These plat the thorns, and pierce the side
  Of Him who, in our souls again,
Is spit upon, and crucified.

The greed for gain, the thirst for power,
  The lust that blackens while it burns :
Ah ! these the whitest souls deflour !
  And one, or all of these by turns,
Rob man of his divinest dower !

Yet man, who shivers like a straw
 Before Temptation's lightest breeze,
Assumes the master—gives the law
 To her who, on her bended knees,
Resists the black-winged thunder-flaw !

To him who deems her weak and vain,
 And boasts his own exceeding might,
She clings through darkest fortune fain ;
 Still loyal, though the ruffian smite ;
Still true, though crime his hands distain !

And is this weakness ? Is it not
 The strength of God, that loves and bears
Though He be slighted or forgot
 In damning crimes, or driving cares,
And closest clings in darkest lot ?

Not many friends my life has made ;
 Few have I loved, and few are they
Who in my hand their hearts have laid ;
 And these were women. I am gray,
But never have I been betrayed.

These words—this tribute—for the sake
  Of truth to God and womankind!
These—that my heart may cease to ache
  With love and gratitude confined,
And burning from my lips to break!

These—to that sisterhood of grace
  That numbers in its sacred list
My mother, risen to her place;
  My wife, but yester-morning kissed,
And folded in Love's last embrace!

This tribute of a love profound
  As ever moved the heart of man,
To those to whom my life is bound,
  To her in whom my life began,
And her whose love my life hath crowned!

Immortal Love! Thou still hast wings
  To lift me to those radiant fields,
Where Music waits with trembling strings,
  And Verse her happy numbers yields,
And all the soul within me sings.

So from the lovely Pagan dream
  I call no more the Tuneful Nine ;
For Woman is my Muse Supreme ;
  And she with fire and flight divine,
Shall light and lead me to my theme.

PART I.

CHILDHOOD AND YOUTH.

Thou lovely vale of sweetest stream that flows:
Winding and willow-fringed Connecticut!
Swift to thy fairest scenes my fancy flies,
As I recall the story of a life
Which there began in years of sinless hope,
And merged maturely into hopeless sin.

O! golden dawning of a day of storms,
That fell ere noontide into rayless night!
O! beautiful initial, vermil-flowered,
And bright with cherub-eyes and effigies,
To the black-letter volume of my life!

O! faery gateway, gilt and garlanded,
And shining in the sun, to gloomy groves
Of shadowy cypress; and to sunless streams,
Feeding with bane the deadly nightshade's roots,-
To vexing labyrinths of doubt and fear,
And deep abysses of despair and death!
Back to thy peaceful villages and fields,
My memory, like a weary pilgrim, comes
With scrip and burdon, to repose awhile,—
To pluck a daisy from a lonely grave
Where long ago, in common sepulture,
I laid my mother and my faith in God;
To fix the record of a single day
So memorably wonderful and sweet
Its power of inspiration lingers still,—
So full of her dear presence, so divine
With the melodious breathing of her words,
And the warm radiance of her loving smile,
That tears fall readily as April rain
At its recall; to pass in swift review
The years of adolescence, and the paths
Of glare and gloom through which, by passion led,

I reached the fair possession of my power,
And won the dear possession of my love,
And then—farewell!

Queen-village of the meads
Fronting the sunrise and in beauty throned,
With jeweled homes around her lifted brow,
And coronal of ancient forest trees—
Northampton sits, and rules her pleasant realm.
There where the saintly Edwards heralded
The terrors of the Lord, and men bowed low
Beneath the menace of his awful words;
And there where Nature, with a thousand tongues
Tender and true, from vale and mountain-top,
And smiling streams, and landscapes piled afar,
Proclaimed a gentler Gospel, I was born.

In an old home, beneath an older elm—
A fount of weeping greenery, that dripped
Its spray of rain and dew upon the roof—
I opened eyes on life; and now return
Among the visions of my early years,

Two so distinct that all the rest grow dim :
My mother's pale, fond face and tearful eyes,
Bent upon me in Love's absorbing trance,
From the low window where she watched my play ;
And, after this, the wondrous elm, that seemed
To my young fancy like an airy bosk,
Poised by a single stem upon the earth,
And thronged by instant marvels. There in Spring
I heard with joy the cheery blue-bird's note ;
There sang rejoicing robins after rain ;
And there within the emerald twilight, which
Defied the mid-day sun, from bough to bough—
A torch of downy flame—the oriole
Passed to his nest, to feed the censer-fires
Which Love had lit for Airs of Heaven to swing.
There, too, through all the weird September-eves
I heard the harsh, reiterant katydids
Rasp the mysterious silence. There I watched
The glint of stars, playing at hide-and-seek
Behind the swaying foliage, till drawn
By tender hands to childhood's balmy rest.

My Mother and the elm! Too soon I learned
That o'er me hung, and o'er the widowed one
Who gave me birth, with broader boughs,
Haunted by sabler wings and sadder sounds,
A darker shadow than the mighty elm!
I caught the secret in the street from those
Who pointed at me as I passed, or paused
To gaze in sighing pity on my play;
From playmates who, forbidden to divulge
The knowledge they possessed, with childish tricks
Of indirection strove in vain to hide
Their awful meaning in unmeaning phrase;
From kisses which were pitiful; from words
Gentler than love's, because compassionate;
From deep, unconscious sighs out of the heart
Of her who loved me best, and from her tears
That freest flowed when I was happiest.

From frailest filaments of evidence,
From dark allusions faintly overheard,
From hint and look and sudden change of theme
When I approached, from widely scattered words

Remembered well, and gathered all at length
Into consistent terms, I know not how
I wrought the full conclusion, nor how young.
I only know that when a little child
I learned, though no one told, that he who gave
My life to me in madness took his own—
Took it from fear of want, though he possessed
The finest fortune in the rich old town.

Henceforth I had a secret which I kept—
Kept by my mother with as close a tongue—
A secret which imbittered every cup.
It bred rebellion in me—filled my soul,
Opening to life in innocent delight,
With baleful doubt and harrowing distrust.
Why, if my father was the godly man
His gentle widow vouched with tender tears,
Did He to whom she bowed in daily prayer—
Who loved us, as she told me, with a love
Ineffable for strength and tenderness—
Permit such fate to him, such woe to us?
Ah! many a time, repeating on my knees

The simple language of my evening prayer
Which her dear lips had taught me, came the
dark
Perplexing question, stirring in my heart
A sense of guilt, or quenching all my faith.
This, too, I kept a secret. I had died
Rather than breathe the question in her ears
Who knelt beside me. I had rather died
Than add a sorrow to the load she bore.

Taught to be true, I played the hypocrite
In truthfulness to her. I had no God,
No penitence, no loyalty, no love,
For any being higher than herself.
Jealous of all to whom she gave her hand,
I clung to her with fond idolatry.
I sat with her; where'er she walked, I walked;
I kissed away her tears; I strove to fill,
With strange precocity of manly pride
And more than boyish tenderness, the void
Which death had made.

I could not fail to see
That ruth for me and sorrow for her loss--

Twin leeches at her heart—were drinking blood
That, from her pallid features, day by day
Sank slowly down, to feed the cruel draught.
Nay, more than this I saw, and sadly worse.
Oft when I watched her, and she knew it not,
I marked a quivering horror sweep her face—
A strange, quick thrill of pain—that brought her hand
With sudden pressure to her heart, and forced
To her white lips a swiftly whispered prayer.
I fancied that I read the mystery ;
But it was deeper and more terrible
Than I conjectured. Not till darker years
Came the solution.

Still, we had some days
Of pleasure. Sorrow cannot always brood
Over the shivering forms that drink her warmth,
But springs to meet the morning light, and soars
Into the empyrean, to forget
For one sweet hour the ring of greedy mouths
That surely wait, and cry for her return.

My mother's hand in mine, or mine in hers,
We often left the village far behind,
And walked the meadow-paths to gather flowers,
And watch the ploughman as he turned the tilth,
Or tossed his burnished share into the sun
At the long furrow's end, the while we marked
The tipsy bobolink, struggling with the chain
Of tinkling music that perplexed his wings,
And listened to the yellow-breasted lark's
Sweet whistle from the grass.

Glad in my joy,
My mother smiled amid these scenes and sounds,
And wandered on with gentle step and slow,
While I, in boyish frolic, ran before,
Chasing the butterflies, or in her path
Tossing the gaudy gold of buttercups,
Till sometimes, ere we knew, we stood entranced
Upon the river's marge.

Ever the spell
Of lapsing water tamed my playful mood,
And I reclined in silent happiness

At the tired feet that rested in the shade.
There through the long, bright mornings we remained,
Watching the noisy ferry-boat that plied
Like a slow shuttle through the sunny warp
Of threaded silver from a thousand brooks,
That took new beauty as it wound away;
Or gazing where at Holyoke's verdant base—
Like a slim hound, stretched at his master's feet—
Lay the long, lazy hamlet, Hockanum;
Or, upward turning, traced the line that climbed
O'er splintered rock and clustered foliage
To the bare mountain top; then followed down
The scars of fire and storm, or paths of gloom
That marked the curtained gorges, till, at last,
Caught by a wisp of white, belated mist,
Our vision rose to trace its airy flight
Beyond the height, into the distant blue.

One morning, while we rested there, she told
Of a dear friend upon the other side—
A lady who had loved her—whom she loved—

And then she promised to my eager wish
That soon, across the stream I longed to pass,
I should go with her to the lady's home.

The wished-for day came slowly—came at last—
My birthday morning—rounding to their close
The fourteen summers of my boyhood's life.
The early mists were clinging to the side
Of the dark mountain as we left the town,
Though all the roadside fields were quick with toil.
In rhythmic motion through the dewy grass
The mowers swept, and on the fragrant air
Was borne from far the soft, metallic clash
Of stones upon the steel.

This was the day
"So memorably wonderful and sweet
Its power of inspiration lingers still,—
So full of her dear presence, so divine
With the melodious breathing of her words,
And the warm radiance of her loving smile,
That tears fall readily as April rain

At its recall." And with this day there came
The revelation and the genesis
Of a new life. In intellect and heart
I ceased to be a child, and grew a man.
By one long leap I passed the hidden bound
That circumscribed my boyhood, and henceforth
Abjured all childish pleasure, and took on
The purpose and the burden of my life.

We crossed the river—I, as in a dream ;
And when I stood upon the eastern shore,
In the full presence of the mountain pile,
Strange tides of feeling thrilled me, and I wept—
Wept, though I knew not why. I could have knelt
On the white sand, and prayed. Within my soul
Prophetic whispers breathed of coming power
And new possessions. Aspiration swelled
Like a pent stream within a narrow chasm,
That finds nor vent nor overflow, but swirls
And surges and retreats, until it floods
The springs that feed it. All was chaos wild,—
A chaos of fresh passion, undefined,

Deep in whose vortices of mist and fire
A new world waited blindly for its birth
I had no words for revelation ;—none
For answer, when my mother pressed my hand,
And questioned why it trembled. I looked up
With tearful eyes, and met her loving smile,
And both of us were silent, and passed on.

We reached at length the pleasant cottage-home
Where dwelt my mother's friend, and, at the gate,
Found her with warmest welcome waiting us.
She kissed my mother's cheek, and then kissed
mine,
Which shrank, and mantled with a new-born shame.
They crossed the threshold : I remained without,
Surprised—half-angry—with the burning blush
That still o'erwhelmed my face.

I looked around
For something to divert my vexing thoughts,
And saw intently gazing in my eyes,
From his long tether in the grass, a lamb—
A lusty, downy, handsome, household pet.
There was a scarlet ribbon on his neck

Which held a silver bell, whose note I heard
First when his eye met mine; for then he sprang
To greet me with a joyous bleat, and fell,
Thrown by the cord that held him. Pitying him,
I loosed his cruel leashing, with intent,
After a half-hour's frolic, to return
And fasten as I found him; but my hand,
Too careless of its charge, slipped from its hold
With the first bound he made; and with a leap
He cleared the garden wall, and flew away.

Affrighted at my deed and its mischance,
I paused a moment—then with ready feet,
And flush and final impulse, I pursued.

He held the pathway to the mountain woods,
The tinkle of his bell already faint
In the long distance he had placed between
Himself and his pursuer. On and on,
Climbing the mountain path, he sped away,
I following swiftly, never losing sight
Of the bright scarlet streaming from his neck,
Or hearing of the tinkle of his bell,

Till, wearied both, and panting up the steep,
Our progress slackened to a walk.

At length
He paused and looked at me, and waited till
My foot had touched the cord he dragged, and then
Bounded away, scaling the shelvy cliffs
That bolder rose along the narrow path.
He had no choice but mount. I pressed him close,
And rocks and chasms were thick on either side.
So, pausing oft, but ever leaping on
Before my hand could reach him, he advanced.
Not once in all the passage had I paused
To look below, nor had I thought of her
Whom I had left. Absorbed in the pursuit
I pressed it recklessly, until I grasped
My fleecy prisoner, wound and tied his cord
Around my wrist, and both of us sank down
Upon the mountain summit.

In a swoon
Of breathless weariness how long I lay

I could not know; but consciousness at last
Came by my brute companion, who, alert
Among the scanty browse, tugged at my wrist,
And brought me startled to my feet. I saw
In one swift sweep of vision where I stood,—
In presence of what beauty of the earth,
What glory of the sky, what majesty
Of lofty loneliness. I drew the lamb—
The dear, dumb creature—gently to my side,
And led him out upon the beetling cliff
That fronts the plaided meadows, and knelt down.

When once the shrinking, dizzy spell was gone,
I saw below me, like a jeweled cup,
The valley hollowed to its heaven-kissed lip—
The serrate green against the serrate blue—
Brimming with beauty's essence; palpitant
With a divine elixir—lucent floods
Poured from the golden chalice of the sun,
At which my spirit drank with conscious growth,
And drank again with still expanding scope
Of comprehension and of faculty.

I felt the bud of being in me burst
With full, unfolding petals to a rose,
And fragrant breath that flooded all the scene.
By sudden insight of myself I knew
That I was greater than the scene,—that deep
Within my nature was a wondrous world,
Broader than that I gazed on, and informed
With a diviner beauty,—that the things
I saw were but the types of those I held,
And that above them both, High Priest and King,
I stood supreme, to choose and to combine,
And build from that within me and without
New forms of life, with meaning of my own.
And there alone, upon the mountain-top,
Kneeling beside the lamb, I bowed my head
Beneath the chrismal light, and felt my soul
Baptized and set apart to poetry.

The spell of inspiration lingered not;
But ere it passed, I knew my destiny—
The passion and the portion of my life:
Though, with the new-born consciousness of power,

And organizing and creative skill,
There came a sense of poverty—a sense
Of power untrained, of skill without resource,
Of ignorance of Nature and her laws,
And language and the learning of the schools.
I could not rise upon my callow wings,
But felt that I must wait until the years
Should give them plumage, and the skill for flight
Be won by trial.

Then before me rose
The long, long years of study, interposed
Between me and the goal that shone afar;
But with them rose the courage to surmount,
And I was girt for toil.

Then, for the first,
My eye and spirit that had drunk the whole
Wide vision, grew discriminate, and traced
The crystal river pouring from the North
Its twinkling tide, and winding down the vale,
Till, doubling in a serpent coil, it paused

Before the chasm that parts the frontal spurs
Of Tom and Holyoke ; then in wreathing light
Sped the swart rocks, and sought the misty South.
Across the meadows—carpet for the gods,
Woven of ripening rye and greening maize
And rosy clover-blooms, and spotted o'er
With the black shadows of the feathery elms—
Northampton rose, half hidden in her trees,
Lifted above the level of the fields,
And noiseless as a picture.

At my feet
The ferry-boat, diminished to a toy,
With automatic diligence conveyed
Its puppet passengers between the shores
That hemmed its enterprise ; and one low barge,
With white, square sail, bore northward languidly
The slow and scanty commerce of the stream.

Eastward, upon another fertile stretch
Of meadow-sward and tilth, embowered in elms,
Lay the twin streets, and sprang the single spire
Of Hadley, where the hunted regicides

Securely lived of old, and strangely died ;
And eastward still, upon the last green step
From which the Angel of the Morning Light
Leaps to the meadow-lands, fair Amherst sat,
Capped by her many-windowed colleges ;
While from his outpost in the rising North,
Bald with the storms and ruddy with the suns
Of the long eons, stood old Sugarloaf,
Gazing with changeless brow upon a scene,
Changing to fairer beauty evermore.

Save of the river and my pleasant home,
I knew not then the names and history
Borne by these visions ; but upon my brain
Their forms were graved in lines indelible
As, on the rocks beneath my feet, the prints
Of life in its first motion. Later years
Renewed the picture, and its outlines filled
With fair associations,—wrought the past
And living present into fadeless wreaths
That crowned each mound and mount, and town
and tower,

The king of teeming memories. Nor could
I guess with faintest foresight of the life
Which, in the years before me, I should weave
Of mingled threads of pleasure and of pain
Into these scenes, until not one of all
Could meet my eye, or touch my memory
Without recalling an experience
That drank the sweetest ichor of my veins,
Or crowded them with joy.

At length I turned
From the wide survey, and with pleased surprise
Detected, nestling at the mountain's foot,
The cottage I had left; and, on the lawn,
Two forms of life that flitted to and fro.
I knew that they had missed me; so I sought
The passage I had climbed, and, with the lamb
Still fastened to my wrist, I hasted down.

Full of the marvels of the hour I sped,
Leaping from rock to rock, or flying swift
The smoother slopes, with arms half wings, and
feet

That only guarded the descent, the while
My captive led me captive at his will.
So tense the strain of sinew, so intense
The mood and motion, that before I guessed,
The headlong flight was finished, and I walked,
Jaded and reeking, in the level path
That led the lambkin home.

My mother saw,
And ran to meet me : then for long, still hours,
Couched in a dim, cool room, I lay and slept.
When I awoke, I found her at my side,
Fanning my face, and ready with her smile
And soothing words to greet me. Then I told,
With youthful volubility and wild
Extravagance of figure and of phrase,
My wild exploit.

At first she questioned me ;
But, as I wrought each scene and circumstance
Into consistent form, she drank my words
In eager silence ; and within her eyes
I saw the glow of pride which gravity

And show of deep concern could not disguise.
I read her bosom better than she knew.
I saw that she had made discovery
Of something unsuspected in her child,
And that, by one I loved,—my dearest, best,—
The fire that burned within me and the power
That morning called to life, were recognized.

When I had told my story, and had read
With kindling pride my praises in her eyes,
She placed her soft hand on my brow, and said:
"My Paul has climbed the noblest mountain hight
"In all his little world, and gazed on scenes
"As beautiful as rest beneath the sun.
"I trust he will remember all his life
"That to his best achievement, and the spot
"Nearest to heaven his youthful feet have trod,
"He has been guided by a guileless lamb.
"It is an omen which his mother's heart
"Will treasure with her jewels."

When the sun

Of the long summer day hung but an hour
Above his setting, and the cool West Wind
Bore from the purpling hills his benison,
The farewell courtesies of love were given,
And we set forth for home.

Not far we fared—
The river left behind—when, looking back,
I saw the mountain in the searching light
Of the low sun. Surcharged with youthful pride
In my adventure, I can ne'er forget
The disappointment and chagrin which fell
Upon me; for a change had passed. The steep
Which in the morning sprang to kiss the sun,
Had left the scene; and in its place I saw
A shrunken pile, whose paths my steps had climbed,
Whose proudest hight my humble feet had trod.
Its grand impossibilities and all
Its store of marvels and of mysteries
Were flown away, and would not be recalled.
The mountain's might had entered into me;
And, from that fruitful hour, whatever scene

Nature revealed to me, she never caught
My spirit humbled by surprise. My thought
Built higher mountains than I ever found;
Poured wilder cataracts than I ever saw;
Drove grander storms than ever swept the sky;
Pushed into loftier heavens and lower hells
Than the abysmal reach of light and dark;
And entertained me with diviner feasts
Than ever met the appetite of sense,
And poured me wine of choicer vintages
Than fire the hearts of kings.

The frolic flame
Which in the morning kindled in my veins
Had died away; and at my mother's side
I walked in quiet mood, and gravely spoke
Of the great future. With a tender quest
My mother probed my secret wish, and heard,
With silence new and strange respectfulness,
The revelation of my plans. I felt
In her benign attention to my words;
In her suggestions, clothed with gracious phrase

To win my judgment; and in all those shades
Of mien and manner which a mother's love
Inspires so quickly, when the form it nursed
Becomes a staff in its caressing hand,
She had made space for me, and placed her life
In new relations to my own. I knew
That she who through my span of tender years
Had counseled me, had given me privilege
Within her councils; and the moment came
I learned that in the converse of that hour,
The appetency of maternity
For manhood in its offspring, had laid hold
Of the fresh growth in me, and feasted well
Its gentle passion.

Ere we reached our home,
The plans for study were matured, and I,
Who, with an aptitude beyond my years,
Had gathered learning's humbler rudiments
From her to whom I owed my earliest words,
Was, when another day should rise, to pass
To rougher teaching, and society

Of the rude youth whose wild and boisterous ways
Had scared my childish life.

I nerved my heart
To meet the change; and all the troubled night
I tossed upon my pillow, filled with fears,
Or fired with hot ambitions; shrinking oft
With girlish sensitiveness from the lot
My manly heart had chosen; rising oft
Above my cowardice, well panoplied
By fancy to achieve great victories
O'er those whose fellows I should be.

At last,
The dawn looked in upon me, and I rose
To meet its golden coming, and the life
Of golden promise whose wide open doors
Waited my feet.

The lingering morning hours
Seemed days of painful waiting, as they fell
In slowly filling numbers from the tower

Of the old village church ; but when, at length,
My eager feet had touched the street, and turned
To climb the goodly eminence where he
In whose profound and stately pages live
His country's annals, ruled his youthful realm,
My heart grew stern and strong ; and nevermore
Did doubt of excellence and mastery
Drag down my soaring courage, or disturb
My purposes and plans.

What boots it here
To tell with careful chronicle the life
Of my novitiate ? Up the graded months
My feet rose slowly, but with steady step,
To tall and stalwart manliness of frame,
And ever rising and expanding reach
Of intellection and the power to call
Forth from the pregnant nothingness of words
The sphered creations of my chosen art.
What boots it to recount my victories
Over my fellows, or to tell how all,
Contemptuous at first, became at length

Confessed inferiors in every strife
When brain or brawn contended? Victories
Were won too easily to bring me pride,
And only bred contempt of the low pitch
And lower purpose of the power which strove
So feebly and so clumsily. When won,
They fed my mother's passion, and she praised;
And her delight was all the boon they brought.
My fierce ambition, ever reaching up
To higher fields and nobler combatants,
Trampled its triumphs underneath its feet;
And in my heart of hearts I pitied her
To whose deep hunger of maternal pride
They bore ambrosial ministry.

In all
These years of doing and development,
My heart was haunted by a bitter pain.
In every scene of pleasure, every hour
That lacked employment, every moment's lull
Of toil or study, its familiar hand
Was raised aloft, to smite me with its pang.

From month to month, from year to year, I saw
That she who bore me, and to whom I owed
The meek and loyal reverence of a child,
Was changing places with me, and that she—
Dependent, trustful and subordinate—
Deferred to me in all things, and in all
Gave me the parent's place and took the child's.
She waited for my coming like a child;
She ran to meet and greet me like a child;
She leaned on me for guidance and defense,
And lived in me, and by me, like a child.
If I were absent long beyond my wont,
She yielded to distresses and to tears;
And when I came, she flew into my arms
With childish impulse of delight, or chid
With weak complainings my delay.

By these,
And by a thousand other childish ways,
I knew disease was busy with her life,
Working distempers in her heart and brain,
And driving her for succor to my strength.

AND WHEN I CAME, SHE FLEW INTO MY ARMS.

The change was great in her, though slowly
wrought,—
Though wrought so slowly that my thought and
life
Had been adjusted to it, but for this :—
One dismal night, a trivial accident
Had kept me from my home beyond the hour
At which my promise stood for my return.
Arriving at the garden gate, I paused
To catch a glimpse of the accustomed light,
Through the cold mist that wrapped me, but in
vain.
Only one window glimmered through the gloom,
Through whose uncurtained panes I dimly saw
My mother in her chamber. She was clad
In the white robe of rest; but to and fro
She crossed the light, sometimes with hands
pressed close
Upon her brow, sometimes raised up toward
heaven,
As if in deprecation or despair;
And through the strident soughing of the elm

I heard her voice still musical in woe,
Wailing and calling.

With a noiseless step
I reached the door, and, with a noiseless key,
Turned back the bolt, and stood within. I could
Have called her to my arms, and quelled her fears
By one dear word, and yet, I spoke it not.
I longed to learn her secret, and to know
In what recess of history or heart
It hid, and wrought her awful malady.

Not long I waited, when I heard her voice
Wail out again in wild, beseeching prayer,—
Her voice so sweet and soulful, that it seemed
As if a listening fiend could not refuse
Such help as in him lay, although her tongue
Should falter to articulate her pain.

I heard her voice—O God! I heard her words!
Not bolts of burning from the vengeful sky
Had scathed or stunned me more. I shook like one

Powerless within the toils of some great sin,
Or some o'ermastering passion ; or like one
Whose veins turn ice at onset of the plague.
"O God," she said, "my Father and my Friend !
"Spare him to me, and save me from myself !
"O ! if thou help me not—if thou forsake—
"This hand which thou hast made, will take the
life
"Thou madst the hand to feed. I cling to him,
"My son,—my boy. If danger come to him,
"No one is left to save me from this crime.
"Thou knowest, O ! my God, how I have striven
"To quench the awful impulse ; how, in vain,
"My prayers have gone before thee, for release
"From the foul demon who would drive my soul
"To crime that leaves no space for penitence !
"O ! Father ! Father ! Hear me when I call !
"Hast thou not made me ? Am I not thy child ?
"Why, why this mad, mysterious desire
"To follow him I loved, by the dark door
"Through which he forced his passage to the
realm

"That death throws wide to all? O why must I,
"A poor, weak woman—"

I could hear no more,
But dropped my dripping cloak, and, with a voice,
Toned to its tenderest cadence, I pronounced
The sweet word, "mother!"

Her excess of joy
Burst in a cry, and in a moment's space
I sat within her room, and she, my child,
Was sobbing in my arms. I spoke no word,
But sat distracted with my tenderness
For her who threw herself upon my heart
In perfect trust, and bitter thoughts of Him
Whose succor, though importunately sought
In piteous pleadings by a gentle saint,
Was grudgingly withheld. Her closing words:
"O! why must I, a poor, weak woman—" rang
Through every chamber of my tortured soul,
And called to conclave and rebellion all
The black-browed passions thitherto restrained.

Ay, why should she, who only sought for God
Be given to a devil? Why should she
Who begged for bread be answered with a stone?
Ay, why should she whose soul recoiled from sin
As from a fiend, find in her heart a fiend
To urge the sin she hated?—questions all
The fiends within me answered as they would.
O God! O Father! How I hated thee!
Nay, how within my angry soul I dared
To curse thy sacred name!

Then other thoughts—
Thoughts of myself and of my destiny—
Succeeded. Who and what was I? A youth,
Doomed by hereditary taint to crime,—
A youth whose every artery and vein
Was doubly charged with suicidal blood.
When the full consciousness of what I was
Possessed my thought, and I gazed down the abyss
God had prepared for me, I shrank aghast;
And there in silence, with an awful oath
I dare not write, I swore my will was mine,

And mine my hand ; and that, though all the fiends
That cumber hell and overrun the earth
Should spur the deadly impulse of my blood,
And heaven withhold the aid I would not ask ;
Though woes unnumbered should beset my life,
And reason fall, and uttermost despair
Hold me a hopeless prisoner in its glooms,
I would resist and conquer, and live out
My complement of years. My bosom burned
With fierce defiance, and the angry blood
Leaped from my heart, and boomed within my brain
With throbs that stunned me, though each fiery thrill
Was charged with tenderness for her whose head
Was pillowed on its riot.

Long I sat—
How long I know not—but at last the sad,
Hysteric sobs and suspirations ceased,
Or only at wide intervals recurred ;
And then I rose, and to her waiting bed

Led my doomed mother. With a cheerful voice—
Cheerful as I could summon—and a kiss,
I bade her a good night and pleasant dreams;
And then, across the hall, I sought my room
Where neither sleep nor dream awaited me,
But only blasphemous, black thoughts, and strife
With God and Destiny.

I saw it all:
The lamp that from my mother's window beamed,
Illumined other nights and other storms,
And by its lurid light revealed to me
The secrets of a life. Her sudden pangs,
Her brooding woes, her terrors when alone,
The strange surrender of her will to mine,
Her hunger for my presence, and her fear
That by some slip of fortune she should lose
Her hold on me, were followed to their home—
To her poor heart, that fluttered every hour
With conscious presence of an enemy
That would not be expelled, and strove to spill
The life it spoiled.

From that eventful night
She was not left alone. I called a friend,
A cheerful lady, whose companionship
Was music, medicine and rest ; and she,
Wanting a home, and with a ready wit
Learning my mother's need and my desire,
Assumed the place of matron in the house ;
And, in return for what we gave to her,
Gave us herself.

My mother's confidence,
By her self-confidence, she quickly won ;
And thus, though sadly burdened at my heart,
I found one burden lifted from my hands.
More liberty of movement and of toil
I needed ; for the time was drawing near
When I should turn my feet toward other halls,
To seek maturer study, and complete
The work of culture faithfully begun.

Into my mother's ear I breathed my plans
With careful words. The university

Was but a short remove—a morning's walk—
Away from her; and ever at her wish—
Nay, always when I could—I would return;
And separation would but sweeten love,
And joy of meeting recompense the pain
Of parting and of absence.

She was calm,
And leaning in her thought upon her friend,
Gave her consent. So, on a summer day,
I kissed her faded cheek, and turned from home
To seek the college halls that I had seen
From boyhood's mount of vision.

Of the years
Passed there in study—of the rivalries,
The long, stern struggles for pre-eminence,
The triumphs hardly won, but won at last
Beyond all cavil, matters not to tell.
It was my grief that while I gained and grew,
My mother languished momently, and lost,—
A grief that turned to poison in my blood.

The college prayers were mummeries to me,
And with disdainful passion I repelled
All Christian questionings of heart and life,
By old and young.

I stood, I moved alone.
I sought no favors, took no courtesies
With grateful grace, and nursed my haughty pride.
The men who kneeled and gloomed, and prayed and sang,
Seemed but a brood of dullards, whom contempt
Would honor overmuch. No tender spot
Was left within my indurated heart,
Save that which moved with ever-melting ruth
For her whose breast had nursed me, and whose love
Had given my life the only happiness
It yet had known.

With her I kept my pledge
With more than faithful punctuality.
Few weeks passed by in all those busy years

In which I did not walk the way between
The college and my home, and bear to her
Such consolation as my presence gave.
In truth, my form was as familiar grown
To all the rustic dwellers on the road
As I had been a post-boy.

Little joy
These visits won for me—little beyond
That which I found in bearing joy to her—
For every year marked on her slender frame,
And on her cheeks, and on her failing brain.
Its record of decadence. I could see
That she was sinking into helplessness,
And that too soon her inoffensive soul,
With all its sweet affections, would go down
To hopeless wreck and darkness.

From her friend
I learned that still the burden of her prayer
Was, that she might be saved from one great sin—
The sin of self-destruction. Every hour

This one petition struggled from her heart,
To reach the ear of heaven ; yet never help
Came down in answer to her cry.

The Spring
That ushered in my closing college year
Came up the valley on her balmy wings,
And Winter fled away, and left no trace,
Save here and there a snowy drift, to show
Where his cold feet had rested in their flight.
But one still night, within the span of sleep,
A shivering winter cloud that wandered late,
Shook to the frosty ground its inch of rime.
So, when the morning rose, the earth was white ;
And shrubs and trees, and roofs and rocks and walls,
Fulgent with downy crystals, made a world
To which a breath were ruin ; and a breath
Wrecked it for me, and, by a few sad words,
Blotted the sunlit splendor from my sight.

As I looked out upon the scene, and mused

Of her to whom I hoped it might impart
Some healthy touch of joy, I heard the beat
Of hoofs upon the trackless blank, and saw
A horseman speeding up the avenue.
I raised my sash, (I knew he came for me,)
And faltered forth my question. From his breast
He drew a folded slip : dismounting then,
He stooped and pressed the missive in a mass
Of clinging snow, and tossed it to my hand.
I closed the window, burst the frosty seal,
And read : "Your mother cannot long survive :
Come home to her to-day." I did not pause
To break the fast of night, but rushing forth,
I followed close the messenger's return.

It was a morning, such as comes but once
In all the Spring,—so still and beautiful,
So full of promise, so exhilarant
With frost and fire, in earth and air, that life
Had been a brimming joy but for the scene
That waited for my eyes—the scene of death--

From which imagination staggered back,
And every sensibility recoiled.

The smoke from distant sugar-camps rolled up
Through the still ether in columnar coils—
Blue pillars of a bluer dome—and all
The resonant air was full of sounds of Spring.
The sheep were bleating round their empty ricks:
Horses let loose were calling from afar,
And winning fierce replies; the axeman's blows
Fell nimbly at the piles which wintry woods
Had lent to summer stores; while far and faint,
The rhythmic ululations of the hound
On a fresh trail, upon the mountain's side,
Added their strange wild music to the morn.

The beauty and the music caught my sense,
But woke within my sick and sinking heart
No motion of response. I walked as one
Condemned to dungeon-glooms might walk
Through shouts of mirth, and festal pageantry,
Hearing and seeing all, yet over all

Hearing the clank of chains and clash of bars,
And seeing but the reptiles of his cell.

How I arrived at home, without fatigue,
Without a thought of effort—onward borne
By one absorbing and impelling thought—
As one within a minute's mete may slide,
O'er leagues of sunny dreamland in a dream,
By magic or by miracle—I found
No time to question.

At my mother's door
I stood and listened : soon I heard my name
Pronounced within in spiteful whisperings.
I raised the latch, and met her burning eyes.
She stared a wild, mad stare, then raised herself,
And in weak fury poured upon my head
The vials of her wrath. I stood like stone,
Without the power to speak, the while she rained
Her maledictions on me, and in words
Fit only for the damned, accused my life
Of crimes my language could not name, and deeds
Which only outcast wretches know.

At length
I gained my tongue, and tried to take her hand;
But with a shriek which cut me like a knife
She shrank from me, and hid her quivering face
Within her pillow.

Then I turned away,
And sought the room where oft in better days
We both had knelt together at my bed,
And, making fast my door, I threw myself
Prone on the precious couch, and gave to grief
My strong and stormy nature. All the day
With bursts of passion I bewailed my loss,
Or lay benumbed in feeling and in thought,
Tasting no food, and shutting out my soul
From all approach of human sympathy,
Till the light waned, and through the leafless boughs
Of the old elm I caught the sheen of stars.

Then sleep descended—such a sleep as comes
To uttermost exhaustion,—sleep with dreams

Wild as the waking fantasies of her
Whose screams and incoherent words gave voice
To all their phantom brood.

At length I woke.
The house was still as death ; and yet I heard,
Or thought I heard, the touch of crafty feet
Upon the carpet, creeping by my door.
It passed away, away ; and then a pause,
Still and presageful as the breathless calm
On which the storm-cloud mounts the pallid West,
Succeeded. I could hear the parlor-clock
Counting the beaded silence, and my bed,
Rustling beneath my breathing and my pulse,
Was sharply crepitant, and gave me pain.

An hour passed by, (it loitered like an age,)
And then came hurried words and hasty fall
Of footsteps in the passage. I could hear
Screams, sobs, and whispered calls and closing
doors,
And heavy feet that jarred my bed, and shook

The windows of my room. I did not stir:
I dared not stir, but lay in deathly dread,
Waiting the dread denouement. Soon it came.
A man approached my door, and tried the latch;
Then knocked, and called. I knew the kindly voice
Of the physician, and threw back the bolt.
Then by the light he held before his face
I read the fact of death.

I took his arm,
And, as I feebly staggered down the stairs,
He broke to me with lack of useless words
The awful truth. . . . The old familiar tale:
She counterfeited sleep: the nurses both,
Weary with over-watching in their chairs,
Under the cumbrous stillness, slept indeed;
And when she knew it, she escaped; and then
She did the deed to which for many years
She had been predisposed. Perhaps I knew
The nature of the case: perhaps I knew
My father went that way. I clutched his arm:
There was no need of words.

—The touch of crafty feet
Upon the carpet, creeping by my door.

The parlor door
Stood open, and a throng of silent friends,
Choking with tears, gazed on a silent form
Shrouded in snowy linen. They made way
For me and my companion. On my knees
I clasped the precious clay, and pouring forth
My pitying love and tenderness for her,
I gave indignant voice to my complaint
Against the Being who, to all her prayers,
For succor and security, had turned
A deaf, dead ear and a repelling hand.

To what blaspheming utterance I gave
My raving passion, may the God I cursed
Forbid my shrinking memory to recall!
I now remember only that when drawn
By strong, determined hands away from her,
The room was vacant. Every pitying friend
Had flown my presence and the room, to find
Release of sensibility from words
That roused their superstitious souls to fear

That God would smite me through the blinding
smoke
Of my great torment.

Silence, for the rest !
It was a dream ; and only as a dream
Do I remember it : the coffined form,
The funeral—a concourse of the town—
The trembling prayer for me, the choking sobs,
The long procession, the descending clods,
The slow return, articulated all
With wild, mad words of mine, and gentle speech
Of those who sought to curb or comfort me—
All was a dream, from which I woke at length
With heart as dead as hers who slept. The heavens
Were brass above me, and the breathing world
Was void and meaningless. When told to pray,
This was the logic of my heart's reply :
If God be Love, not such is he to me
Nor such to mine. If He heard not the voice
Of such a lovely saint as she I mourned,
Mine would but rouse His vengeance.

So I closed
With Reason's hand the adamantine doors
Which only Faith unlocks, and shut my soul
Away from God, the warder of a gang
Of passions that in darkness stormed or gloomed ;
And with each other fought, or on themselves
Gnawed for the nourishment which I denied.

COMPLAINT.

RIVER, sparkling river, I have fault to find with
thee:
River, thou dost never give a word of peace to me!
Dimpling to each touch of sunshine, wimpling to
each air that blows,
Thou dost make no sweet replying to my sighing
for repose.

Flowers of mount and meadow, I have fault to find
with you;
So the breezes cross and toss you, so your cups are
filled with dew,
Matters not though sighs give motion to the ocean
of your breath;
Matters not though you are filling with the chilling
drops of death!

Birds of song and beauty, lo! I charge you all with
blame :—
Though all hapless passions thrill and fill me, you
are still the same.
I can borrow for my sorrow nothing that avails
From your lonely note, that only speaks of joy that
never fails.

O! indifference of Nature to the fact of human pain!
Every grief that seeks relief entreats it at her hand
in vain;
Not a bird speaks forth its passion, not a river seeks
the sea,
Nor a flower from wreaths of Summer breathes in
sympathy with me.

O! the rigid rock is frigid, though its bed be sum-
mer mould,
And the diamond glitters ever in the grasp of
changeless gold;
And the laws that bring the seasons swing their
cycles as they must,

Though the ample road they trample blind the
eyes with human dust.

Moons will wax in argent glory, though man wane
to hopeless gloom ;
Stars will sparkle in their splendor, though he
darkle to his doom ;
Winds of heaven he calls to fan him, ban him with
an icy chill,
And the shifting crowds of clouds go drifting o'er
him as they will.

Yet within my inmost spirit I can hear an under-
tone,
That by law of prime relation holds these voices as
its own,—
The full tonic whose harmonic grandeurs rise
through Nature's words,
From the ocean's thundrous rolling to the trolling
of the birds.

Spirit, O ! my spirit ! Is it thou art out of tune ?

Art thou clinging to December while the earth is
in its June ?
Hast thou dropped thy part in nature ? Hast thou
touched another key ?
Art thou angry that the anthem will not, cannot,
wait for thee ?

Spirit, thou art left alone—alone on waters wild ;
For God is gone, and Love is dead, and Nature
spurns her child.
Thou art drifting in a deluge, waves below and
clouds above,
And with weary wings come back to thee, thy
raven and thy dove.

PART II.

LOVE.

As from a deep, dead sea, by drastic lift
Of pent volcanic fires, the dripping form
Of a new island swells to meet the air,
And after months of idle basking, feels
The prickly feet of life from countless germs
Creeping along its sides, and reaching up
In fern and flower to the life-giving sun,
So from my grief I rose, and so at length
I felt new life returning : so I felt
The life already wakened stretching forth
To stronger light and purer atmosphere.
But most I longed for human love—the source

(So sadly closed,) from which my life had drawn
Its sweetest inspiration and reward.
I could not pray, nor could my spirit win
From sights and sounds of nature the response
It vainly yearned for. They assailed my sense
With senseless seeming of the hum and whirl
Of vast machinery, whose motive power
Sought its own ends, or wrought for ministry
To other life than mine.

I could stand still,
And see the trains sweep by; could hear the roar
Of thundering wheels; could watch the pearly plumes
That floated where they flew; could catch a glimpse
Of thousand happy faces at the glass;
But felt that all their freighted life and wealth
Were naught to me, and moved toward other souls
In other latitudes.

A year had flown,
And more, when, on a Sunday morn in June,

I wandered out to wear away the hours
Of growing restlessness. The worshipers
Were thronging to the service of the day,
And gave me sidelong stare, or shunned me quite,
As if they knew me for a reprobate,
And feared a taint of death.

I took the road
That eastward cleft the town, and sought the bridge
That spanned the river, reaching which I crossed.
Then deep within the stripes of springing corn
I found the shadow of an elm, and lay
Stretched on the downy grass for listless hours,
Dreaming of days gone by, or turning o'er
With careless hand the pages of a book
I had brought with me.

Tired at length I rose,
And, touched by some light impulse, moved along
The old familiar road. I loitered on
In a blind revery, nor marked the while
The furlongs or the time, until the spell

In a full burst of music was dissolved.
I startled as one startles from a dream,
And saw the church of Hadley, from whose doors,
Opened to summer air, the choral hymn
Poured out its measured tides, and rose and fell
Upon the silence in broad cadences,
As from a far, careering sea, the waves
Lift into silver swells the sleeping breasts
Of land-locked bays.

I heard the sound of flutes,
And hoarse, sonorous viols, in accord
With happy human voices,—and one voice—
A woman's or an angel's—that compelled
My feet to swift approach. A thread of gold,
Through all the web of sound, I followed it
Till, by the stress of some strange sympathy,
And by no act of will, I joined my voice
To that one voice of melody, and sang.

The heart is wiser than the intellect,
And works with swifter hands and surer feet

Toward wise conclusions. So, without resort
To reason, in my heart I knew that she
Who sang had suffered—knew that she had grieved,
Had hungered, struggled, kissed the cheek of death,
And ranged the scale of passions till her soul
Was deep, and wide, and soft with sympathy ;—
Nay, more than this : that she had found at last
Peace like a river, on whose waveless tide
She floated while she sang. This was the key
That loosed my prisoned voice, and filled my eyes
With tender tears, and touched to life again
My better nature.

When the choral closed,
And the last chord in silence lapsed away,
I raised my eyes, and, nodding to the beck
Of the old, slippered sexton, I went in,—
Not (shall it be confessed ?) to find the God
At whose plain altar bowed the rural throng ;
But, through a voice, to follow to its source
The influence that moved me.

I was late ;
And many eyes looked up as I advanced
Through the broad aisle, and took a seat that turned
My face to all the faces in the house.
I scanned the simpering girls within the choir,
But found not what I sought ; and then my eyes
With rambling inquisition swept the pews,
Pausing at every maiden face in vain.
One head, that crowned a tall and slender form,
Was bowed with reverent grace upon the rail
Before her ; and, although I caught no glimpse
Of her sweet face, I knew such face was there,
And there the voice.

It was Communion Day.
The simple table underneath the desk
Was draped with linen, on whose snow was spread
The feast of love—the vases filled with wine,
The separated bread and circling cups.
The venerable pastor had come down
From his high pulpit, and assumed the seat
Of presidence, and, with benignant eyes,

Sat smiling on his flock. The deacons all
Rose from their pews—four old, brown-handed
men,
With frosty hair—and took the ancient chairs
That flanked the table. All the house was still,
Save here and there the rustle of a silk
Or folding of a fan ; and over all
Brooded the dove of peace. I had no part
In the fair spectacle, but I could feel
That it was beautiful and sweet as heaven.

When the old pastor rose, with solemn mien,
I looked to see the lady lift her head ;
But still she bowed ; and then I heard these words:
"The person who unites with us to-day
"Will take her place before me in the aisle,
"To give her answer to our creed, and speak
"The pledges of our covenant."

Then first
I saw her face. With modest grace she rose,
Lifted her hat, and gave it to the hand

Of a companion, and within the aisle
Stood out alone. My heart beat thick and fast
With vision of her perfect loveliness,
And apprehension of the heroism
That shone within her eyes, and made her act
A Christ-like sacrifice.

O ! eyes of blue !
O ! lily throat and cheeks of faintest rose !
O ! brow serene, enthroned in holy thought !
O ! soft, brown sweeps of hair ! O ! shapely grace
Of maidenhood, enrobed in virgin white !
Why, in your rapt unconsciousness of me
And all around you—in the presence-hall
Of God and angels—at the marriage-feast
Of Jesus and his chosen—did my eyes
Profane the hour with other feast than yours ?

I heard the "You Believe" of the old creed
Of Puritan New England ; and I heard
The old "You Promise" of its covenant.
Her bow of reverent assent to all

The knotty dogmas, and her silent pledge
Of faithfulness and fellowship, I saw.
These formularies were the frame of oak--
Gnarled, strongly carved, and swart with age and
use—
Which held the lovely picture of my saint,
And showed her saintliness and beauty well.

At close of the recital and response,
The pastor raised the plain, baptismal bowl,
And she, the maiden devotee, advanced
And knelt before him. Lifting then her eyes
To him and heaven, with look of earnest faith
And perfect consecration, she received
Upon her brow the water from his hand.
The trickling chrism shone on her cheeks like tears,
The while he joined her lovely name with God's :

"KATHRINA, I BAPTIZE THEE IN THE NAME
"OF FATHER, SON, AND HOLY GHOST, AMEN !"

Still kneeling like a saint before a shrine,

STILL KNEELING LIKE A SAINT.

She closed her eyes. Then lifting up toward heaven
His hands, the pastor prayed,—prayed that her soul
Might be forever kept from stain and sin;
That Christ might live in her, and through her life
Shine into other souls; might give her strength
To master all temptation, and to keep
The vows that day assumed; might comfort her
In every sorrow, and, in death's dread hour,
Bear her in hopeful triumph to the rest
Prepared for those who love him.

All this scene
I saw through blinding tears. The poetry
That like a soft aureola embraced
Within its cope those two contrasted forms;
The eager observation and the hush
That reigned through all the house; the breathless spell
Of sweet solemnity and tender awe
Which held all hearts, when she, The Beautiful,
Received the sign of marriage to The Good,
O'erwhelmed me, and I wept. Shall I confess

That in the struggle to repress my tears
And hold my swelling heart, I grudged her gift.
And felt that, by the measure she had risen,
She had put space between herself and me,
And quenched my hope ?

She stood while courtesy
Of formal Christian welcome was bestowed ;
Then straightway sought her seat, as though no eyes
But those of One unseen observed her steps.
I saw her taste the sacramental bread,
And touch the silver chalice to her lips ;
And while she thought of Him, the Spotless One
Whose flesh and blood were symbolled to her heart,
And worshiped in her thought, I ate and drank
Her virgin beauty—with what guilty sense
Of profanation !

Last, the closing hymn
Gave me her voice again ; and this I drank ;
Nay, this invaded and pervaded me.
Its subtile search found out the sleeping chords

Of sympathy ; and on the bridge of sound
It built between our souls, I crossed, and saw
Into the depths of purity and love—
The full, pathetic power of womanhood—
From which the structure sprang. Just once
I caught her eyes. She blushed with consciousness
Of my strong gaze ; but paused not in her hymn
Till she had given to every word the wings
That bore it, like a singing bird, toward heaven.

The benediction fell ; and then the throng
Passed slowly out. I was the last to go.
I saw a man whom I had known, and shrank
Both from his greetings and his questionings.
One thing I learned : that she who thus had joined
This cluster of disciples was not born
And reared among their number : that was plain.
I saw it in her bearing and her dress ;
In that unconsciousness of self that comes
Of gentle breeding, and society
Of gentle men and women ; in the ease
With which she bore the awkward deference

Of those who spoke with her adown the aisle;
In distant and admiring gaze of men,
And the cold scrutiny of village girls
Who passed for belles.

I stood upon the steps—
The last who left the door—and there I found
The lady and her friend. The elder turned,
And with a cordial greeting took my hand,
And rallied me on my forgetfulness.
Her eyes, her smile, her manner and her voice
Touched the quick springs of memory, and I spoke
Her name.

She was my mother's early friend,
Whose face I had not seen in all the years
That had flown over us, since, from her door,
I chased her lamb to where I found—myself.
She spoke with tender words and swimming eyes
Of her I mourned, and questioned me like one
Who felt a mother's anxious interest
In all my cares and plans. Why did I not

In all my maunderings and wanderings
Remember I had friends, and visit them—
Not missing her? Her niece was with her now;
Would live with her, perhaps—("a lovely girl!"—
In whisper;) and they both would so much like
To see me at their house! (whisper again:
"Poor child! I fear it is but dull for her,
Here in the country.") Then with sudden thought—
"Kathrina!"

With a blushing smile she turned,
(She had heard every word,) and then her aunt—
Her voluble, dear aunt—presented me
As an old friend—the son of an old friend—
Whose eyes had promised he would visit them,
Although, in her monopoly of speech,
She had quite shut him from the chance to say
So much as that.

I caught the period
Quick as it dropped, and spoke the happiness
I had in meeting them, and gave the pledge—

No costly thing to give—to end my walks
On pleasant nightfalls at the little house
Under the mountain.

I had spoken more,
But then the carriage, with its single horse,
For which they waited, rattled to the steps,
And we descended. To their lofty seats
I helped the pair, and in my own I held
For one sweet moment, hand of all the hands
In the wide world I longed to clasp the most.
A plain "Good Evening Sir," was all I won
From its possessor ; but her lively aunt
With playful menace shook her fan at me,
And said : "Remember, Paul !" and rode away.

"A worldly woman, Sir !" growled a grum throat.
I turned and saw the sexton. *Query:* "Which ?"
"I mean the aunt." . . . "And what about
the niece ?"
"Too fine for common people !" (with a shrug.)
"I think she is," I said, with quiet voice,

And turned my feet toward home.

A pious girl!
And what could I be to a pious girl?
What could she be to me? Weak questions, these,
And vain, perhaps; but such as young men ask
On slighter spur than mine.

She had bestowed
Her love, her life, her goodly self on Heaven,
And had been nobly earnest in her gift.
Before all lovers she had chosen Christ;
Before all idols, God; before all wish
And will of loving man, her heart and hand
Were pledged to duty. Could she be a wife?
Could she be mine, with such unstinted wealth
Of love, and love's devotion, as I craved?
Would she not leave me for a Sunday School
Before the first moon's wane? Would she not seek
The cant and snuffle of conventicles
"At early candle-light," and sing her hymns
To driveling boors, and cheat me of her songs?

Would she exhaust herself in "doing good"
After the modern styles—in patching quilts,
And knitting socks, and bearing feeble tracts
To dirty little children—not to speak
Of larger work for missionary folk?
Would there not come a time (O! fateful time!)
When Dorcas and her host would fill my house,
And I by courtesy be held at home
To entertain their twaddle, and to smile,
While in God's name and lovely Charity's
They would consume my substance? Would she not
Become the stern and stately president
Of some society, or figure in the list
Of slim directresses in spectacles?

So much for questions: then reflections came.
These pious women make more careful wives
Than giddy ones. They do not run away,
Though, doubtless, husbands live whose hearts would heal,
Broken by such a blow! The time they give

To worship and to pious offices
Defrauds the mirror mainly; and the gold
That goes for charity goes not for gems.

Besides, these pious and believing wives
Make gentle mothers, who, with self-control
And patient firmness, train their children well—
A fact to be remembered. But, alas!
They train their husbands, too, and undertake
A mission to their souls, so gently pushed,
So tenderly, they may not take offence,
Or punish with rebuff; and yet, dear hearts!
With such persistence, that they reach the raw
Before they know it; so it comes to tears
At last, with comfort in an upper room.
But then—a seal is sacred to them, and a purse
Or pocket-book, though in a dressing-room
With shutters and a key!

Thus wrapped in thought
And selfish calculation of the claims
Of one my peer, or my superior,

In every personal and moral grace,
I walked along, till, on my consciousness,
Flashed the absurdity of my conceits
And my assumptions, and I laughed outright—
Laughed at myself, so loudly and so long
That I was startled. Not for many months
Had sound of mirth escaped me ; and my voice
Rang strangely in my ears, as if the lips
Of one long dead had spoken.

I received
The token of returning healthfulness
With warm self-gratulation. I had touched
The magic hand that held new life for me ;
The cloud was lifted, and the burden gone.
The leaf within my book of fate, that gloomed
With awful records, washed and blotched by tears—
Blown by a woman's breath from finger-tips
That knew not what they did—was folded back ;
And all the next white page held but one word—
One word of gold and flame—its title-crown,

That wrought a rosy nimbus for itself;
And that one word was LOVE.

The laggard days
My pride or my propriety imposed
Upon desire, before my eyes could see
The object of my new-born passion, passed
And in the low hours of an afternoon,
Bright with the largess of a kingly shower
Whose chariot-wheels still thundered in the East,
Leaving the West aflame, I sought the meads,
And once again, thrilled by fore-tasted joy,
Walked toward the mountain.

While I walked, the rain
Fell like a veil of gauze between my eyes
And the blue wall; and from the precious spot
That held the object of my thought, there sprang
An iridal effulgence, faint at first,
But brightening fast, and leaping to an arch
That spanned the heavens—a miracle of light!

"There's treasure where the rainbow rests," I said.
Would it evade me, as, for years untold,
It had evaded every childish dupe
Whose feet had chased the bright, elusive cheat ?
Would it evade me ? Question that arose,
And loomed with darker front and huger form
Than the dark mountain, and more darkly loomed
And higher rose as the long path grew short !
Would it evade me ? Like a passing smile
The rainbow faded from the mountain's face ;
And Hope's resplendent iris, which illumed
My question grew phantasmal, and at length
Evanished, leaving but a doubtful blur.
Would it evade me ? Gods ! what wealth or waste
Of precious life awaited the reply !
Was it a coward's shudder that o'erswept
My frame at thought of possible repulse
And possible relapse ?

"Oh ! there he comes !"
I heard the mistress of the cottage say
Behind a honeysuckle. Did I smile ?

It was because the fancy crossed me then
That the announcement was like one which rings
Over the polar seas, when, from his perch,
The lookout bruits a long-expected whale!
Then sweeping the piazza from the spot
Where with her niece she sat, she hailed me with:
"So you are come at last! How very sad
These men have so much business! Tell me how
You got away; how soon you must return;
Who suffers by your absence; what the news,
And whether you are well?"

Brisk medicine
These words to me, and timely given. They broke
The spell of fear, and banished my restraint.
She took my arm, and led me to her niece,
Who greeted me as if some special grace
Of courtesy were due, to make amends
For the familiar badinage her aunt
Had poured upon me.

They had come without—
One with her work, the other with her book—

To taste the freshness of the evening air,
Washed of the hot day's dust by rain ; to hear
The robin's hymn of joy ; and watch the clouds
That canopied with gold the sinking sun.
The maiden in a pale blue muslin robe—
Dyed with forget-me-nots, I fancied then,
And sweet with life in every fold, I knew—
A blush-rose at her throat, and in her hair
A sprig of green and white, was lovelier
Than sky or landscape ; and her low words fell
More musically than the robin's hymn.
So, with my back to other scene and sound,
I faced the faces, took the proffered chair,
And looked and listened.

"Tell us of yourself,"
Spoke the blunt aunt, with license of her years.
"What are you doing now?"

"Nothing," I said.

"And were you not the boy who was to grow

Into a great, good man, and write fine books,
And have no end of fame ?"

The question cut
Deeper than she intended. The hot blush
And stammering answer told her of the hurt,
And tenderly she tried to heal the wound :
"I know that you have suffered ; but your hours
Must not be told by tears. The life that goes
In unavailing sorrow goes to waste."

"True," I replied, "but work may not be done
Without a motive. Never worthy man
Worked worthily who was not moved by love.
When she I loved, and she who loved me died,
My motive died ; and it can never rise
Till trump of love shall call it from the dust
To resurrection."

I spoke earnestly,
Without a thought that other ears than hers
Were listening to my words ; but when I looked,

I saw the maiden's eyes were dim with tears.
I knew her own experience was touched,
And that her heart made answer to my own
In perfect sympathy.

To change the drift,
I took her book, and read the title-page :
"So you like poetry," I said.

"So well my aunt
Finds fault with me."

"You write, perhaps ?"

"Not I."

"A happy woman !" I exclaimed ; "in truth,
The first I ever found affecting art
Who shunned expression by it. If a girl
Like painting, she must paint ; if poetry,
She must write verses. Can you tell me why
(For sex marks no distinction in this thing.)

Men with a taste for art in finest forms
Cherish the fancy that they may become,
Or are, Art's masters ? You shall see a man
Who never drew a line or struck an arc
Direct an architect, and spoil his work,
Because, forsooth ! he likes a tasteful house !
He likes a muffin, but he does not go
Into his kitchen to instruct his cook,—
Nay, that were insult. He admires fine clothes,
But trusts his tailor. Only in those arts
Which issue from creative potencies
Does his conceit engage him. He could learn
The baker's trade, and learn to cut a coat,
But never learn to do that one great deed
Which he essays."

"'Tis not a strange mistake
These people make"—she answered, thoughtfully.
"Art gives them pleasure ; and they honor those
Whose heads and hands produce it. If they see
The length and breadth and beauty of a thought
Embodied by another,--if they hold

The taste, the culture, the capacity,
To measure values in the things of art,
Why cannot they create? Why cannot they
Win to themselves the honor they bestow
On those who feed them? Is it very strange
That those who know how sweet the gratitude
Which the true artist stirs, should burn to taste
That gratitude themselves?"

"Not strange, perhaps,"
I said, "and yet it is a sad mistake;
For countless noble lives have gone to waste
In work which it inspired."

Here spoke the aunt:
"You are a precious pair; and if you know
What you are talking of, you know a deal
More than your elders. By your royal leave,
I will retire; for I can lay the cloth
For kings and queens, though I may fail to know
Their lore and language. You can eat, I think;
And hear a tea-bell, though you hear not me."

Thus speaking in her crisp, good-natured way,
The lady left us.

When she passed the door,
And laughter at her jest had had its way,
I said: "It takes all sorts to make a world."

"How many, think you? Only one, two, three,"
The maiden said. "Here we have all the world
In this one cottage—artist, teacher, taught,
In—not to mar the order of the scale
For courtesy—yourself, myself, my aunt.
You are an artist, so my aunt reports;
But, as an artist, you are naught to her.
And now, to broach a petted theory,
Let me presume too boldly, while I say
She cannot understand you, though I can;
You cannot measure her, though she is wise.
You have not much for her, and that you have
You cannot teach her; but I, knowing her,
Can pick from your creations crumbs of thought
She will find manna. In the hands of Christ
The five loaves grew, the fishes multiplied;

And He to his disciples gave the feast—
They to the multitude. Artists are few,
Teachers are thousands, and the world is large.
Artists are nearest God. Into their souls
He breathes his life, and from their hands it comes
In fair, articulate forms to bless the world;
And yet, these forms may never bless the world
Except its teachers take them in their hands,
And give each man his portion."

As she spoke
In earnest eloquence, I could have knelt,
And worshiped her. Her delicate cheek was flushed,
Her eyes were filled with light, and her closed book
Was pressed against her heart, whose throbbing tide
Thridded her temples. I was half amused,
Half rapt in admiration; and she saw
That in my eyes at which she blushed and paused.
"Your pardon, Sir," she said. "It ill becomes
A teacher to instruct an artist."

"Nay,
It does become you wondrously," I said,
With light but earnest words. "Pray you go on;
And pardon all that my unconscious eyes
Have done to stop you."

"I have little more
That I would care to say: you have my thought,"
She answered; "yet there's very much to say,
And you should say it."

"Not I, lady, no:
A poet is not practical like you,
Nor sensible like you. You can teach him
As well as tamer folk. In truth, I think
He needs instruction quite as much as they
For whom he writes."

"That's possible," she said,
With an arch smile.

"Will you explain yourself?"

"Well—if you wish it—yes:" she made reply.
"And first, my auditor must know that I
Believe in inspiration, though he knows
So much as that already, from my words,—
Believe that God inspires the poet's soul,—
That He gives eyes to see, and ears to hear
What in his realm holds finest ministry
For highest aptitudes and needs of men,
And skill to mould it into forms of art
Which shall present it to the world he serves.
Sometimes the poet writes with fire; with blood
Sometimes; sometimes with blackest ink:
It matters not. God finds his mighty way
Into his verse. The dimmest window-panes
Let in the morning light, and in that light
Our faces shine with kindled sense of God
And his unwearied goodness; but the glass
Gets little good of it; nay, it retains
Its chill and grime beyond the power of light
To warm or whiten. E'en the prophet's ass
Had better eyes than he who strode his back,
And, though the prophet bore the word of God,

Did finer reverence. The Psalmist's soul,
Was not a fitting place for psalms like his
To dwell in over-long, while waiting words,
If I read rightly. As for the old seers,
Whose eyes God touched with vision of the life
Of the unfolding ages, I must doubt
Whether they comprehended what they saw,
Or knew what they recorded. It remains
For the world's teachers to expound their words;
To probe their mysteries; and relegate
The truth they hold in blind significance
Into the fair domains of history
And human knowledge. Am I understood?"

"You are," I answered; "and I cannot say
You flatter me. God takes within his hand
A thing of his contrivance which we call
A poet; then He puts it to his lips,
And speaks his word, and puts it down again—
The instrument not better and not worse
For being handled;—not improved a whit
In quality, by quality of that

Which it conveys. Do I report aright?
Or do you prompt me?"

"You are very apt,"
She said, "at learning, but a little bald
In statement. Nathless, be it as you say;
And we shall see how it is possible
That poets need instruction quite as much
As those for whom they write. What sad, bad men
The brightest geniuses have been! How weak,
How mean in character! how foul in life!
How feebly have the best of them retained
The wealth of good and beauty which has flowed
In crystal streams from God, the fountain-head,
Through them to fertilize the world! Nay, worse:
How many of them have infused the tide
With tincture of their own impurity,
To poison sweetest, unsuspecting lips,
And breed diseases in the finest blood!
And poets not alone, and not the worst;
But painters, sculptors—those whose kingly power

And aptitude for utterance divine
Have made them artists :—how have these contemned
In countless instances the God of Heaven
Who filled them with his fire ! Think you that these
Could compass their achievements of themselves ?
Can streams surpass their fountains ?"

"Nay," I said,
In quick response. "Your argument is good ;
But is the artist nothing ? Is he naught
But an apt tool—a mouth-piece for a voice ?
You make him but the spigot of a cask
Round which you, teachers, wait with silver cups
To bear away the wine that leaves it dry.
You magnify your office."

"We do all
Wait upon God for every grace and good,"
She then rejoined. "You take it at first hands,
And we from yours : the multitude from ours.

It may leach through our souls, if our poor wills
Retain it not, and drench the fragrant sand.
And if I magnify my office—well!
Tis a great office. What would come of all
The music of the masters, did not we
Wait at their doors, to publish to the world
What God has told them? They would be as
mute
As the dumb Sphinx. They write a symphony,
An opera, an oratorio,
In language that the teacher understands,
And straight the whole world echoes to its strains.
It shrills and thunders through cathedral glooms
From golden organ-tubes and voiceful choirs;
The halls of art of both the hemispheres
Resound with its divinest melodies;
The street stirs with the impulse, and we hear
The blare of martial trumpets, and the tramp
Of bannered armies swaying to its rhythm;
The hurdy-gurdies and the whistling boys
Adopt the lighter strains: and round and round
A million souls its hovering fancies float,

Like butterflies above a fair parterre,
Till, settling one by one, they sleep at last;
And lo! two petals more on every flower!
And this not all; for though the master die,
The teacher lives forever. On and on,
Through all the generations, he shall preach
The beautiful evangel;—on and on,
Till our poor race has passed the tortuous years
That lie prevening the millennium,
And slide into that broad and open sea,
He shall sail, singing still the songs he learned
In the world's youth, and sing them o'er and o'er
To lapping waters, till the thousand leagues
Are overpast, and argosy and crew
Ride at their port."

"True as to facts," I said;
"And as to prophecies, most credible;
But, as an illustration, false, I think.
That which the voice and instrument may do
For the composer, types may do for those
Who mint their thoughts in verse. Music is writ

In language that the people do not read—
Is lame in that—and needs interpreters;
While poetry, e'en in its noblest forms
And boldest flights, speaks their vernacular.
Your aunt can read the book within your hand
As well as you, if she desires, yet finds
Your score all Greek, until you vocalize
Its wealth of hidden meaning. As for arts
Which meet the eye in picture and in form,
They ask no mediator but the light—
No grace but privilege to shine with naught
Between them and the light. They are themselves
Expositors of that which they expose,
Or they are nothing. All the middle-men—
The fools profound—who take it on their tongues
To play the showmen, strutting up and down,
And mouthing of the beauty that they hide,
Are an impertinence."

"You leave no room
For critics," she suggested, with a smile.

"We must not spoil a trade, or starve the wives
And innocent babes it feeds."

"No care for them!"
I made reply. "They do not need much room—
Men of their build—and what they need they take
The feeble conies burrow in the rocks;
But the trees grow, and we are not aware
Of space encumbered by them."

"Yet the fact
Still stands untouched," she added, thoughtfully.
"That greatest artists speak to fewest souls,
Or speak to them directly. They have need
Of no such ministry as waits the beck
Of the composer; but they need the life,
If not the learning, of the cultured few
Who understand them. If from out my book
I gather that which feeds me, and inspires
A nobler, sweeter beauty in my life,
And give my life to those who cannot win
From the dim text such boon, then have I borne

A blessing from the book, and been its best
Interpreter. The bread that comes from heaven
Needs finest breaking. Some there doubtless are—
Some ready souls—that take the morsel pure
Divided to their need; but multitudes
Must have it in admixtures, menstruums,
And forms that human hands or human life
Have moulded. Though the multitudes may find
Something to stir and lift their sluggish souls
In sight of great cathedrals, or in view
Of noble pictures, yet they see not all,
And not the best. That which they do not see
Must enter higher souls, and there, by art
Or life, be fashioned to their want."

"Your thought
Grows subtle," I responded, "and I grant
Its force and beauty. If the round truth lie
Somewhere between us, and I see the face
It turns to me in stronger light than you
Reveal its opposite, why, let the fault be mine;

It is not yours. You have instructed me,
And won my thanks."

"Instructed you?" she said,
With a fine blush: "you mock, you humble me.
And have I talked so much, with such an air,
That, either earnestly or in a jest,
You can say this to me?"

"'Tis not a sin,
In latitude of ours," I made reply,
"To talk philosophy; 'tis only rare
For beardless lips to do so. I have caught
From yours a finer, more suggestive scheme
Than all the wise have taught me by their books,
Or by their voices. I will think of it."

"Now may you be forgiven!" the aunt exclaimed,
Approaching unobserved. "There never lived
A quieter, more plainly speaking girl
Than my Kathrina. All these weeks and months,
I have heard naught from her but common sense;

But when you came, why, off she went; though
where
It's more than I know. You, sir, have the blame;
And you must lift your spell, and give her back
Just as you found her."

"She has practised well
Her scheme on us. She breaks to you the bread
That meets your want; to me, that meets my
own,"
I said, in answering.

"Well," spoke the aunt,
"I think I'll try my hand at breaking bread:
So follow me."

We followed to her board,
And there, in converse suited to the hour
And presence of our hostess, proved ourselves—
Quite to that lady's liking—of the earth.
We ate her jumbles for her, sipped her tea,
And revelled in the spicy succulence
Of her preserves.

While still I sat at ease,
The maiden's eye, with quick, uneasy glance,
Sought the clock's dial. Then she turned to me,
And said, with sweet, respectful courtesy:
"Pray you excuse my presence for an hour.
A duty calls me out; and that performed,
I will return."

I saw she marked my look
Of disappointment—that it staggered her—
The while with words of stiffest commonplace
I gave assent. But she was on her feet;
And soon I heard her light step on the stair,
Seeking her chamber.

"Whither will she go
At such an hour as this, from you and me?"
I coldly questioned of the keen-eyed aunt.
"You men are very curious," she said.
"I knew you'd ask me. Can't a lady stir,
But you must call her to account? Who knows
She may not have some rustic lover here
With whom she keeps her tryst? 'Tis an old trick,

Not wholly out of fashion in these parts.
What matters it? She orders her own ways,
And has discretion."

With lugubrious voice
I said: "You trifle, madam, with my wish.
I know the lady has no lover here,
And so do you."

"I am not sure of that!"
My hostess made response; and then she laughed
A rippling, rollicking roulade, and shook
Her finger at me, till my temples burned
With the hot shame she summoned.

"There!" I said;
"You've done your worst, and learned so much, at least—
That I admire your niece. *I* curious!
Well, you are curious and cunning too.
Now, in the moment of your victory,
Be generous; and tell me what may call
The lady from us."

"It is Thursday night,"
She answered soberly,—"the weekly hour
At which our quiet neighborhood convenes
For social worship. You may guess the rest
Without my telling; but you cannot know
With what anticipated joy she leaves
Our company, or with what shining face
She will return."

At that I heard her dress
Sliding the flight, and rising, made my way
To meet her at its foot. A happy smile
Illumed her features, as she gave her hand
With thought of parting. I had rallied all
My self-control and gallantry meanwhile,
And said: "Not here. I'll with you, by your leave,
So far as you may walk."

There was a flash
Of gladness in her eyes, and in her thanks
A subtler charm than gratitude.

I bade
My hostess a "good-night," and left her door,
Declining her entreaty to return.
We walked in silence, side by side, a space,
And then, with feigned indifference, I spoke:
"Your aunt has told me of your errand; else
It had been modest in me to withhold
This tendance on your steps. She tells me you
Are quite a devotee. Whom do you meet,
In neighborhood like this, to give a zest
To hour like this?"

"Brothers and sisters all,"
She said in low reply; "and as for zest,
There's never lack of it where there is love.
When families convene, they have no need
Of more than love to give them festal joy;
Nor do they with discrimination judge
Between the high and humble. These are one;
Love makes them one."

"And you are one with these?"

"Though most unworthy of such fellowship,
I trust that I am one with these;—that they
Are one with me, and reckon me among
Their number."

"Can they do you any good?"

"They can," she said; "but were it otherwise,
I can serve them; and so should seek them still.
I help them in their songs."

We reached too soon
The open doorway of the humble hut
Which, for long years, had held the village school,
And, at a little distance, paused. The room,
Battered and black by wantonest abuse
Of the rude youth, was lit by feeble lamps,
Brought by the villagers; and scattered round
Upon the high, hacked benches, hardly less
Rude and rough-worn than they, the worshipers
In silence sat. It was no place for words.
I took the lady's hand, and said "good-night!"

In whisper. Then she turned, and disappeared
Within the sheltered gloom ; but I could see
The care-worn cheeks light up with pleasant fire
As she passed in ; and e'en the fainting lamps
Flared with new life, the while they caught the
breath
Of her sweet robe. Then with an angry heart
I turned away, and, wrapped in selfish thought,
Took up the walk toward home.

This homely group
Of Yankee lollards she preferred to me !
These poor, pinched boobies, with their silly
wives—
Ah ! these were they who gave her overmuch
In the bestowal of their fellowship !
These crowned her with a peerless privilege,
Permitting her to sit with them an hour
As a dear sister ! How my sore self-love
Burned with the hot affront !

With lips compressed,

I TOOK THE LADY'S HAND AND SAID, "GOOD NIGHT!

Or blurting forth their anger and disgust,
I strode the meadows, stalked the silent town,
And growled and groaned in sullen helplessness
About the streets, until the midnight bell
Tolled from the old church tower;—in helplessness,
For mattered nothing what or who she was,
(I had not dared or cared to question that,)
Or how offensive in her piety
And her devotion to the tasteless cult
Of the weak throng, I was her slave; and she—
Her own and God's. The miserable strife
Between my love of self and love of her
I knew was bootless; and the trenchant truth
Cut to the quick. She held within her hand
My heart, my life, my doom, yet knew it not;
And had she known, her soul was under vows
Which would forever make subordinate
Their recognized possession,

But the morn
Brought with it better mood and calmer thoughts.
I had the grace to gauge the heartlessness

Of my exactions, and the power to crush
The tyrant wish to tear her from the throne
To which she clung. I said: "So she love me
As a true woman loves, and give herself—
Her sweet, pure self—to me, and fill my home
With her dear presence, loyal still to me
In wifely love and wifely offices,
Though she abide in Christian loyalty
By Christian vows, she shall have liberty,
And hold it as her right."

She was my peer:
No weakling girl, who would surrender will
And life and reason, with her loving heart,
To her possessor;—no soft, clinging thing
Who would find breath alone within the arms
Of a strong master, and obediently
Wait on his whims in slavish carefulness;—
No fawning, cringing spaniel, to attend
His royal pleasure, and account herself
Rewarded by his pats and pretty words,
But a round woman, who, with insight keen,

Had wrought a scheme of life, and measured well
Her womanhood ; had spread before her feet
A fine philosophy to guide her steps ;
Had won a faith to which her life was brought
In strict adjustment—brain and heart meanwhile
Working in conscious harmony and rhythm
With the great scheme of God's great universe,
On toward her being's end.

I could but know
Her motive was superior to mine.
I could but feel that in her loyalty
To God and duty, she condemned my life.
Into her woman's heart, thrown open wide
In holy charity, she had drawn all
Of human kind, and found no humblest soul
Too humble for her entertainment,—none
So weak it could return no grateful boon
For what she gave ; and standing modestly
Within her scheme, with meekest reverence
She bowed to those above her, yet with strong
And hearty confidence assumed a place

In service of the world, as minister
Ordained of Heaven to break to it the bread
She took from other hands. And she was one,
Who could see all there was of good in me,—
Could measure well the product of my power,
And give it impulse and direction ; nay,
Could supplement my power ; and help my heart
Against its foes.

The moment that I thrust
The selfish thirsting for monopoly
Of her affections from my godless heart,
She entered in, and reigned a goddess there.
If she had fascinated me before,
And fired my heart with passion, now she bent
My spirit to profound respect. I bowed
To the fair graces of her character,
Her queenly gifts, and the beneficence
Of her devoted life, with humbled heart
And self-depreciation. All of God
That the world held for me, I found in her ,
And in her, all the God I sought. She was

My saviour from myself and from my sins ;
For, with my worship of the excellence
Which she embodied, came the purity
And peace to which, through all my troubled life,
I had been stranger. Thoughts and feelings all
Were sublimated by the subtle flame
Which wrapped and warmed me ; and I walked as one
Might walk on air, with things of earth beneath,
Breathing a rare, supernal atmosphere
Which every sense and faculty informed
With light and life divine.

What need to tell
Of the succeeding summer days, and all
Their deeds and incidents ? They floated by
Like silent sails upon a summer sea,
That, sweeping in from farthest heaven at morn,
Traverse the vision, and at evening slide
Out into heaven again, their pennant-flames
The rosy dawns and day-falls. O'er and o'er
I walked the path, and crossed the stream, that lay

Between me and the idol of my heart;
And every day, in every circumstance,
I found her still the same, yet not the same;
For, every day, some unsuspected grace,
Or some fresh revelation of her wealth
Of character and culture, touched my heart
To new surpsise, and overflowed the cup
Whose wine was life to me.

Though I could see
That I was not unwelcome; though I knew
I gave a zest to her sequestered life,
I had built up so high my only hope
On her affection—I had given myself
So wholly to the venture for her hand,
I did not dare to speak of love, or ask
The question which, unasked, held hopefully
My destiny; which answered, might bring doom
Of madness or of death.

Meanwhile, I learned
The lady's history from other lips

Than hers—her aunt's. Alas! the old, old tale!
She had been bred to luxury; and all
That wealth could purchase for her, or the friends
Swarmed by its golden glamour could bestow,
She had possessed. But he who won the wealth,
Reaching for more, slipped from his height and fell,
Dragging his house to ruin. Then he died—
Died in disgrace; and all his thousand friends
Fell off, and left his pampered family,
The while the noisy auctioneer knocked down
His house and household gods, and set adrift
The helpless life thus cruelly bereft.
The mother lived a month: the rest went forth,
Not knowing whither; but they found among
The poor a shelter for their poverty,—
Kathrina with her aunt. Thus, in few words,
A tragedy of heart-breaks and of death,
Such as the world abounds with.

But this girl,
With her quick instincts and her brave, good heart,

Determined she would live a while, and learn
What lesson God would teach her. This she sought,
And, seeking, found, or thought she found. How well
She learned the lesson—what the lesson was—
Her life, thus far revealed, and waiting still
My feeble record, shall disclose. Enough,
Just now and here, that out of it she bore
A noble womanhood, accepting all
Her great misfortunes as the discipline
Of a paternal hand, in love prescribed
To lead her to her place, and whiten her
For Christian service.

All the summer fled;
And still my heart delayed. One pleasant eve,
When first the creaking of the crickets told
Of Autumn's opening door, I went with her
To ramble in the fields. We touched the hem
Of the dark mountain's robe, that falls in folds
Of emerald sward around his feet, and there

Upon its tufted velvet we sat down.
It was my time to speak, but I was dumb;
And silence, painful and portentous, hung
Upon us both. At length, she turned and said:
"Some days have passed since you were latest here.
Have you been ill?"

"No, I have been at work,"
I answered,—"at my own delightful work;
The first since first we met. The record lies
Where I may reach it at a word from you.
Command, and I will read it."

"I command,"
She said, responding with a laugh. "Nay, I
Entreat. I used your word, but this is mine,
And has a better sound from lips of mine.
I am your waiting auditor."

I read:

"Was it the tale of a talking bird?

Was it a dream of the night?
When have I seen it? Where have I heard
Of the haps of a dainty craft, that stirred
My spirit with affright?

"The shallop stands out from the sheltered bay
With a burden of spirits twain,—
A woman who lifts her sad eyes to pray,
A tall youth, trolling a roundelay,
And before them night, and the main!

"O! Star of The Sea! They will come to harm:
Nor master nor sailor is there!
The youth clasps the mast with his sinewy arm,
And laughs! Does he hold in his bosom a charm
That will baffle the sprites of the air?

"O! woe to the delicate ship! O! woe!
For the sun is sunk, and behold!
The trooping phantoms that come and go
In the sky above and the waves below!
Ho! The wind blows wild and cold.

"The woman is weeping in weak despair;
The youth still clings to the mast,
With cheeks all aflame, and with eyes that stare
At the phantoms hovering everywhere;
And the storm-rack rises fast!

"The phantoms close on the flying bark;
They flutter about her peak;
They sweep in swarms from the outer dark;
But the youth at the mast stands still and stark,
While they flap his stinging cheek.

"They shiver the bolts that the lightning flings;
They bellow and roar and hiss;
They splash the deck with their slimy wings
Monstrous, horrible, ghastly things—
That climb from the foul abyss.

"No star shines out at the woman's prayer;
O! madly distraught is she!
And the bark drives on with her wild despair,

With shrieking fiends in the crowded air,
And fiends on the swarming sea.

"Then out of the water before their sight
A shape loomed bare and black!
So black that the darkness bloomed with white;
So black that the lightning grew strangely bright;
And it lay in the shallop's track!

"O! fierce was the shout of the goblins then!
How the gibber and laugh went round!
The shout and the laugh of a thousand men,
Echoed and answered, and echoed again,
Had given a feebler sound.

"Straight toward the blackness drove the ship;
But the youth still clung to the mast:
'I have read,' quoth he, with a proud, cold lip,
'That the devil gets never a man on the hip
Whom he scares not first or last.'

"Nearer the blackness loomed; and the bark

Scudded before the breeze;
Nearer the blackness loomed, and hark!
The crash of breakers out of the dark,
And the shock of plunging seas!

"O! woe! for the woman's wits ran daft
With the fearful bruit and burst;
She sprang to her feet, and flitting aft,
She plunged in the sea, and the black waves quaffed
The sweet life they had cursed.

"Light leaped the bark on the mountain-breast
Of a tenth-wave out to land;
While the sprites of the sea fell off to rest,
And the youth, unharmed, became the guest
Of the elves of the silent land.

"With banter and buffet they pressed around;
They tied his strong hands fast;
But he laughed, and said, 'I have read and found
That the devil throws never a man to the ground
Whom he scares not, first or last.'

"Under the charred and ghastly gloom,
Over the flinty stones,
They led him forth to his terrible doom,
And, plunged in a deep and noisome tomb,
They sat him among the bones.

"They left him there in the crawling mire:
They could neither maim nor kill:
For fiends of water, and earth, and fire,
Are baffled and beaten by the ire
Of a dauntless human will.

"Days flushed and faded, months passed away,
He knew by the golden light
That shot, through a loop in the wall, the ray
Which parted the short and slender day
From the long and doleful night.

"Was it a vision that cheated his eyes?
Was he awake, or no?
He stared through the loop with keen surprise;

For he saw a sweet angel from the skies,
    With white wings, folded low.

"Could she not loose him from his thrall,
    And lead him into the light ?
'Ah me !' he murmured, 'I dare not call,
Lest she may doubt it a goblin's waul,
    And leave me in swift affright !'

"She plumed her wings with a noiseless haste ;
    He could neither call nor cry :
She vanished into the sunny waste,
Into far blue air that he longed to taste ;
    And he cursed that he could not die.

"But she came again, and every day
    He worshiped her where she shone ;
And again she left him and floated away,
But his faithless tongue refused to pray
    For the boon she could give alone.

"And there he sits in his dumb despair,

And his watching eyes grow dim :
Would God that his coward lips might dare
To utter the word to the angel fair,
That is life or death to him !"

I marked her as I read, a furtive glance
Filling each pause. The passion of the piece,
Flaming and fading, ever and anon,
Mirrored itself within her tender eyes,
Themselves the mirror of her tender soul,
And fixed attent upon my face the while.
She had not caught my meaning, but had heard
Only a weird, wild story. When I paused,
Folding the manuscript, I saw a shade
Of disappointment sweep her face, and marked
A question rising in her eyes. She knew
That I was waiting for her words. and turned
Her look away, and for long moments gazed
Into the brooding dusk.

"Speak it !" I said.

"'Twas very strange and sad," she answered me.
"Why do you write such things?—or, writing such,
Leave them so incomplete? The prisoned youth,
Thus unreleased, will haunt me while I live;
I shudder while I think of him."

Then I:

"The poem will be finished by-and-by,
For this is history, and antedates
No fact that it records. Whether this youth
Shall live entombed, or reach the blessed air,
Depends upon his angel; for he calls—
I hear him call, and call again her name
Kathrina! O! Kathrina!"

Like the flash

Of the hot lightning, the significance
Of the strange vision gleamed upon her face
In a bright, throbbing flame, that fell full soon
To ashen paleness. By unconscious will
We both arose. She vainly tried to speak,
And gazed into my eyes with such a look

Of tender questioning, of half-reproach,
Of struggling, doubting, hesitating joy,
As few men ever see, and none but once.

Are there not lofty moments, when the soul
Leaps to the front of being, casting off
The robes and clumsy instruments of sense,
And, postured in its immortality,
Reveals its independence of the clod
In which it dwells ?—moments in which the earth
And all material things, all sights and sounds,
All signals, ministries, interpreters,
Relapse to nothing, and the interflow
Of thought and feeling, love and life go on
Between two spirits, raised to sympathy
By an inspiring passion, as, in heaven,
The body dust within an orb outlived,
It shall go on forever ?

Moments like these—
Nay, these in very truth—were given us then.
Who shall expound !—ah ! who but God alone,

The everlasting mystery of love ?
She spoke not, but I knew that she was mine.
I breathed no word, but she was well assured
That I was wholly hers.

In what disguise
Our love had hid, and wrought its miracle ;
Behind what semblance of indifference,
Or play of courtesy, it spun the chords
That bound our hearts in one, was mystery
Like love itself. The swift intelligence
Of interchange of perfect faith and troth,
Of gift of life and person, of the thrill
Of triumph in my soul, and gratitude
In hers, without a gesture, or a word,
Was like the converse of the continents—
Tracking with voiceless flight the slender wire
That underlay the throbbing mystery
Between our souls, and made our heart-beats one.
I opened wide my arms, and she, my own,
Sobbed on my breast with such excess of joy,
In such embrace of passionate tenderness,

As heaven may yield again, but never earth.
Slow in the golden twilight, toward her home,
Her hand upon my arm, we loitered on,
Silent at first, and then with quiet speech
Broaching our plans, or tracing in review
The history of our springing love, when she,
Lifting her soft blue eyes to mine :

"Dear Paul!
There are some things, and some I will not name,
That make me sad, e'en in this height of joy.
In the wild lay that you have read to-night,
You make too much of me. No heart of man,
Though loving well and loving worthily,
Can be content with any human love.
No woman, though the pride and paragon
Of all her sex, can take the place of God.
No angel she ; nor is she quite a man
In power and courage,—gifts which charm her most,
And which, possessing most, disrobe her charms,
And make her less a woman. If she stand

SLOW IN THE GOLDEN TWILIGHT TOWARD HER HOME,
HER HAND UPON MY ARM, WE LOITERED ON.

In fair equality with man—his mate—
Each unto each the rounded complement
Of their humanity, it is enough;
And such equality must ever lie
In their unequal gifts. This thing, at least,
Is true as God: she is not more than he,
And sits upon no throne. To be adored
By man, she must be placed upon a throne
Built by his hands, and sit an idol there,
Degraded by the measure of the flight
Between God's thought and man's."

Responding I:

"Fix your own place, my love; it is your right.
'Tis well to have a theory, and sit
In the centre of it, mistress of its law,
And subject also;—to set men up here
And woman there, in a fine equipoise
Of gift and grace and import. It conveys
To nicely-working minds a pleasant sense
Of order, like a well-appointed room,
Where one may see, in various stuffs and wares,

Forethoughts of color brought to harmony;
Strict balancings of quantity and form;
Flowers in the centre, and, beside the grate,
A rack for shovel and tongs. But minds like these
(Your pardon, love!) are likely to arrange
The window-lights to save the furniture,
And spoil the pictures on the wall. And you,
In the adjustment of your theory,
Would shut the light from her whose mind informs
Its harmonies. All worship, in my thought,
Goes hand in hand with love. We cannot love,
And fail to worship what we love. While you
Worship the strength and courage which you find
In him who has your heart, he bows to all
Of faith and sweetness which he finds in you.
If, in our worship, we have need to build
Noblest ideals, taking much from God
With which to make them perfect in our eyes,
Shall God mark blame? We worship Him the while,
In attributes His own, or attributes

With which our thought invests him. As for me—
It is no secret—I am what you call
A godless man; yet what is worshipful,
Or seems to be so, that with all my heart
I worship; and I worship while I love.
You deem yourself the dwelling-place of God,
And keep your spirit cleanly for His feet.
All merit you abjure, ascribing all
To Him who dwells within you. How can you
Forbid that I fall down and worship you,
When what I find to worship is not yours,
But God's alone? I know the ecstasy
Enlarges, strengthens, purifies my soul,
And blesses me with peace. My love, my life,
You are my all. I have no other good,
And, in this moment of my happiness,
I ask no other."

Tears were in her eyes,
Her clasped hands clinging fondly to my arm,
While under droop of lashes she replied:
"I feel, dear Paul, that this is sophistry.

It does not touch my judgment or my heart
With motive of conviction. In what way
God may be working to reclaim your will
And worship to Himself, I cannot know.
If through your love for me, or mine for you,
Then as his grateful, willing instrument,
I yield myself to Him. But this is true:
God is not worshiped in his attributes.
I do not love your attributes, but you.
Your attributes all meet me otherwhere,
Blended in other personalities,
Nor do I love, nor do I worship them,
Or those who bear them. E'en the spotted pard
Will dare a danger which will make you pale,
But shall his courage steal my heart from you?
You cheat your conscience, for you know that I
May like your attributes, yet love not you;
Nay, worship them indeed, despising you.
I do not argue thus to damp your joy,
But make it rational. If you presume
Perfection in me,—if you lavish all
The largess of your worship and your love

On me, imposing on my head a crown
Stolen from God's, there surely waits your heart
The pang of disappointment. There will come
A sad, sad time, when, in your famished soul.
The cry for something more, and more divine,
Will rise, nor be repressed."

There is a charm
In earnestness, when it inspires the lips
Of one we love, that spoils their argument,
And yields so much of pleasure and of pride,
That the conviction which they seek evades
Their eager fingers, and with throbbing wings
Crows from its covert.

She was casuist,
Cunning and clear, and I was proud of her;
And though I knew that she had swept away
My refuges of lies like chaff, and proved
My fair words fustian, I was moved to mirth
Over the solemn ruin. Had it been
A decent thing to do, I should have laughed

Full in her face ; but knowing that her words
Were offspring of her conscience and her love,
I could no less than hold respectfully
Her earnest warning.

"Well, I'll take the risk,"
I said. "While you shall have the argument,
I will have you, whom, on the whole, I like
Better than that. And you shall have your way,
And I my own, in common liberty,
With things like these. You, doubtless, are to me
What I am not to you. We are unlike
In life and circumstance—alike alone
In this : that better than all else on earth
We love each other. This is basis broad
For happiness, or broad enough for me.
If you build better, you are fortunate,
Ay, fortunate indeed ; and some fine day
We'll talk about it. Let us have to-night
Joy in our new possessions, and defer
This little joust of wits and consciences
To more convenient season."

We had reached
The cottage door at this; and there her aunt
Awaited our return. So, hand in hand,
Assuming show of rustic bashfulness,
We paused before her, and with bows profound
Made our obeisance.

"Well?" she said at length
"Well?—and what of it?"

"Are you not surprised?"
I asked.

"Surprised, indeed! Surprised at what?"

"At what you see: and this! and this!" I said,
Planting a kiss upon each lovely cheek
Of my betrothed, that straightway bloomed with rose.
"What! are you blind, my aunt?"

"You silly fools!

I've seen it from the first," she answered me.
"No doubt you thought that you were very deep,
Very mysterious—all that sort of thing.
I've watched you, and if you, young man, had been
Aught but a coward, it had come before,
And saved some sleep o'nights to both of you.
But down upon your knees, for benison
Of one who loves you both."

We knelt, and then
She kissed us, leaving on our cheeks the tears
That sprang to brim the moment. Her shrewd eyes,
That melted in the sympathy of love,
Would not meet ours again, but turned away,
And sought in solitude to drain themselves
Of their strange passion.

God forbid that I,
With weak and sacrilegious lips, betray
The confidence of love; or tear aside

The secrecy behind whose snowy folds
Honor and virgin modesty retire
For holiest communion! For the fire
Which burns upon that altar is of God.
Its tongues of flame, throughout all time and space,
Speak but one language, understood by all,
But sacred ever to the wedded hearts
That listen to their breathings.

In the deep hours of night
I left the cottage, brain and heart o'erfilled
With the ethereal vintage I had quaffed.
Disturbing not the drowsy ferryman,
I slipped his little wherry from the sand,
And in the star-sprent river lipped the oars
That pulled me homeward. The enchanting tide
Was smooth continuation of the dream
On which my spirit, holily afloat,
Had glided through long hours of happiness.
Earth, by the strange, delicious ecstasy,
Was changed to paradise; and something kin
To gratitude arose within my soul—

A fleeting passion, dying all too soon,
Lacking the root which faith alone can feed.

I touched the shore; but when my hasting feet
Started the homeward walk, there came a change.
Down from the quiet stars there fell a voice,
Heard in the innermost, that troubled me:
"She is not more than you: why worship her?
"And she will die; what will remain for you?
"You may die first, indeed: then what resource?
"You have no sympathy with her in things
"Ordained within her conscience and her life,
"The things supreme: can there be marriage
thus?
"Is e'en such bliss as may be possible
"Sure to be yours? Fate has a thousand hands
"To dash your lifted cup."

With thoughts like these,
A vague uneasiness pervaded me,
And toned the triumph of my passion, till,
Almost in anger, I exclaimed at last:

"This is reaction. I have flown too high
"Above the healthy level, and I feel
"The press of denser air. The equipoise
"Of circumstance and feeling will be reached
"All in good time. Rest and to-morrow's sun
"Will bring the remedy, and, with the mists,
"This cloud will pass away."

Then with clenched hands
I swore I would be happy,--that my soul
Should find its satisfaction in her love ;
And that, if ever there should come a time
Of cold satiety, or I should find
Weakness or fault where I had thought strength
And full perfection, I would e'en endow
Her poverty with all the hoarded wealth
Of my imagination, making her
The woman of my want, in plenitude
Of strength and loveliness.

The breezy days

Over whose waves my buoyant life careered,
Rolled to October, falling on its beach
With bursts of mellow music; and I leaped
Upon the longed for shore, for in that month
My dear betrothed, deferring to the stress
Of my impatient wish, had promised me
Her hand in wedlock.

Ere the happy day
Dawned on the world, the world was draped in robes
Meet for the nuptials. Baths of sunny haze,
Steeping the ripening leaves from day to day,
And dainty kisses of the frost at night,
Joined in the subtile alchemy that wrought
Such miracles of change, that myriad trees
Which pranked the meads and clothed the forest glooms
Bloomed with the tints of Eden. Had the earth
Been splashed with blood of grapes from every clime,
Tinted from topaz to dim carbuncle,

Or orient ruby, it would not have been
Drenched with such waste of color. All the hues
The rainbow knows, and all that meet the eye
In flowers of field and garden, joined to tell
Each tree's close-folded secret. Side by side
Rose sister maples, some in amber gold,
Others incarnadine or tipped with flame;
And oaks that for a hundred years had stood,
And flouted one another through the storms—
Boasting their might—proclaimed their pique or pride
In dun, or dyes of Tyre. The sumach-leaves
Blazed with such scarlet that the crimson fruit
Which hung among their flames was touched to guise
Of dim and dying embers; while the hills
That met the sky at the horizon's rim—
Dabbled with rose among the evergreens,
Or stretching off in sweeps of clouted crimson–glowed
As if the archery of sunset clouds,
By squads and fierce battalions, had rained down

Its barbed and feathered fire, and left it fast
To advertise th' exploit.

In such a pomp
Of autumn glory, by the simplest rites,
Kathrina gave her hand to me, and I
Pledged truth and life to her. I bore her home
Through shocks of maize, revealing half their gold,
Past gazing harvesters with creaking wains
That brimmed with fruitage—my adored, my wife,
Fruition of my hope—the proudest freight
That ever passed that way!

My troops of friends,
Grown strangely warm and strangely numerous
With scent of novelty and pleasant cheer,
Assisted me to place upon her throne
My household queen. Right royally she sat
The new-born dignity. Most graciously
She spoke and smiled among the silken clouds
That, fold on perfumed fold, like frankincense
Enveloped her, through half the festal night,

With welcome and good wishes. I was proud;
For was not I a king where she was queen?
And queen she was—though consort in my home,
Queen regnant in the realm of womanhood,
By right of every charm.

Into her place,
As mistress of all home economies,
She slid without a jar, as if the Fates,
By concert of foreordinate design,
Had fitted her for it, and it for her,
And, having joined them well, were satisfied.
Obedient to the orbit of our love,
We came and went, revolving round our home
In spheral harmony—twin stars made one,
And loyal to one law.

When at our board,
All viands lifted by her hand became
Ambrosial; and her light, elastic step
From room to room, in busy household cares,
Timed with my heart, and filled me with a sense

Of harmony and peace. Days, weeks, and months
Lapsed like soft measures, rhyming each with
each,
All charged with thoughtful ministries to me,
And not to me alone ; for I was proud
To know that she was counted by the good
As a good power among them,—by the poor,
As angel sent of God, on whom they called
His blessing down.

She held her separate life
Of prayer and Christian service, without show
Of sanctity, without obtrusiveness ;
And, though I could but know she never sought
A blessing for herself, forgetting me
In her petition, not in all those months
Did word of difference betray the gulf
Between our souls and lives. She had her plan :
I guessed it, and respected it. She felt
That if her life were not an argument
To move me, nothing that her lips might say
Could win me to her wish. Pride would repel

What it could not refute, and pleasantry
Parry the thrusts that love could not resent.

A whole year sped, yet not a line of verse
Had grown beneath my pen. When I essayed
To brace my powers to effort, and to call
Forth from their camp and covert the bright ranks
Of tuneful numbers, no responsive shout
Answered the bugle-blast, and from my hand—
Irresolute and nerveless as a babe's—
My falchion fell.

She rallied me on this;
But I had naught to say, save this, perhaps:
That she, being all my world, had left no room
For other occupation than my love.
She did not smile at this: it was no jest,
But saddest truth. I had grown enervate
In the warm atmosphere which I had breathed:
And this, with consciousness that in her soul—
As warm with love as mine—each gentle power

Was kindling with new life from day to day,
Growing with my decline.

Well, in good time
There came to us a child, the miniature
Of her on whose dear breast my babyhood
Was nursed and cradled ; and my happy heart,
Charged with a double tenderness, received
And blessed the precious gift. Another fount
Of human love gurgled to meet my lips.
Another store of good, as rich and pure,
In its own kind, as that from which I drank,
Was thus discovered to my taste, and I
Feasted upon its fulness.

With the gift
That brimmed my cup of joy, there came a grace
To her who bore it of fresh loveliness.
If I had loved the maiden and the bride,
The mother, through whose pain my heart had won
Its new possession, fastened to my heart

With a new sympathy. Whatever dross
Our months of intimacy had betrayed
Within her character, was purged away,
And she was left pure gold. Nay, I should say,
Whatever goodness had not been revealed
Through the relations of her heart to mine
As loving maid and mistress, found the light
Through her maternity. A heavenly change
Passed o'er her soul and o'er her pallid face,
As if the unconscious yearning of a life
Had found full satisfaction in the birth
Of the new being. Her long weariness
Was but a trance of peace and gratitude ;
And as she lay—her babe upon her breast,
Her eyelids closed—I could but feel that heaven,
Should it hold all the good of which she dreamed,
Had little more for her.

And when again
She moved about the house, in ministry
To me and to her helpless child, I knew
That I had tasted every precious good

That woman bears to man. Ay, more than this:
That not one man in thousands had received
Such largess of affection, and such prize.
Of womanhood, as I had found in her,
And made my own. The whole enchanting round
Of pure domestic commerce had been mine
A lover blest, a husband satisfied,
A father crowned! Love had no other boon
To offer me, and held within its gift
No other title.

Thus within the space
Of two swift years, I traversed the domain
Of novelty, and learned that I must glean
The garnered fields of my experience
To gratify the greed that still possessed
My sateless heart. The time had come to me—
Which I had half foreseen—when, by my will,
My interest in those I loved should live
Predominant in all my life. I nursed
With jealous care my passion for my wife.
I raised her to an apotheosis

In my imagination, where I bowed
And paid my constant homage. I was still
Her fond and loyal lover; but my heart,
That had so freely drunk, with full content,
Had seen the bottom of the cup she held;
And what remained but tricks to eke it out,
And artifice to give it piquancy,
And sips to cool my tongue, the while my heart
Was hollow with its thirst? My little child
Was precious to my soul beyond all price;
Mother and babe were all that they could be
To any heart of man; and yet—and yet!

Of all the dull, dead weights man ever bore,
Sure, none can wear the soul with discontent
Like consciousness of power unused. To feel
That one has gift to move the multitude,—
To act upon the life of humankind
By force of will, or fire of eloquence,
Or voice of lofty art, and yet, to feel
No stir of mighty motive in the soul
To action or endeavor; to behold

The fairest prizes of this fleeting life
Borne off by patient men who, day by day,
By bravest toil and struggle, reach the heights
Of great achievement, toiling, struggling thus
With a strong joy, and with a fine contempt
For soft and selfish passion ; to see this,
Yet cling to such a passion, like a slave
Who hugs his chains in sluggish impotence,
Refusing freedom lest he lose the crust
The chain of bondage warrants him—ah ! this
Is misery indeed !

Such misery
Was mine. I held the consciousness of power
To labor even-headed with the best
Who wrought for fame, or strove to make themselves
Felt in the world's great life ; and yet, I felt
No lift to enterprise, from heaven above
Or earth beneath ; for neither God nor man
Lived in my love. My home held all my world ;
Yet it was evident—I felt, I knew—

MY HOME HELD ALL MY WORLD.

That naught could fill my opening want but toil;
And there were times when I had hailed with joy
The curse of poverty, compelling me
To labor for my bread, and for the bread
Of those I loved.

My neighbors all around
Were happy in their work. The plodding hind
Who served my hand, or groomed my petted horse,
Whistled about his work with merry heart,
And filled his measure of content with toil.
In all the streets and all the busy fields
Men were astir, and doing with their might
What their hands found to do. They drove the plough,
They trafficked, builded, delved, they spun and wove,
They taught and preached, they hasted up and down
Each on his little errand, and their eyes
Were full of eager fire, as if the earth

And all its vast concerns were on their hands.
Their homes were fresh with guerdon every night,
And ripe with impulse to new industry
At each new dawn.

I saw all this, but knew
That they were not like me—were most unlike
In constitution and condition. Thus,
My power to do, and do the single thing
My power was shaped to do, became, instead
Of wings to bear me, weights to burden me.
The moiling multitude for little tasks
Found little motives plenty; but for me,
Whom in my indolence they all despised—
Not understanding me—no motive rose
To lash or lead. Even the love I dreamed
Would give me impulse had defrauded me.
Feeble and proud; strong, yet emasculate;
Centred in self, and still despising self;
Goaded, yet held; convinced, but never moved;
Such conflict ofttimes held and harried me
That death had met with welcome. If I read,

I read to kill my time. No interest
In the great thoughts of others moved my soul,
Because I had no object : useless quite
The knowledge and the culture I possessed ;
And if I rode, the stale monotony
Of the familiar landscapes sickened me.

In these dull years, my toddling little wean
Grew into prattling childhood, and I gained
Such fresh delight from her as kept my heart
From fatal gloom ; but more and more I shunned
The world around me, more and more drew in
The circle of my life, until, at last,
My home became my hermitage. I knew
The dissolution of the spell would come,
And, though I dreaded it, I longed to greet
The crash and transformation. If my pride
Forbade the full confession to my wife
That time had verified her prophecy,
It failed to hold the truth from her. She read,
With a true woman's insight, all my heart ;
But, with a woman's sensitiveness, shrank

From questions which might seem to carry blame ;
And so, for years, there lay between our souls
The bar of silence.

One sweet summer eve,
After my lamb was folded, and before
The lamps were lighted, as I sat alone
Within my room, I heard reluctant feet
Seeking my door. They paused, and then I heard:

" May I come in ?"

" Ay, you may always come ;
And you are welcome always," I replied.
The room was dim, but I could see her face
Was pale, and her long lashes wet. " Your seat,"—
I said, with open arms. Upon my knee,
One hand upon my shoulder, she sank down
As if the heart within her breast were lead,
And she were weary with its weight.

"My wife,
What burden now?" I asked her tenderly.
She fixed her swimming eyes on mine, and said:
"My dear, you are not happy. Years have gone
Since you have been content. I bring no words
Of blame against you: you have been to me
A comfort and a joy. Your constancy
Has honored me as few of all my sex
Are honored by your own; but while you pine
With secret pain, I am so wholly yours
That I must pine with you. I've waited long
For you to speak; and now I come to you
To ask you this one question: is there aught
Of toil or sacrifice within my power
To ease your heart, or give you liberty
Beyond the round to which you hold your feet?
Speak freely, frankly, as to one who loves
Her husband better than her only child,
And better than herself."

I drew her head
Down to my cheek, and said: "My angel wife!

Whatever torment or disquietude
I may have suffered, you have never been
Its cause, or its occasion. You are all—
You have been all—that womanhood can be
To manhood's want; and in your woman's love
And woman's pain, I have found every good
My life has known since first our lives were joined.
You knew me better than I knew myself;
And your prophetic words have haunted me
Like thoughts of retribution: '*There will come*
'*A sad, sad time, when in your famished soul*
'*The cry for something more, and more divine*
'*Will rise, nor be repressed.*' For something more
My spirit clamors: nothing more divine
I ask for."

"What shall be this 'something more?'"

"Work," I replied; "ay, work, but never here;
Work among men, where I may feel the touch
Of kindred life; work where the multitudes
Are surging; work where brains and hands

Are struggling for the prizes of the world;
Work where my spirit, driven to its bent
By competitions and great rivalries,
Shall vindicate its own pre-eminence,
And wring from a reluctant world the meed
Of approbation and respect for which
It yearns with awful hunger; work, indeed,
Which shall compel the homage of the souls
That creep around me here, and pity you
Because, forsooth, the Fates have hobbled you
With a dull drone. I know how sweet the love
Of two fond souls; and I will have the hearts
Of millions. These shall satisfy my greed,
And round the measure of my life; and these
My work shall win me."

At these childish words
She raised her head, and with a sweet, sad smile
Of love and pity blent, made her response:
"Not yet, my husband—if your wife may speak
A thought that crosses yours—not yet have you

Found the great secret of content. But work
May help you toward it, and in any case
Is better far than idleness. For this,
You ask of me to sacrifice this home
And all the truest friends my life has gained.
I do it from this moment; glad to prove,
At any tender cost, my love for you,
And faith in your endeavor. I will go
To any spot of earth where you may lead,
And go rejoicing. Let us go at once!"

"I burn my ships behind me." I replied.
"Measure the cost: be sure no secret hope
Of late return be found among the flames;
For if I go, I leave no single thread,
Save that which binds me to my mother's grave,
To draw me back."

"My love shall be the torch
To light the fire," she answered.

Then we rose,
And, with a kiss, marked a full period
To love's excess, and with a sweet embrace
Wrote the initial of a stronger life.

A REFLECTION.

Oh! not by bread alone is manhood nourished
    To its supreme estate!
By every word of God have lived and flourished
    The good men and the great.
      Ay, not by bread alone!

"Oh! not by bread alone!" the sweet rose breathing
    In throbs of perfume, speaks;
"But myriad hands, in earth and air, are wreathing
    The blushes for my cheeks.
      Ay, not by bread alone!"

"Oh! not by bread alone!" proclaims in thunder
The old oak from his crest;
"But suns and storms upon me, and deep under,
The rocks in which I rest.
Ay, not by bread alone!"

"Oh! not by bread alone!" The truth flies singing
In voices of the birds;
And from a thousand pastured hills is ringing
The answer of the herds:
"Ay, not by bread alone!"

Oh! not by bread alone! for life and being
Are finely complex all,
And increment, with element agreeing,
Must feed them, or they fall.
Ay, not by bread alone!

Oh! not by love alone, though strongest, purest,
That ever swayed the heart;
For strongest passion evermore the surest

Defrauds each manly part.
Ay, not by love alone!

Oh! not by love alone is power engendered.
Until within the soul
The gift of every motive has been rendered,
It is not strong and whole.
Ay, not by love alone!

Oh! not by love alone is manhood nourished
To its supreme estate:
By every word of God have lived and flourished
The good men and the great.
Ay, not by love alone!

PART III.

LABOR.

TEN years of love !--a sleep, a pleasant dream
That passed its culmen in the early half,
Concluding in confusion—a wild scene
Of bargains, auctions, partings, and what not ?
And an awaking !

I was in Broadway,
A unit in a million. Like a bath
In ocean surf, blown in from farthest seas
Under the August ardors, the grand rush
Of crested life assailed me with its waves,
And cooled me while it fired. With sturdy joy
I sought its broadest billows, and resigned

My spirit to their surge and sway; and stood
In sheltered coves, reached only by the spume
And crepitant bubbles of the yesty floods,
Drinking the roar, the sheen, the restlessness,
As inspiration, both of sense and soul.

I saw the waves of life roll up the steps
Of great cathedrals and retire; and break
In charioted grandeur at the feet
Of marble palaces, and toss their spray
Of feathered beauty through the open doors,
To pile the restless foam within; and burst
On crowded caravansaries, to fall
In quick return; and in dark currents glide
Through sinuous alleys and the grimy loops
Of reeking cellars; and with softest plash
Assail the gilded shrines of opulence,
And slide in musical relapse away.

With senses dazed and stunned, and soul o'erfilled
With chaos of new thoughts, I turned away,
And sought my city home. There all was calm,

With wife and daughter waiting my return,
And eager with their welcome. That was life !—
An interest in the great world of life,
A place for toil within a world of toil,
And love for its reward. "Amen !" I said,
"And twice amen ! I've found my life at last,
And we will all be happy."

Day by day—
The while I sought adjustment to the life
Which I had chosen, and with careful thought
Gathered to hand the fair material
Elect by Fancy for the organism
Over whose germ she brooded—I went out,
To bathe again upon the shore of life
My long-enfeebled nature.

Every day
I met some face I knew. My college friends
Came up in strange disguises. Here was one,
With a white neck-cloth and a saintly face,
Who had been rusticated and disgraced

For lawlessness. Now he administered
A charge which proved that he had been at work,
And made himself a man. And there was one—
A lumpy sort of boy, as memory
Recalled him to me—grown to portliness
And splendid spectacles. He drove a chaise,
And practised surgery,—was on his way
To meet a class of youth, who sought to be
Great surgeons like himself, and took full notes
Of all his stolen wisdom. By his watch—
A gold repeater, with a mighty chain—
He gave me just five minutes; then rolled off—
Pretension upon wheels. Another grasped
My hand as if I were his bosom friend,
Just in from a long voyage. He was one
Who stole my wood in college, and received
With grace the kick I gave him. He had grown
To be the tail of a portentous firm
Of city lawyers: managed, as he said,
The matter of collections; and had made
In his small way—to use his modest phrase:
Truthful as modest—quite a pretty plum.

He was o'erjoyed to see me in the town:
Hoped I would call upon him at his den:
If I had any business in his line,
Would do it for me promptly; as for price,
No need to talk of that between two friends!

But these, and all—the meanest and the best—
Were hard at work. They always questioned me
Before we parted, touching my pursuits;
And though they questioned kindly, I grew sore
Under the repetition, and ashamed
To iterate my answer, till I burned
To do some work, so lifted into fame,
That shame should be to him whose ignorance
Compelled a question.

Simplest foresters
Have learned the trick of woodland broods, that fly
In radiant divergence from the flash
Of death and danger, and, when all is still,
Steal back to where their fellows bit the dust
For rendezvous. And thus society

Follows the brutal instinct. When the friends,
Who from her father's ruin fled amain,
Found out my wife, and learned that it was safe
To gather back to the old feeding-ground,
They came. Her old home had become my own
And they were all delighted. It was sweet
To have her back again ; and it was sad
To know that those who once were happy there,
Dispensing happiness, could come no more.

It had its modicum of earnestness,—
This talk of theirs—and she received it all
With hearty courtesy, and yielded it
The unction of her charity, so far
That it was smooth and redolent to her.
The difference—the world-wide difference—
Between my wife and them was obvious ;
But she was generous through nature's gift
I fancied—could not well be otherwise ;
Although their fawning filled me with disgust.
Oh ! fool and blind : not to perceive the Christ
That shone and spoke in her !

The hour approached—
The pre-determined time—when I should close
My study-door, and wrap my kindling brain
In the poetic dream which, day by day,
Was swiftly gathering consistence there.
The quick, creative instinct in me plumed
Its pinions for the flight, and I could feel
The influx of fresh power; but whence it came,
I did not question; though it fired my heart
With the assurance of success.

I told
My dear companion of my hopeful plans
For winning fame, and making for myself
A lofty place; but I could not inspire
Her heart with my ambition, or win o'er
Her judgment to my motive. She adhered
To her old theory, and gave no room
To any motive it did not embrace.
We argued much, but always argued wide,
And ended where we started. Postulates
On which we stood in perfect harmony,

Were points of separation, out from which
We struck divergently, till sympathy,
That only lives by rhythm of thoughts and hearts,
Lay dead between us.

"Man loves praise," I said.
"It is an appetence which He who made
The human soul, made to be satisfied.
It is a tree He planted. If it grow
On that which feeds it, and become at last
Thrifty and fruitful, it is still His own,
With usury. And if, in His intent,
This passion have no place among the powers
Of active life, why is it mighty there
From youngest childhood? Pray you what is fame
But concrete praise?—the universal voice
Which bears, from every quarter of the earth,
Its homage to a name, that grows thereby
To be its own immortal monument,
Outlasting all the marble and the bronze
Which cunning fingers, since the world began,

Have shaped or stamped with story? What is
fame
But aggregate of praise? And if it be
Legitimate to win, for sake of praise,
The praise of one, why not of multitudes?"

"Ay," she replied; "'tis true that men love
praise;
And it is true that He who made the soul
Planted therein the love of praise, to be
A motive in its life—all true so far;
And so far we agree. But motives all
Have their appropriate sphere and sway, like men
Who bear them in their breasts. The love of
praise
Fills life with fine amenities. Not all
Who live have pleasant tempers, and not all
The gift of gracious manners, or the love
Of nobler motive, higher meed than praise.
The world is full of bears, who smooth their hair,
And glove their paws, and put on manly airs,
And hold our honey sacred, and our lives

Our own, because they hunger for our praise.
'Tis a fine thing for bears—this love of praise—
And those who deal with them ; and a good thing
For children, and for parents, teachers—all
Who have them in their keeping. It may hold
A little mind to rectitude, until
It grow, and grow ashamed to yield itself
To such a petty motive. Children all
Like sugar, and it may admit of doubt
Whether our praise or sugar sweetens more
Their petulant sub-acids ; but a man
Would choke in swallowing the compliment
Which we should pay him, were we but to say
'Go to ! Do some great deed, and you shall have
Your pay in sugar :—maple, mind you, now,
So you shall do it featly.' "

"Very good !"
I answered, " very good, indeed ! if we
Engage in talk for sport ; but argument
On themes like these must have the element
Of candor. Highest truth, in certain lights,

May be ridiculous, and yet be truth.
Women are angels : just a little weak
And just a little wicked, it may be,
Yet still the sweetest beings in the world ;
But when one stands with apprehensive gasp
At verge of sternutation, or leaps off,
Projecting all her being in a sneeze,
Or snores with lips wide-parted, or essays
The 'double-quick,' we turn our eyes away
In sadness, that a creature so divine
Can be so shockingly ridiculous :
Yet who shall say she's not an angel still ?
Now you present to me the meanest face
Of a most noble truth. I laugh with you
Over its sorry semblance ; but the truth
Is still divine, and claims our reverence.
The great King Solomon—and you believe
In Solomon—has said that a good name
Is more to be desired than much fine gold.
If a good name be matter of desire
Beyond all wealth—and you will pardon me
For holding to the record—it may stand

As a grand motive in the life of man,
To grand endeavor. I have yet to learn
That Solomon addressed his words to bears,
Or little children. I am forced to think
That you and I, and all who read his words,
Are those for whom he wrote."

Rejoining she !
"A good may be the subject of desire,
And not be motive to achievement. Life,
If I may speak the riddle, is a scheme
Of indirections. My own happiness
Is something to desire ; and yet, I know
That I must win it by forgetting it
In ministry to others. If I make
My happiness the motive of my work,
I spoil it by the taint of selfishness.
But are you sure that you do not presume
Somewhat too much, in claiming the desire
For a good name as motive of your life ?
Greatness, not goodness, is the end you seek,
If I mistake you not ; and these are held,

In the world's thought, as two, and most distinct.
King Solomon was wise, but wiser He
Who said to those that loved and followed him,
'Who would be great among you, let him serve.'
The greatest men—and artists should be such,
For they are God's nobility and man's—
Should work from greatest motives. Selfishness
Is never great, and moves to no great deeds.
To honor God, to benefit mankind,
To serve with lofty gifts the lowly needs
Of the poor race for which the God-man died,
And do it all for love—oh ! this is great !
And he who does this will achieve a name
Not only great but good."

"Not in this world,"
I answered her. "I know too much of it.
The world is selfish ; and it never gives
Due credit to a motive which assumes
To be above its own. If a man write,
It takes for granted that he writes for fame,
And judges him accordingly. It holds

Of no account all other aims and ends ;
And visits with contempt the man who bears
A mission to his kind. The critic pens
That twiddle with his work, or play with it
As cats with mice, are not remarkable
For gentle instincts ; and my name must live
By pens like these. I choose to take the world
Just as I find it, and I pitch my tune
To the world's key, that it may sing my tune,
And sing for me. Ay, and I take myself
Just as I find myself. I do not love
The human race enough to work for it.
Having no motive of philanthropy,
I'll make pretence to none. The love of praise
I count legitimate and laudable.
'Tis not the noblest motive in the world,
But it is good ; and it has won more fames
Than any other. Surely, my good wife,
You would not shut me from it, and deprive
My power of its sole impulse."

"No ; oh ! no,

She answered quickly. "I am only sad
That it should be the captain of your host.
All creatures of the brain are the result
Of many motives and of many powers.
All life is such, indeed. The power that leads—
The motive dominant—this stamps the work
With its own likeness. Throughout all the world
Are careful souls, with careful consciences,
That pierce themselves with questionings and fears
Because that, with the motives which are good,
And which alone they seek, a hundred come
They do not seek, and aye sophisticate
Their finest action. They are wrong in this:
All motives bowing to one leadership,
And aiding its emprise, are one with it—
The same in trend, the same in terminus.
All the low motives that obey the law,
And aid the work, of one above them all,
Do holy service, and fulfil the end
For which they were designed. The love of praise
Is not the lowest motive which can move
The human soul. Nay, it may do good work

As a subordinate, and leave no soil
On whitest fabric, at whose selvage shines
The Master's broidered signature. Although
You write for fame, think not you will escape
The press of other motives. You love me;
You love your child; you love your pleasant home;
You love the memory of one long dead.
These, joined with all those qualities of heart
Which make you dear to me, will throng around
The leader you appoint, and come and go
Under his banner; and the work of God
Will thrive through these, the while your own goes on.
God will not be defrauded, nor yet man;
And you, who like the Pharisees make prayer
At corners of the streets, for praise of men,
Will have reward you seek."

"Ay, verily!"
Responded I with laughter. "Verily!
Though not a saint, I'll do a saintly work
For my own profit, and in spite of all

The selfishness that moves me. Better, this,
Than I suspected. My sweet casuist—
My gentle, learned, lovely casuist—
I thank you ; and I'll pay you more than thanks.
I'll promise that when these fine motives come,
And volunteer their service, they shall find
Welcome and entertainment, and a place
Within the rank and file, with privilege
Of quick promotion, so they show themselves
Motives of mettle."

This the type of talk
That passed between us. I was not a fool
To count her wisdom worthless ; nor a God,
To work regeneration in myself.
That something which I longed for, to fill up
The measure of my good, was human praise ;
Yet I could see that she was wholly right,
And that she held within herself resource
Of satisfaction better than my own.
But I was quite content—content to know
I trod the average altitude of those

Within the paths of art, and had no aims
To be misconstrued or misunderstood
By Pride and Selfishness—that these, in truth,
Expected of me what I had to give.

Strange, how a man may carry in his heart,
From year to year—through all his life, indeed—
A truth, or a conviction, which shall be
No more a part of it, and no more worth
Than to his flask the cork that slips within!
Of this he learns by sourness of his wine,
Or muddle of its color; by the bits
That vex his lips while drinking; but he feels
No impulse in his hand to draw it forth,
And bid it crown and keep the draught it spoils.

I write this, here, not for its relevance
To this one passage of my story, but
Because there slipped into my consciousness
Just at this juncture, and would not depart,
A truth I carried there for many years,
Each minute seeing, feeling, tasting it,

Yet never touching it with an attempt
To draw it forth, and put it to its place.

One evening, when our usual theme was up,
I asked my wife in playful earnestness
How she became so wise. "You talk," I said,
"Like one who has survived a thousand years,
And drunk the wisdom of a thousand lives."

"Who lacketh wisdom, let him ask of God,
Who giveth freely and upbraideth not,"
Was her reply.

"I never ask of God,"
I said. "So, while you take at second hand
His breathings to the artist, I will take
At second hand the wisdom that He gives
To you, His teacher."

"Do you never pray?"

"Never," I answered her. "I cannot pray:
You know the reason. Never since the day

God shut his heart against my mother's prayer
Have I raised one petition, or been moved
To reverence."

Her long, dark lashes fell,
And from her eyes there dropped two precious tears
That bathed her folded hands. She pitied me,
With tenderness beyond the reach of words.
I did not seek her pity. I was proud,
And asked her if she blamed me.

"No," she said;
"I have no right to blame you, and no wish.
I marvel only that a man like you
Can hold so long the errors of a boy.
I've looked—with how much longing, words of mine
Can never tell—for reason to restore
That priceless thing which passion stole from you,
And looked in vain."

Though piqued by the reproach
Her words conveyed, (unwittingly I knew,)
I wished to learn where, in her theory
Of human life, my case had found a place ;
So, bidding pride aback, I questioned her.
"You are so wise in other things," I said,
"And read so well God's dealings with His own,
Perhaps you can explain this mystery
That clouds my life."

"I know that God is good,"
She answered, "and, although my reason fail
To explicate the mystery that wraps
His providence, it does not shake my faith.
But this sad case of yours has seemed so plain,
That Reason well may spare the staff of Faith
To climb to its conclusions. You are loved,
My husband : can you tell your wife for what ?'

"Oh ! modesty ! my dear ; hem ! modesty !
Spare me these blushes ! I have not at hand
The printed catalogue of qualities

Which give you inspiration, and decline
The personal rehearsal."

"You mistake,"
She answered, smiling. "Not for modesty;
And as for blushes, they're not patent yet.
But frankly, soberly, I ask you this:
Have you a quality of heart or brain
Which makes you lovable, and in my eyes
A man to be admired, that was not born
Quick in your blood? Pray, have you anything
Which you did not inherit? Who to me
Furnished my husband? By what happy law
Was all that was the finest, noblest, best
In those who gave you life, bestowed on you?
You have your father's form, your father's brain;
You have your mother's eyes, your mother's heart.
Those twain produced a man for me to love,
Out of themselves. I am obliged to them
For the most precious good the round earth holds,
Transmitted by a law that slew them both.
It was not sin, or shame, for them to die

Just as they died. They passed with whiter hands
Up to The Throne than he who wantonly
Murders a sparrow. When your mother prayed,
She prayed for the suspension of the law
By which from Eve, the mother of the race,
She had received the grace and loveliness
Which made her precious to your heart—the law
By which alone she could convey these gifts
To others of her blood. Your daughter's face
Is beautiful, her soul is pure and sweet,
By largess of this law. Could God subvert,
To meet her wish, though shaped in agony,
The law which, since the life of man began
In life of God, has kept the channel clear
For His own blood, that it might bless the last
Of all the generations as the first?
What could He more than give her liberty—
When reason lay in torture or in wreck,
And life was death—to part with stainless hand
The tie that held her from his loving breast?"

If God himself had dropped her words from heaven,

They had not reached with surer plummet-plunge
The depths of my conviction. I was dumb ;
I opened not my mouth ; but left her side,
And sought the crowded street. I felt that all
Delusions, subterfuges, self-deceits,
By which my soul had shut itself from God,
Were stripped away, and that no barrier
Was interposed between us which was not
My own hand's building. Never, nevermore,
Could I hold God in blame, or deem myself
A guiltless, injured creature. I could see
That I was hard, implacable, unjust ;
And that by force of wilful choice I held
Myself from God ; for no impulsion came
To seek His face and favor. Nay, I feared
And fought such incidence, as enemy
Of all my plans.

So it became thenceforth
A problem with me how to separate
My new conviction from my life—to hold
A revolutionizing truth within,

And hold it yet so loosely, it should be
Like a dumb alien in a mural town—
No guest, but an intruder, who might bide,
By law or grace, but win no domicile,
And hold no power.

When I returned, that night,
My course was chosen, with such sense of guilt
I blushed before the calm, inquiring eyes
That met me at my threshold ; but the theme
Was dropped just there. My gentle mentor read
The secret of the struggle and the sin,
And left me to myself.

At the set time,
I entered on my task. The discipline
Of early years told feebly on my work,
For dissipation and disuse of power
Had brought me back to infancy again.
My will was weak, my patience was at fault,
And in my fretful helplessness, I stormed
And sighed by turns ; yet still I held in force

Determination, as reserve of will;
And when I flinched or faltered, always fell
Back upon that, and saved my powers from rout.
Casting, recasting, till I found the germ
Of my conception putting forth its whorls
In orderly succession round the stem
Of my design, that straight and strong shot up
Toward inflorescence, my long work went on,
Till I was filled with satisfying joy.
This lasted for a little time, and then
There came reaction. I grew tired of it.
My verses were as meaningless and stale
As doggrel of the stalls. I marvelled much
That they could ever have beguiled my pride
Into self-gratulation, or done aught
But overwhelm me with contempt for them,
And the dull pen that wrote them.

I had hoped

To form and finish my projected work
Within, and by, myself,—to tease no ear
With fragmentary snatches of my song,

And call for no support from friendly praise
To reinforce my courage; but the stress
Of my disgust and my despair—the need,
Imperative and absolute, to brace myself
By some opinion borrowed for the nonce,
And bathe my spirit in the sympathy
Of some strong nature—mastered my intent,
And sent me for resource to her whose heart
Was ever open to my call.

She sat
Through the long hour in which I read to her,
Absorbed, entranced, as one who sits alone
Within a dim cathedral, and resigns
His spirit to the organ-theme, that mounts,
Or sinks in tremulous pauses, or sweeps out
On mighty pinions and with trumpet voice
Through labyrinthine harmonies, at last
Emerging, and through silver clouds of sound
Receding and receding, till it melts
Into the empyrean and is lost.
It was not needful she should say a word;

For in her glowing eyes and kindling face,
I caught the full assurance that my heart
Had yearned for ; but she spoke her hearty praise;
And when I asked her for her criticism,
Bestowed it with such modest deference
To my opinion, as to spare my pride ;
Yet, with such subtle sense of harmony,
And insight of proportion, that I saw
That I should find no critic in the world
More competent or more severe. I said,
Gulping my pride : "Better this ordeal
In friendly hands, before the time of types,
Than afterward, in hands of enemies."

So, from that reading, it was understood
Between us that, whenever I essayed
Revising and retouching, I should know
Her intimate impressions, and receive
Her frank suggestions. In this oversight
And constant interest of one whose mind
Was excellent and pure, and raised above

All motive to beguile me, I secured
New inspiration.

Weeks and months passed by
With gradient hopefulness, and strength renewed
At each renewal of the confidence
I had reposed in her ; till I perceived
That I was living on her praise—that she
Held God's place in me and the multitude's.
And now, as I look back upon these days
Of difficult endeavor, I confess
That had she not been with me, I had failed—
Ay, foundered in mid-sea—my hope, my life,
The spoil of deep oblivion.

At last
The work was done—the labored volume closed.
"I cannot make it better," I exclaimed.
"I can write better, but, before I write,
I must have recognition in the voice
Of public praise. A good paymaster pays
When work is finished. Let him pay for this,

And I will work again; but, till he pay,
My leisure is my own, and I will wait."

"And if he grudge your wage?" suggested she
To whom I spoke.

"I shall be finished too."

Came then the proofs and latest polishing
Of words and phrases—work I shared with her
To whom I owed so much; and then the fear,
The deathly heart-fall, and the haunting dread
That go before exposure to the world
Of inmost life, and utmost reach of power
Toward revelation;—then the shrinking spell
When morbid love of self awaits in pain
The verdict it has courted.

But at last
The book was out. My daughter's hand in mine—
Her careless feet, that thrilled with springing life,

Skipping the pavement—I walked down Broadway
To ease the restlessness and cool the heat
That vexed my idle waiting. As we passed
A showy window, filled with costly books,
My little girl exclaimed : "Oh father ! See !
There is your name !"

Straight all the bravery
Within my veins, at one wild heart-thump, dropped,
And I was limp as water ; but I paused,
And read the poster. It announced my book
In characters of flame, with adjectives
My daring publisher had filched, I think,
From an old circus-broadside.

"Well !" thought I—
Biting my lip—"I'm in the market now !
How much—O ! rattling, roaring multitude !
O ! selfish, cheating, lying multitude !
O ! hawking, trading, delving multitude !—
How much for one man's hope, for one man's life ?
What for his toil and pain ?—his heart's red blood ?

What for his brains and breeding? Oh how much
For one who craves your praises with your pence,
And dies with your denial?"

I went in,
And bought my book—not doubting I was first
To give response to my apostrophe.
The smug old clerk, who found his length of ear
Convenient as a pencil-rack, and thus
Made nature's wrath proclaim the praise of trade,
Wrapped my dear bantling well; and, as he dropped
My dollar in his till, smiled languidly
Upon my little girl, and said to me—
To cheer me in my purchase—that the book
Was thought to be a deuced clever thing.
He never read such books: he had no time.
Indeed, he had no interest in them.
Still, other people had, and it was well,
For it helped trade along.

It was for him—

Well, thought I, biting my lip, "I'm in the market now."

A vulgar fraction of the integral
We speak of as "the people," and "the world"—
I had been writing! Had he read my book,
And given it his praise, I should have been
Delighted, though I knew that his applause
Was worthless as his brooch. I was a fool
Undoubtedly; yet I could understand,
Better than e'er before, how separate
The artist is from such a soul as his—
What need of teachers and interpreters
To crumble in his pewter porringer
The rounded loaf, whose crust was adamant
To his weak fingers.

The next morning's press
Was purchased early. though I read in vain
To find my reputation. But at night,
My door-bell rang; and I received a note
From one who edited an evening print,
(I had dined with him at my publisher's,)
Inclosing a review, and venturing
The hope that I should like it.

Cunning man!
He knew the tricks of trade, and was adroit.
My poem was "a revelation." I had "burst
Like thunder from a calm and cloudless sky."
Well, not to quote his language, this the drift?
A man of fortune, living at his ease,
But fond of manly effort, had sat down,
And turned his culture to supreme account;
And he—the editor—took on himself
To thank him on the world's behalf. Withal,
The poet had betrayed the continence
Of genius. He had held, undoubtedly,
The consciousness of power from early youth;
But, yielding never to the itch for print,
Had nursed and chastened and developed it,
Until his hand was strong, and swept his lyre
With magic of a master.

Followed here
Sage comments on the rathe and puny brood
Of poet-sucklings, who had rushed to type

Before their time—pale stems that spun their flowers
In the first sunshine, but, when Autumn came,
Were fruitless. It was pleasant, too, to see,
In such an age of sentimental cant,
One man who dared to hold up to the world
A creature of his brain, and say: "Look you!
This is my thought; and it shall stand alone.
It has no moral, bears no ministry
Of pious teaching, and makes no appeal
To sufferance or suffrage of the muffs
Who, in the pulpit or the press, prepare
The nation's pap. The fiery-footed barb
That pounds the pampas, and the lily-bells
That hang above the brooks, present the world
With no apology for being there,
And no attempt to justify themselves
In uselessness. It is enough for God
That they are beautiful, and hold His thought
In fine embodiment; and it shall be
Enough for me that, in this book of mine,
I have created somewhat that is strong

And beautiful, which, if it profit,—well:
If not, 'tis no less strong and beautiful,
And holds its being by no feebler right."

Ay, it was glorious to find one man
Who piled no packs upon his Pegasus,
Nor chained him to a rag-cart, loaded down
With moral frippery, and strings of bells
To call the people to their windows.

Then
There followed extracts, with a change of type
To mark the places where the editor
Had caught a fancy hiding, which he feared
Might slip detection under slower eyes
Than those he carried ; or to emphasize
Felicities of diction that were stiff
In Roman verticals, but grew divine
At the Italic angle ; then apology,
Profoundly humble, to his patrons all
For quoting at such length, and one to me
For quoting anything, and deep regrets,

In quite a general way, that lack of space
Forbade the reproduction of the book
From title-page to tail-piece, winding up
With counsel to all lovers of pure art,
Patrons of genius, all Americans,
All friends of cis-Atlantic literature,
To buy the book, and read it for themselves.

I drank the whole, at one long, luscious draught,
Tipping the tankard high, that I might see
My features at the bottom, and regale
My pride, after my palate. Then I tossed
The paper to my wife, and bade her read.
I watched her while she read, but failed to find
The sympathy of pleasure in her face
I had expected. Finishing at last,
She raised her eyes, and, fixing them on me,
Said thoughtfully: "You like this, I suspect."

"Well, granted!" I responded, "since it seems."
To be the first instalment of the wage
Which you suggested might come grudgingly.

Ay, it is sweet to me. I know it fails
In nice discrimination,—that it slurs
Defects which I perceive as well as you;
But it is kind, and places in best light
Such excellences as we both may find—
May claim, indeed."

"And yet, it is a lie,
Or what the editor would call 'a puff,'
From first to last. The 'continence,' my dear,
'Of genius!' What of that? And what about
The 'manly effort,' for whose exercise
He thanked you on the world's behalf? And so
Your nursing, chastening and developing
Of power!—Pray what of these?"

"Oh! wife!" I said;
"Don't spoil it all! Be pitiful, my love!
I am a baby—granted: so I need
The touch of tender hands, and something sweet
To keep me happy."

"Babies take a bath,
Sometimes, from which the hand of warmest love
Filches the chill, and you must have one dash,"
She answered me, "to close your complement.
The weakest spot in all your book, he found
With a quick instinct; and on that he spent
His sharpest force and finest rhetoric,
Shoring and bracing it on every side
With bold assumptions and affirmatives,
To blind the eyes of novices, and scare
With fierce forestalment all the critic-quills
Now bristling for their chance. He saw at once
Your poem had no mission, save, perhaps,
The tickle of the taste, and that it bore
Upon its glowing gold small food for life.
He saw just there the point to be attacked;
And there threw up his earth-works, and spread
out
His thorny abatis. Ay, he was kind
Undoubtedly, and very cunning, too;
For well he knew that there are earnest souls
In the broad world, who claim that highest art

Is highest ministry to human need;
And that the artist has no Christian right
To prostitute his art to selfish ends,
Or make it vehicle alone of plums
For the world's pudding."

"These will speak in time,"
Responded I; "but they have not the ear
Of the broad world, I think. The Christian right
Of which you speak is hardly recognized
Among the multitude, or by the guild
In which I claim a place. The sectaries
Who furnish folios, quartos, magazines,
To the religious few, are limited
In influence; and these, my wife, are all
I have to fear;—nay, could I but arouse
Their bitter enmity, I might receive
Such superflux of praise and patronage
As would o'erwhelm my sweetly Christian wife
With shame and misery. But we shall see;
And, in the meantime, let us be content
That, if one man shall praise me overmuch,

Ten, at the least, will fail to render me
Befitting justice."

As the days went on,
Reviews and notices came pouring in.
I was notorious, at least ; and fame,
I whispered comfortably to myself,
Is only notoriety turned gray,
With less of fire, if more of steadiness.
The adverse verdicts were not numerous ;
And these were rendered, as I fancied then,
By sanctimonious fools who deemed profane
All verse outside their thumb-worn hymnodies.
My book received the rattling fusilade
Of all the dailies : then the artillery
Of the hebdomadals, whose noisy shells,
Though timed by fuse to burst on Saturday
Exploded at the middle of the week ;
And last, a hundred-pounder quarterly
Gave it a single missive from its mask
Of far and dark impersonality.
The smoke cleared up, and still my colors flew,

And still my book stood proudly in the sun,
Nor breached nor battered.

I had won a place ;
That I was sure of. All had said of me
That I was "brilliant :" was not that enough ?
The petty pesterers, with card and stamp,
Who hunt for autographs, were after me,
In packages by post ; and idle men
Held me at corners by the button-hole,
And introduced me to their friends. I dined
With meek-eyed men, whose literary wives
Were dying all to know me, as they said ;
And the lyceums, quick at scent and sight—
Watching the jungles for a lion—all
Courted the delectation of my roar
Upon their platforms, pledging to my hand
(With city reference to stanchest names,)
Such honoraria as would have been
The lion's share of profits. These were straws ;
But they had surer fingers for the wind
Than withes or weathercocks.

The book sold well,
My publisher (who published at my risk,)
And first put on the airs of one who stooped
To grant a favor, brimmed and overflowed
With courtesy ; and ere a year was gone,
Became importunate for something more.
This was his plea : I owed it to myself
To write again. The time to make one's hay
Is when the sun shines : time to write one's books
Is when the public humor turns to them.
The public would forget me in a year,
And seek another idol ; or, meanwhile,
Another writer might usurp my throne,
And I be hooted from my own domain
As a pretender. Then the market's maw
Was greedy for my poems. Just how long
The appetite would last, he could not tell,
For appetite is subject of caprice,
And never lasts too long.

The man was wise,
I plainly saw, and gave me the results

Of observation and experience.
I took his hint, accepting with a pang
The truths that came with it; for instance,
these :—
That he who speaks for praise of those who live,
Must keep himself before his audience,
Nor look for "bravas," cheers, and cries of "hear!"
And clap of hands and stamp of feet, except
With fresh occasion ; that applause of crowds,
Though fierce, runs never to the chronic stage ;
That good paymasters, having paid for work
The doer's price, expect receipt in full
At even date ; and that if I would keep
My place, as grand purveyor to the greed
For novelties of literary art,
My viands must be sapid, and abound
With change, to wake or whet the appetite
I sought to feed.

I say I took his hint,
Bestowed in selfishness, without a doubt,
Though in my interest. For ten long years

It was the basis of my policy.
I poured my poems with redundancy
Upon the world, and won redundant meed.
If I gave much, the world was generous,
Paying me more than justice ; but, at last,
Tired and disgusted, I laid down my pen.
I knew my work would not outlast my life,
That the enchantments which had wreathed themselves
Around my name were withering away,
With every breath of fragrance they exhaled ;
And that, too soon, the active brain and hand
Whose skill had conjured them, would faint and fail
Under the press of weariness and years.
My reputation piqued me. None believed
That it was in me to write otherwise
Than I had written. All the world had laughed,
Or shaken its wise head, had I essayed
A work beyond the round of brilliancies
In which my pen had revelled, and for which
It gave such princely guerdon. If I looked,

Or came to look, with measureless contempt
On those who gave with such munificence
The boon I sought, I had provoking cause
I fooled them all with patent worthlessness,
And they insisted I should fool them still.
The wisdom of a whole decade had failed
To teach them that the thing my hand had done
Was not worth doing.

More and worse than this:
I found my character and self-respect
Eroded by the canker of conceit,
Poisoned by jealousy, and made the prey
Of meanest passions. Harlequins in mask,
Who live upon the laughter of the throng
That crowds their reeking amphitheatres;
Light-footed dancing-girls, who sell their grace
To gaping lechers of the pit, to win
That which shall feed their shameless vanity;
The mimics of the buskin—baser still,
The mimics of the negro—minstrel-bands,
With capital of corks and castanets

And threadbare jests—Ah! who and what was I
But brother of all these—in higher walk,
But brother in the motive of my life,
In jealousy, in recompense for toil,
And, last, in destiny?

My wife had caught
Stray silver in her hair in these long years;
And the sweet maiden springing from our lives
Had grown to womanhood. In my pursuits,
Which drank my time and my vitality,
I had neglected them. I worked at home,
But lived in other scenes, for other lives,
Or, rather, for my own; and though my pride
Shrank from the deed, I had the tardy grace
To call them to me, and confess my shame,
And beg for their forgiveness.

Once again—
All explanations passed—I sat beside
My faithful wife, and canvassed as of old
New plans of life. I found her still the same

In purpose and in magnanimity;
For she dealt no upbraidings and no blame;
Cast in my teeth no old-time prophecies
Of failure; felt no triumph which rejoiced
To mock me with the words, "I told you so."
Calmly she sat, and tried, with gentlest speech,
To heal the bruises of my fall; to wake
A better feeling in me toward the world,
And soothe my morbid self-contempt.

The world,
She said, is apt to take a public man
At his own estimate, and yield him place
According to his choice. I had essayed
To please the world, and gather in its praise;
And, certainly, the world was pleased with me,
And had not stinted me in its return
Of plauditory payment. As the world
Had taken me according to my rate,
And filled my wish, it had a valid claim
On my good nature.

Then, beyond all this,
The world was not a fool. Those books of mine,
That I had come to look upon as trash,
Were not all trash. My motive had been poor,
And that had vitiated them for me;
But there was much in them that yielded strength
To struggling souls, and, to the wounded, balm.
Indeed, she had been helped by them, herself.
They were all pure; they made no foul appeal
To baseness and brutality; they had
An element of gentle chivalry,
Such as must have a place in any man
Shrinking with sensitiveness, like myself,
From a fine reputation, scorning it
For motive which had won it.

Words like these,
From lips like hers, were needed medicine.
They clarified my weak and jaundiced sight,
And helped to juster vision of the world,
And of myself. But there was no return
Of the old greed; and fame, which I had learned

To be an entity quite different
From my conceit of it in other days,
Was something much too far and nebulous
To be my star of life.

"You have some plan?"—
Statement and query in same words, which fell
From lips that sought to rehabilitate
My will and self-respect.

"I have," I said.

"Else you were dead," responded she. "To live,
Men must have plans. When these die out of men
They crumble into chaos, or relapse
Into inanity. Will you reveal
These plans of yours to me?"

"Ay, if I can,"
I answered her; but first I must reveal
The base on which I build them. I have tried
To find the occasion of my discontent,

And found it, as I think, just here: In quest
Of popularity, I have become
Untrue both to myself and to my art.
I have not dared to speak the royal truth
For fear of censure: I have been a slave
To men's opinions. What is best in me
Has been debauched by the pursuit of praise,
As life's best prize. Conviction, sentiment,
All love and hate, all sense of right and wrong,
I have held in abeyance, or compelled
To work in menial subservience
To my grand purpose. If my sentiment
Or my conviction were but popular,
It flowed in hearty numbers: otherwise,
It slept in silence.

"Now as to my art:
I find that it has suffered like myself,
And suffered from same cause. My verse has been
Shaped evermore to meet the people's thought.
That which was highest, grandest in my art,
I have not reached, and have not tried to reach.

I have but touched the surfaces of things
That meet the common vision ; and my art
Has only aimed to clothe them gracefully
With fancy's gaudy fabrics, or portray
Their patent beauties and deformities.
Above the people in my gift and art,
Both gift and art have had a downward trend
And both are prostitute.

"Discarding praise
As motive of my labor, I confess
My sins against my art, and so, henceforth,
As to my goddess, give myself to her.
The chivalry which you are pleased to note
In me and works of mine, turns loyally
To her and to her service. Nevermore
Shall pen of mine demean itself by work
That serves not first, and with supreme intent,
The art whose slave it is."

"I understand,
I think, the basis of your plan," she said ;

"And e'en the plan itself. You now propose
To write without remotest reference
To the world's wishes, prejudices, needs,
Or e'en the world's opinions,—quite content
If the world find aught in you to applaud ;
Quite as content if it condemn. With full
Expression of yourself, in finest terms
And noblest forms of art, so far as God
Has made you masterful, you give yourself
Up to yourself and to your art. Is this
Fair statement of your purpose ?"

"Not unfair,"
I answered. "Tell me what you think of it."

"Suppose," she said, "that all the artist-souls
That God has made since time and art began
Had acted on your theory ; suppose
In architecture, picture, poetry,
Naught had found utterance but works that sprang
To satisfy the worker, and reveal

That bundle of ideas which, to him,
Is instituted art; but which, in truth,
Is figment of his fancy, or his thought, --
His creature, made his God—say where were all
The temples, palaces and homes of men;
The galleries that blaze with history,
Or bloom with landscape, or look down
With smile of changeless love or loveliness
Into the hearts of men? And where were all
The poems that give measure to their praise
Voice to their aspirations, forms of light
To homely facts and features of their life,
Enveloping this plain, prosaic world
In an ideal atmosphere, in which
Fair angels come and go? All gifts of men
Were made for use, and made for highest use.
If highest use be service of one's self,
And highest standard, one's embodiment
Of dogmas, theories and thoughts of art,
As art's identity, then are you right;
But if a higher use of gift and art
Be service of mankind, and higher rule

God's regal truth, revealed in words or worlds,
And verified by life, then are you wrong."

"But art?"—responded I—"you do not mean
That art is nothing but a thing of thought,
Or, less than that, of fancy? Nay, I claim
That it is somewhat—a grand entity—
An organism of lofty principles,
Informed with subtlest life, and clothed upon
With usage and tradition of the men
Who, working in those sunny provinces
Where it holds eminent domain, have brought
To build its temple and adorn its walls
The usufruct of countless lives. So far
Is art from being creature of man's thought
That it is subject of his knowledge—stands
In mighty mystery, and challenges
The study of the world; rules noblest minds
Like law or like religion: is a power
To which the proudest artist-spirits bow
With humblest homage. Is astronomy
The creature of man's thought? Is chemistry?

Yet these hold not, in this our universe,
A form more definite, nor yet a place
In human knowledge more beyond dispute,
Than art itself. To this embodiment
Of theory—of dogmas, if you will—
This body aggregate of truth revealed
In growing light of ages to the eyes
Touched to perception, I devote my life."

"Nay, you're too fast," she said: "let alchemy
And old astrology present your thought.
These were somewhat; these were grand entities;
But they went out like candles in thin air
When knowledge came. The sciences are things
Of law, of force, relations, measurements,
Affinities and combinations, all
The definite, demonstrable effects
Of first and second causes. Between these
And men's opinions, braced by usages,
The space is wide. The thing which you call art,
Is anything but definite in form,
Or fixed in law. It has as many shapes

As worshipers. The world has many books,
Written by earnest men, about this art;
But having read them, we are no more wise
Than he whose observation of the sun
Is taken by kaleidoscope. The more
He sees in it, the more he is confused.
The sun works, doubtless, many fine effects
With what he sees, but he sees not the sun."

"But art is art," I said. "You'd cheat my sense,
And mock my reason too. Ay, art is art.
Things must have being that have history."

Then she: "Yes, politics has history,
And therefore has a being,—has, in truth,
Just such a being as I grant to art—
A being of opinions. Every state
Has origin and ends of government
Peculiarly its own, and so, from these,
Constructs its theory of politics,
And holds this theory against the world;
And holds it well. There is no fixedness

Or form of politics for all mankind;
And there is none of art. Each artist-soul
Is its own law; and he who dares to bring
From work of other man, to lay on yours,
His square and compasses—declaring him
The pattern man—and tells, by him, you lack
Just so much here, or wander so much there,
Thereby confesses just how much he lacks
Of wisdom and plain sense. For every man
Has special gift of power and end of life.
No man is great who lives by other law
Than that which wrapped his genius at his birth.
The Lind is great because she is the Lind,
And not the Malabran. Recorded art
Is yours to study—e'en to imitate,
In education—imitate or shun,
As the case warrants; but it has destroyed,
Or toned to commonplace, more gifts of God
Than it has ever fanned to life or fed.
Who never walks save where he sees men's tracks,
Makes no discoveries. Show me the man
Who, leaving God and nature and himself,

Sits at the feet of masters, stuffs his brain
With maxims, notions, usages and rules,
And yields his fancy up to leading-strings,
And I shall see a man who never did
A deed worth doing. So, in the name of art--
Nay, in the name of God—do no such thing
As smutch your knees by bowing at a shrine,
Whose doubtful deity, in midst of dust,
Sits in the cast-off robes of devotees,
And lives on broken victuals!"

"Drive, my dear!
Drive on, and over me! You're on the old
High-stepping horse to-night; so give him rein,
For exercise is good," I said, in mirth.
"You sit your courser finely. I confess
I'm very proud of you, and too much pleased
With your accomplishments to check your speed.
Drive on, my love! drive on!"

"I thank you, sir!
No one so gracious as your grudging man

Under compulsion! With your kind consent
I'll drive a little further," she replied,—
"For I enjoy it quite as much as you—
The more because you've given me little chance
In these last years. . . . Now, soberly, this art—
Of which we talk so much, without the power
To tell exactly what we understand
By the hack term—suppose we take the word,
And try to find its meaning. You recall
Old John who dressed the borders in our court:
You called him, hired him, told him what to do.
He and his rake stood interposed between
You and your work. You chose his skilful hands,
Endowing them with pay, or pledge of pay,
And set him at his labor. Now suppose
Old John had had a philosophic turn
After you left him, and had thought like this:
'I am called here to do a certain work—
My rake tells what; and he who called me here
Has given me the motive for the job.
The work is plain. These borders are to be

Levelled and cleaned of weeds : my hand, my rake
Are fitted for the service ;—this my art ;
And it is first of all the arts. There's none
More ancient, useful, worshipful, indeed,
Than agriculture. Adam practised it ;
Poets have sung its praises ; and the great
Of every age have loved and honored it.
This art is greater than the man I serve,
And greater than his borders. Therefore I
Will serve my art, and let the borders lie,
And my employer whistle. True to that,
And to myself, it matters not to me
What weeds may grow, or what the master think
Of my proceeding !'

"So, intent on this,
He hangs his rake upon your garden wall,
And steals your clematis, with which to wind
The handle upward ; then o'erfills his hands
With roses and geraniums, and weaves
Their beauty into laurel, for a crown
For his slim god, completing his *devoir*

By buttering the teeth, and kneeling down
In abject homage. Pray, what would you say,
At close of day, when you should go to see
Your untouched borders, and your gardener
At genuflexion, with your mignonnette
In every button-hole? Remember, now,
He has been true to art and to himself,
According to his notion; nor forget
To take along a dollar for his hire,
Which he expects, of course! What would you say?"

"Oh don't mind that: you've reached your 'fifthly' now,
And here the 'application' comes," I said.

"I think," responded she, with an arch smile,
"The application's needless: but you men
Are so obtuse, when will is in the way,
That I will do your bidding. Every gift
That God bestows on men holds in itself
The secret of its office, like the rake

The gardener wields. The rake was made to till—
Was fashioned, head and handle, for just that;
And if, by grace of God, you hold a gift
So fashioned and adapted, that it stands
In like relation of supremest use
To life of men, the office of your gift
Has perfect definition. Gift like this
Is yours, my husband. In your facile hand.
God placed it for the service of Himself,
In service of your kind. Taking this gift,
And using it for God and for the world,
In your own way, and in your own best way;
Seeking for light and knowledge everywhere
To guide your careful hand; and opening wide
To spiritual influx all your soul,
That so your Master may breathe into you,
And breathe His great life through you, in such forms
Of pure presentment as He gives you skill
To build withal—that's all of art—for you.
Art is an instrument, and not an end—
A servant, not a master, nor a God

To be bowed down to. Shall we worship rakes?
Honor of art, by him whose work is art,
Is a fine passion: but he honors most
Whose use and end are best."

"Use! Use! Use!"
I cried impatiently;—"nothing but use!
As if God never made a violet,
Or hung a harebell, or in kindling gold
Garnished a sunset, or upreared the arch
Of a bright rainbow, or endowed a world—
A universe, indeed—stars, firmament,
The vastitudes of forest and of sea,
Swift brooks and sweeping rivers, virid meads
And fluff of breezy hills—with tints that range
The scale of spectral beauty, till they leave
No glint or glory of the changeful light
Without a revelation! Is this use—
I beg your pardon, love: you say 'this art'—
The sum and end of art? If it be so,
Then God's no artist. Are the crystal brooks
Sweeter for singing to the thirsty brutes

That dip their beaded muzzles in the foam?
Burns the tree better that its leaves are green?
Sleeps the sun sounder under canopy
Of gold or rose?"

"Yet beauty has its use,"
Responded she. "Whatever elevates,
Inspires, refreshes, any human soul,
Is useful to that soul. Beauty has use
For you and me. The dainty violet
Blooms in our thought, and sheds its fragrance
there:
And we are gainers through its ministry.
All God's great values wear the drapery
That most becomes them. Beauty may, in truth,
Be incident of art and not be end—
Its form, condition, features, dress, and still
The humblest value of the things of art.
This truth obtains in all God's artistry.
Does God make beauty for himself, alone?
He is, and holds, all beauty. Has He need
To kindle rushes that He may behold

The glory of His thoughts ? or need to use
His thoughts as plasms for the amorphous clay
That He may study models ? For an end
Outside himself, he ever speaks Himself ;
And end, with Him, is use."

"Well, I confess
There's truth in what you utter," I replied ;—
"A modicum of truth, at least ; and still
There's something more which this our subtle talk
Has failed to give us. I will not affirm
That art, recorded in its thousand forms,
And clothed with usages, traditions, rules,—
The thing of history—the mighty pile
Of drift that sweep of ages has brought down
To heap the puzzled present—is the sum
And substance of all art. I will not claim—
Nay, mark me now—I will not even claim
That beauty is art's end, or has its end
Within itself. Our tedious colloquy
Has cleared away the rubbish from my thought,
And given me cleaner vision. I can see

Before, around me, underneath, above,
The great unrealized; and while I bow
To the traditions and the things of art,
And hold my theories, I find myself
Inspired supremely by the Possible
That calls for revelation—by the forms
That sleep imprisoned in the snowy arms
Of still unquarried truth, or stretch their hands
At sound of sledge and drill and booming fire,
Imploring for release. I turn from men,
And stretch my hands toward these. I feel—I know—
That there are mighty myriads waiting there,
And listening for my steps. Suppose my age
Should fail to give them welcome; ay, suppose
They may not help a man to coin a dime
Or cook a dinner: they will fare as well
As much of God's truth fares, though clothed in forms
Divinely chosen. Does God ever stint
His utterance because no creature hears?
Is it a grand and goodly thing, to spend

Brave life and precious treasures in a search
For palpitating water at the pole,
That so the sum of knowledge may be swelled,
Though pearls are not increased; and something
less
To probe the Possible in art, or sit
Through months of dreary dark to catch a glimpse
Of the live truth that quivers with the jar
Of movement at its axle? Is it good
To garner gain beyond the present need,
Won by excursive commerce in all seas;
And something less to pile redundantly
The spoil of thought?"

"These latest words of yours,"
She answered musingly, "impress me much;
And yet, I think I see where they will lead,
Or, rather, fail to lead. Your fantasy
Is beautiful but vague. The Possible
Is a vast ocean, from which one poor soul,
With its slight oars, can float but flimsy freight;
Yet I would help your courage, for I see

Where your sole motive lies. Go on, and prove
Whether your scheme or mine holds more of good;
And take my blessing with you."

Then she rose,
And kissed my forehead. Looking in her face,
By the sharp light that touched her, I was thrilled
By her flushed cheeks and strangely lustrous eyes.
She spoke not; but I heard the sigh she breathed—
The long-drawn, weary sigh—as she retired;
And then the Possible, which had inspired
So wondrously my hope, drooped low around,
And filled me with foreboding.

Had her life
Been chilled by my neglect? Was it on wane?
Could she be lost to me? Oh! then I felt,
As I had never felt before, how mean
Beside one true affection is the best
Of all earth's prizes, and how little worth
The world would be without her love—herself!

But sleep refreshed her, and next morn she sat
At our bright board, in her accustomed place;
And sunlight was not sweeter than her smile,
Or cheerfuller. My quick fears died away;
And though I saw that she had lost the fire
Of her young life, I comforted myself
With thinking that it was the same with me—
The sure result of years.

My time I gave
To my new passion, rioting at large
In the fresh realm of fancy and of thought
To which the passion bore me, and from which
I strove to gather for embodiment
Material of art.

The more I dreamed,
The broader grew my dream. The further on
My footsteps pushed, the brighter grew the light;
Till, half in terror, half in reverence,
I learned that I had broached the Infinite!
I had not thought my Possible could bear

Such name as this, or wear such attribute ;
And shrank befitting distance from the front
Of awful secrets, hid in awful flame,
That scorched and scared me.

So, more humble grown,
And less adventurous, I chose at last,
My theme and vehicle of song, and wrote.
My faculties, grown strong and keen by use,
Bent to their task with earnest faithfulness,
And glowed with high endeavor. All of power
I had within me flowed into my hand ;
And learning, language—all my life's resource—
Lay close around my enterprise, and poured
Their hoarded wealth of imagery and words
Faster than I could use it. For long weeks,
My ardent labor crowded all my days,
Invaded sleep, and haunted e'en my dreams :
And then the work was done.

I left it there,
And sought for recreative rest in scenes

That once had charmed me—in society
Where I was welcome: but the common talk
Of daily news—of politics and trade—
Was senseless as the chatter of the jays
In autumn forests. No refreshing balm
Came to me in the sympathy of men.
In my retirement, I had left the world
To go its way; and it had gone its way,
And left me hopelessly.

I told my wife
Of my dissatisfaction and disgust,
But found small comfort in her words. She said:
"The world is wide, and woman's vision short;
But I have never seen a man who turned
His efforts from his kind, and failed to spoil
All men for him—himself, indeed, for them;
And he who gives nor sympathy nor aid
To the poor race from which he seeks such boon,
Must be rejoiced if it be generous;
Content, if it be just. Society
Is a grand scheme of service and return.

We give and take ; and he who gives the most,
In ways directest, wins the best reward."

By purpose, I closed eyes upon my work
For many weeks, resisting every day
The impulse to review the glowing dream
My fancy had engendered : for I wished
To go with faculty and fancy cooled
To its perusal. I had strong desire,
So far as in me lay, to see the work
With the world's eyes, for reasons—ah ! I shrink
From writing them ! All men are sometimes weak,
And some are inconsistent with their wills.
If I were one of these, think not I failed
To justify my weakness to myself,
In ways that saved my pride.

Yet this was true :
I had an honest wish to learn how far
My work of heat had power to re-inspire
The soul that wrought it, and how well my verse
Had clothed and kept the creature of my thought ;

For memory still retained the loveliness
That filled the fresh conceit.

When, in good time,
Rest and diversion had performed their work,
And the long fever of my brain was gone,
I broached my feast, first making fast my door,
That so no eye should mark my greedy joy
Or my grimaces,—doubtful of the fate
That waited expectation.

It were vain
To try in these tame words to paint the pang,
The faintness and the chill, which overwhelmed
My disappointed heart. My welded thoughts
Which, in their whitest heat, had bent and bound
My language to themselves, imparting grace
To stiffest words, and meanings fresh and fine
To simplest phrases, interfusing all
With their own ardency, and shining through
With smoothly rounded beauty, lay in heaps
Of cold, unmeaning ugliness. My words

Had shrunk to old proportions, and stood out
In hard, stiff angles, challenging a guess
Of what they covered.

Meaningless to me,
Who knew the meaning that had once informed
Its faithless numbers, what way could I hope
That, to my own, or any future age,
My work should speak its full significance ?
My latest child, begot in manly joy,
Conceived in purity, and born in toil,
Lay dead before me,—dead, and in the shroud
My hopeful hands had woven and bedecked
To be its chrisom.

Then the first I learned
Where language finds its bound,—learned that beyond
The range of human commerce, save by force,
It never moves, nor lingers in the realm
It thus invades, a moment, if the voice
Of human commerce speak not the demand ;–

That language is a thing of use;—that thought
Which seeks a revelation, first must seek
Adjustment in the scale of human need,
Or find no fitting vehicle.

And more:
That the great Possible which lies outside
The range of commerce is identical
With the stupendous Infinite of God,
Which only comes in glimpses, or in hints
Of vague significance, so dim, so vast,
That subtlest, most prehensile language, shrinks
From plucking of its robes, the while they sweep
The perfumed air.

I closed my manuscript,
And locked it in my desk. Then stealing forth,
I sought the bustle of the street, to drown
In the great roar of careless toil, the pain
That brings despair. My last resource was gone;
And as I brooded o'er the awful blank
Of hopeless life that waited for my steps,

A fear which I had feared to entertain
Found entrance to my heart, and held it still,
Almost to bursting.

Not alone my life
Was sliding from me; for my better life,
My pearl of price, the jewel in my crown,
My wife Kathrina, growing lovelier
With every passing day, arose each morn
From wasting dreams to paler loveliness,
And sank in growing weariness each night,
And hotter hectic, to her welcome bed.
Her bed! The sweet, the precious nuptial bed!
Bed sanctified by love! Bed blest of God
With fruit immortal! Bed too soon to be
Crowned with the glory of a Christian death!
Ah God! How it brought back the agony,
And the rebellious hate of other years—
The hopeless struggle of my will with Him
Whose will is law.

Thus torn with mingled thoughts

Of fear, despair and spite, I wore away
Miles of wild wandering about the streets,
Till weariness at last compelled my feet
To drag me to my home.

Before my door
Stood the familiar chair of one whose call
Was ominous of ill. My heart grew sick
With flutter of foreboding and foredoom ;
But in swift silence I flew up the steps,
And, blind with stifled frenzy, reached the side
Of my poor wife. She smiled at seeing me,
But I could only kneel, and bathe her hands
With tears and kisses. In her gentle breast—
True home of love, and love and home to me—
The blood had burst its walls, and flowed in flame
From lips it left in ashes.

In her smile
Of perfect trustfulness, I caught first glimpse
Of that aureola of fadeless light
Which spans my lonely couch, and kindles hope

That when my time shall come to follow her,
My spirit may go out, enwreathed and wrapped
By the familiar glory, which to-night
Shall brood o'er all my vigils and my dreams !

DESPAIR.

Ah! what is so dead as a perished delight!
  Or a passion outlived! or a scheme overthrown!
Save the bankrupt heart it has left in its flight,
  Still as quick as the eye, but as cold as a stone!

The honey-bee hoards for its winter-long need,
  The treasure it gathers in joy from the flowers;
And drinks in each sip of its silvery mead
  The flavor and flush of the sweet summer hours.

But a pleasure expires at its earliest breath;
  No labor can hoard it, no cunning can save;
For the song of its life is the sigh of its death,
  And the sense it has thrilled is its shroud and its
    grave.

Ah! what is our love, with its tincture of lust,
And its pleasure that pains us and pain that endears,
But joy in an armful of beautiful dust
That crumbles and flies on the wings of the years?

And what is ambition for glory and power,
But desire to be reckoned the uppermost fool
Of a million of fools, for a pitiful hour,
And be cursed for a tyrant, or kicked for a tool?

Nay, what is the noblest that art can achieve,
But to conjure a vision of light to the eyes,
That will pale ere we paint it, and pall ere we leave
On the heart it betrays and the hand it defies?

We love, and we long with an infinite greed
For a love that will fill our deep longing, in vain;
The cup that we drink of is pleasant, indeed,
Yet it holds but a drop of the heavenly rain.

We plan for our powers the divinest we can;
We do with our powers the supremest we may;
And, winning or losing, for labor and plan
The best that we garner is—rest and decay!

Content — satisfaction— who wins them? Look down!
They are held without thought by the dolts and the drones:
'Tis the slave who in carelessness carries the crown;
And the hovels have kinglier men than the thrones.

The maid sings of love to the hum of her wheel;
And her lover responds as he follows his team;
They wed, and their children come quickly to seal
In fulfilment the pledge of their loftiest dream.

With humblest ambitions and homeliest fare,
Contented, though toiling, they travel abreast,
Till the kind hand of death lifts their burden of care,

And they sink, in the faith of their fathers, to
rest.

Did I beg to be born? Did I seek to exist?
Did I bargain for promptings to loftier gains?
Did I ask for a brain, with contempt of the fist
That could win a reward for its labor and pains?

Was it kind—the strong promise that girded my
youth?
Was it good—the endowment of motive and
skill?
Was it well to succeed, when success was in truth,
But the saddest of failure? Make answer, who
will!

Do I rave without reason? Why, look you, I pray!
I have won all I sought of the highest and best;
But it brings me no guerdon; and hopeless to-day,
I am poorer than when I set out on the quest.

Oh! emptiness! Life, what art thou but a lie,

Which I greeted and honored with hopefullest
trust?
Pah! the beautiful apples that tempted my eye
Break dead on my tongue into ashes and dust!

"A Father who loves all the children of men?"
"A future to fill all these bottomless gaps?"
But one life has failed: can I fasten again
With my faith and my hope to a specious Perhaps?

O! man who begot me! O! woman who bore!
Why, why did you call me to being and breath?
With ruin behind me, and darkness before,
I have nothing to long for, or live for, but death!

PART IV.

CONSUMMATION.

A GUEST was in my house—a guest unbid—
Who stayed without a welcome from his host;—
So loathed and hated, on such errand bent,
And armed with such resistless power of ill,
I dared not look him in the face. I heard
His tireless footsteps in the lonely halls,
In the chill hours of night; and, in the day,
They climbed the stairs, or loitered through the rooms
With lawless freedom. Ever when I turned
I caught a glimpse of him. His shadow stalked
Between me and the light, and fled before
My restless feet, or followed close behind.
Whene'er I bent above the couch that held

My fading wife, though looking not, I knew
That he was bending from the other side,
And mocking me.

Familiar grown, at last,
He came more closely—came and sat with me
Through hours of revery ; or, as I paced
My dimly-lighted room, slipped his lank arm
Through mine, and whispered in my shrinking ear
Such fearful words as made me sick and cold.
He took the vacant station at my board,
Sitting where she had sat, and mixed my cup
With poisoned waters, saying in low tones
That none but me could hear:

"This little room,
Where you have breakfasted and dined and supped,
And laughed and chatted in the days gone by,
Will be a lonely place when we are gone.
Those roses at the window, that were wont
To bloom so freely with the lady's care,
Already miss her touch. That ivy-vine

Has grown a yard since it was tied, and needs
A training hand."

Rising with bitter tears
To flee his presence, he arose with me,
And wandered through the rooms.

"This casket here"—
I heard him say: "Suppose we loose the clasp.
These are her jewels—pretty gifts of yours.
There is a diamond: there a string of pearls.
That paly opal holds a mellow fire
Which minds me of the mistress, whose bright soul
Glows through the lucent whiteness of her face
With lambent flicker. These are legacies:
She will not wear them more. Her taste and mine
Are one in this, that both of us love flowers.
Ay, she shall have them, too, some pleasant day,
When she goes forth with me!

"So? what is this?
Her wardrobe! Let the door be opened wide!

This musk, so blent with scent of violets,
Revives one. You remember when she wore
That lavender ?—a very pretty silk !
Here is a *moire antique.* Ah ! yes—I see !
You did not like her in it. 'Twas too old,
And too suggestive of the dowager.
There is your favorite—that glossy blue—
The sweet tint stolen from the skies of June—
But she is done with it. I wonder who
Will wear it, when your grief shall find a pause !
Your daughter—possibly ? . . You shiver, sir !
Is it the velvet ? Like a pall, you think !
Well, close the door !

"Those slippers on the rug :
The time will come when you will kiss their soles
For the dear life that pressed them. Their rosettes
Will be more redolent than roses then.
You did not know how much you loved your wife ?
I thought so !

"This way ! Let us take our stand

Beside her bed. Not quite so beautiful
To your fond eyes as when she was a bride,
Though still a lovely woman ! Seems it strange
That she is yours no longer ?—that her band
Is given to another—to the one
For whom she has been waiting all her life,
And ready all her life ? Your power is gone
To punish rivals. There you stand and weep,
But dare not lift a finger, while with smiles
And kindly welcome she extends her hands
To greet her long-expected friend. She knows
Where I will take her—to what city of God,
What palace there, and what companionship.
She knows what robes will drape her loveliness,
What flowers bedeck her hair, and rise and fall
Upon the pulses of her happy breast.
And you, poor man ! with all your jealous pride,
Have learned that she would turn again to you,
And to your food and furniture of life,
With disappointment.

"Ay, she pities you—

Loves you, indeed; but there is One she loves
With holier passion, and with more entire
And gladder self-surrender. She will go—
You know that she will go—and go with joy;
And you begin to see how poor and mean,
When placed beside her joy, are all your gifts,
And all that you have won by them.

"Poor man!
Weeping again! Well, if it comfort you,
Rain your salt tears upon her waxen hands,
And kiss them dry at leisure! Press her lips,
Hot with the hectic! Lay your cold, wet cheek
Against the burning scarlet of her own:
Only remember that she is not yours,
And that your paroxysms of grief and tears
Are painful to her."

Ah! to wait for death!
To see one's idol with the signature
Of the Destroyer stamped upon her brow,
And know that she is doomed, beyond all hope;

To watch her while she fades ; to see the form
That once was beauty's own become a corpse
In all but breathing, and to meet her eyes
A hundred times a day—while the heart bleeds—
With smiles of smooth dissembling, and with words
Cheerful as morning, and to do all this
Through weeks and weary months, till one half longs
To see the spell dissolved, and feel the worst
That death can do : can there be misery
Sadder than this ?

My time I passed alone,
And at the bedside of my dying wife.
She talked of death as children talk of sleep,
When—a forgetful blank—it lies between
Their glad impatience and a holiday.
The morrow—ah ! the morrow ! That was name
For hope all realized, for work all done,
For pain all past, for life and strength renewed,
For fruitage of endeavor, for repose
For heaven !

What would the morrow bring to me?
The morrow—ah! the morrow! It was blank—
Nay, blank and black with gloom of clouds and
night.
Never before had I so realized
My helplessness. I could not find relief
In love or labor. I could only sit,
And gaze against a wall, without the power
To pierce or climb. My pride of life was gone,
My spirit broken, and my strife with God
Was finished. If I could not look before,
I dared not look above; and so, whene'er
I could forget the present, I went back
Upon the past.

One soft June day, my thoughts,
Touched by some song of bird, or glimpse of green,
Returned to life's bright morning, and the Junes
That flooded with their wealth of life and song
The valley of my birth. Again I walked the
meads,
Brilliant with beaded grass, and heard the shrill,

AGAIN I TROD THE FOREST PATHS.

Sweet jargon of the meadow-birds. Again
I trod the forest paths, in shade of trees
With foliage so tender that the sun
Shot through the soft, thin leaves its virid sheen,
As through the emerald waters of the sea.
The scarlet tanager—a flake of fire,
Blown from the tropic heats upon the breath
That brought the summer—caught upon a twig,
Or quenched its glow in some remote recess.
The springing ferns unfolded at my feet
Their tan-brown scrolls, the tiny star-flower shone
Among its leaves: the insects filled the air
With a monotonous, reedy resonance
Of whir and hum, and I sat down again
Upon a bank to gather violets.

From dreams of retrospective joy I woke
At last, to the quick tinkle of a bell.
My wife had touched it. She had been asleep,
And, waking, called me to her side. The note,
Familiar as the murmur of her voice,
For the first time was strange. Another bell,

With other music, rang adown the years
That lay between me and the golden day
When, up the mountain-path, I followed far
The lamb that bore it. All the scene came back
In a broad flash; and with it came the same
Strange apprehension of a mighty change—
A vague prevision of transition, born
Of what, I knew not; on what errand sent,
I could not guess.

I rose upon my feet,
Responsive to the summons, when I heard,
Repeated in the ear of memory,
The words my mother spoke to me that day;

"My Paul has climbed the noblest mountain-height
"In all his little world, and gazed on scenes
"As beautiful as rest beneath the sun.
"I trust he will remember all his life
"That, to his best achievement, and the spot
"Closest to heaven his youthful feet have trod,
"He has been guided by a guileless lamb.

"It is an omen which his mother's heart
"Will treasure with her jewels."

Had her tongue
Been moved to prophecy? Omen of what?—
Of a new height of life to be achieved
By my lamb's leading? Ay, it seemed like this?
An answer to a thousand prayers, up-breathed
By her whom I had lost, repeated long
By her whom I was losing? Was it this?
Thus charged with premonition, when I stepped
Into the shaded room, my cheeks were pale,
And every nerve was quivering with the stress
Of uncontrolled emotion. Ah! my lamb!
How white! How innocent! My lamb, my lamb!
Even the scarlet ribbon which adorned
The lambkin of my chase was at her throat,
Repeated in a bright geranium-flower!

"Loop up the curtains, love! Let in the light!"
The words came strong and sweet, as if the life
From which they breathed were at its tidal flood.

"Oh ! blessed light !" she added, as the sun
Flamed on the velvet roses of the floor,
And touched to life the pictures on the wall,
And smote the dusk with bars of amber.

"Paul !"

I turned to answer, and beheld a face
That glowed with a celestial fire like his
Who talked with God in Sinai.

"Paul," she said,
"I have been almost home. I may not tell,
For language cannot paint, what I have seen.
The veil was very thin, and I so near,
I caught the sheen of multitudes, and heard
Voices that called and answered from afar
Through spaces inconceivable, and songs
Whose harmonies responsive surged and sank
On the attenuate air, till all my soul
Was thrilled and filled with music, and I prayed
To be let loose, that I might cast myself

Upon the mighty tides, and give my life
To the supernal raptures. Ay, I prayed
That death might come, and give me my release
From this poor clay, and that I might be born
By its last travail into life."

"Dear wife," I said,
"You have been wildly dreaming, and your brain,
Quickened to strange vagaries by disease,
Has cheated you. You must not talk like this:
'Twill harm you. I will hold your hand awhile,
And you shall have repose."

She smiled and said,
While her eyes shone with an unearthly light:
"You are not wise, my dear, in things like these.
The vision was as real as yourself;
And it will not be long before I go
To mingle in the life that I have seen.
I know it, dearest, for she told me this."

"She told you this?" I said,—"Who told you this?
Did you hold converse with the multitude?"

"Not with the multitude," she answered me;
"But while I gazed upon the throng, and prayed
That death might loose me, there appeared a group
Of radiant ones behind the filmy veil
That hung between us, looking helplessly
Upon my struggle, but with eyes that beamed
With love ineffable. I knew them too—
Knew all of them but one—and she the first,
And sweetest of them all. Pure as the light,
And beautiful as morning, she advanced;
And, at her touch, the veil was parted wide,
While she passed through, and stood beside my bed.
She took my hand, she kissed my burning cheek,
And then, in words that calmed my spirit, said:

"Your prayer will soon be answered; but one prayer,
Breathed many years by you, and many years
By one you know not, must be answered first.
You must go back, though for a little time,
And reap the harvest of a life. To him

Whom you and I have loved, say all your heart
Shall move your lips to speak, and he will hear.
The strength, the boldness, the persuasive power
Which you may need for this, shall all be yours;
For you shall have the ministry of those
Whom you have seen. Speak as a dying wife
Has liberty to speak to him she leaves;
And tell him this—that he may know the voice
That gives you your commission—tell him this:
The lamb has slipped the leash by which his hand
Held her in thrall, and seeks the mountain-height;
And he, if he reclaim her to his grasp,
Must follow where she leads, and kneel at last
Upon the summit by her side. And more:
Give him my promise that if he do this,
He shall receive from that fair altitude
Such vision of the realm that lies around,
Cleft by the river of immortal life,
As shall so lift him from his selfishness,
And so enlarge his soul, that he shall stand
Redeemed from all unworthiness, and saved
To happiness and heaven."

Her words flowed forth
With the strong utterance, in truth, of one
Inspired from other worlds; while pale and faint,
I drank her revelations. Unbelief
Had given the lie to her abounding faith,
And held her vision figment of disease,
Until the message of my mother fell
Upon my ears. Then overcome, I wept
With deep convulsions, rose and walked the room,
Wrung my clasped hands, and cried with choking voice,
"My mother! O! my mother!"

"Gently, love!
For she is with you," said my dying wife.
"Nay, all of them are with us. This small room
Is now the gate of heaven; and you must do
That which befits the presence and the place.
Come! sit beside me; for my time is short,
And I have much to say. What will you do
When I am gone? Will the old life of art

Content you? Will you fill your waiting time
With the old dreams of fame and excellence?"

"Alas!" I answered, "I am done with life:
My life is dead; and though my hand has won
All it has striven to win, and all my heart
In its weak pride has prompted it to seek
Of love and honor; though success is mine
In all my eager enterprise, I know
My life has been a failure. I am left
Or shall be left, when you, my love, are gone,
Without resource—a hopeless, worthless man,
Longing to hide his shame and his despair
Within the grave."

"I thank thee, Lord!" she said:
"So many prayers are answered! . . . You knew not
That I had asked for this. You did not know,
When you were striving with your feeble might
For the great prizes that beguiled your pride,
That at the hand of God I begged success.

Ay, Paul, I prayed that you might gather all
The good that you have won, and that, at last,
You might be brought to know the worthlessness
Of every selfish meed, and feel how weak—
How worse than helpless—is the highest man
Who lives within, and labors to, himself.
Not one of all the prizes you have gained
Contains the good that lies in your despair."

"Teach me," I said, "for I am ignorant;
Lead me, for I am blind. Explain the past,
With all its errors. Why am I so low,
And you so high?"

She pressed my hand, and said:
"You have been hungry all your life for God,
And known it not. You lavished first on me
Your heart's best love. You poured its treasured wealth
At an unworthy shrine. You made a God
Of poor mortality; and when you learned
Your love was greater than the one you loved—

The one you worshiped—you invoked the aid
Of your imagination, to enrich
Your pampered idol, till at last you bowed
Before a creature of your thought. You stole
From excellence divine the grace and good
That made me worshipful; and even these
Palled on your heart at last, and ceased to yield
The inspiration that you craved. You pined,
You starved for something infinitely sweet;
And still you sought it blindly, wilfully,
In your poor wife,—sought it, and found it not,
Through wasted years of life.

"And then you craved
An infinite return. You asked for more
Than I could give, although I gave you all
That woman can bestow on man. You knew
You held my constant love, unlimited
Save by the bounds of mortal tenderness;
And still you longed for more. Then sprang your scheme
For finding in the love of multitudes,

And in their praise, that which had failed in me.
You wrote for love and fame, and won them both
By manly striving—won and wore them long.
All good there is in love and praise of men,
You garnered in your life. On this reward
You lived, till you were sated, or until
You learned it bore no satisfying meed—
Learned that the love of many was not more
Than love of one. With all my love your own,
With love and praise of men, your famished soul
Craved infinite approval—craved a love
Beyond the love of woman and of man.

"Then with new hope, you apotheosized
Your cherished art, and sought for excellence
And for your own approval; with what end,
Your helplessness informs me. You essayed
The revelation of the mighty forms
That dwell in the unrealized. You sought
To shape your best ideals, and to find
In the grand scheme your motive and reward.
All this blind reaching after excellence,

Was but the reaching of your soul for God.
Imagination could not touch the height,
And you were baffled. So, you failed to find
The God your spirit yearned for in your art,
And failed of self-approval.

"You have now
But one resource,—you are shut up to this:
You must bow down and worship God; and give
Your heart to Him, accept His love for you,
And feast your soul on excellence in Him.
So, a new life shall open to your feet,
Strown richly with rewards; and when your steps
Shall reach the river, I will wait for you
Upon the other shore, and we shall be
One in the life immortal as in this.
O! Paul! your time is now. I cannot die
And leave you comfortless. I cannot die
And enter on the pleasures that I know
Await me yonder, with the consciousness
That you are still unhappy."

All my life
Thus lay revealed in light which she had poured
Upon its track. I learned where she had found
Her peaceful joy, her satisfying good,
And where, in my rebellious pride of heart,
Mine had been lost. She, by an instinct sure,
Or by the grace of Heaven, had in her youth,
Though sorely chastened, given herself to God;
And through a life of saintly purity—
A life of love to me and love to all—
Had feasted at the fountain of all love,
Had worshiped at the Excellence Divine,
And only waited for my last adieu
To take her crown.

I sat like one struck dumb.
I knew not how to speak, or what to do.
She looked at me expectant; while a thrill
Of terror shot through all my frame.

"Alas!"
She said, "I thought you would be ready now."

At this, the door was opened silently,
And our dear daughter stood within the room.
Alarmed at vision of the sudden change
That death had wrought upon her mother's face,
She hastened to her side, and kneeling there,
Bowed on her breast with tears and choking sobs,
Her heart too full for speech.

"Be silent, dear!"
The dying mother said, resting her hand
Upon her daughter's head. "Be silent, dear!
Your father kneels to pray. Make room for him,
That he may kneel beside you."

At her words,
I was endowed with apprehensions new;
And somewhere in my quickened consciousness,
I felt the presence of her heavenly friends,
And knew that there were spirits in the room.
I did not doubt, nor have I doubted since,
That there were loving witnesses of all
The scenes enacted round that hallowed bed.

Ay, and they spoke. Deep in the innermost
I heard the tender words, "O! kneel my son!—"
A sweet monition from my mother's lips.

"Kneel! kneel!" It was the echo of a throng.

"Kneel! kneel!" The gentle mandate reached my heart
From depths of lofty space. It was the voice
Of the Good Father.

From the curtain folds,
That rustled at the window, in the airs
That moved with conscious pulse to passing wings,
Came the same burden, "Kneel!"

"Kneel! kneel! O! kneel!"
In tones of earnest pleading, came from lips
Already pinched by death.

A hundred worlds,
Imposed upon my shoulders, had not bowed

And crushed me to my knees with surer power.
The hand that lay upon my daughter's head
Then passed to mine; but still my lips were dumb.

"Pray!" said the spirit of my mother.

"Pray!"
The word repeated, came from many lips.

"Pray!" said the voice of God within my soul;
While every whisper of the living air
Echoed the low command.

"Pray! pray! O! pray!"
My dying wife entreated.

Words were given,
And I poured out like water all my heart.
"O! God!" I said, "be merciful to me
A reprobate! I have blasphemed Thy name,
Abused Thy patient love, and held from Thee

My heart and life; and now, in my extreme
Of need and of despair, I come to Thee.
O! cast me not away, for here, at last,
After a life of selfishness and sin,
I yield my will to Thine, and pledge my soul—
All that I am, all I can ever be—
Supremely to Thy service. I renounce
All worldly aims, all selfish enterprise,
And dedicate the remnant of my power
To Thee and those Thou lovest. Comfort me!
O! come and comfort me, for I despair!
Give me Thy peace, for I am rent and tossed!
Feed me with love, else I shall die of want!
Behold! I empty out my worthlessness,
And beg Thee to come in, and fill my soul
With Thy rich presence. I adore Thy love;
I seek for Thy approval; I bow down,
And worship Thee, the Excellence Supreme.
I've tasted of the sweetest that the world
Can give to me; and human love and praise,
And all of excellence within the scope
Of my conception, and my power to reach

And realize in highest forms of art,
Have left me hungry, thirsty for Thyself.
O! feed and fire me! Fill and furnish me!
And if Thou hast for me some humble task--
Some service for Thyself, or for Thy own—
Reveal it to Thy sad, repentant child,
Or use him as Thy willing instrument.
I ask it for the sake of Jesus Christ,
Henceforth my Master!"

Multitudes, it seemed,
Responded with "Amen!" as if the word
Were caught from mortal lips by swooping choirs
Of spirits ministrant, and borne away
In sweet reverberations into space.

I raised my head at last, and met the eyes
Bright with the light of death, and with the dawn
Of opening heaven. The smile that overspread
The fading features was the peaceful smile
Of imanmortal,—full of faith and love—

A satisfied, triumphant, shining smile,
Lit by the heavenly glory.

"Paul," she said,
"My work is done; but you will live and work
These many years. Your life is just begun,
Too late, but well begun; and you are mine,
Now and forevermore. . . . Dear Lord! my thanks
For this Thy crowning blessing!"

Then she paused,
And raised her eyes in a seraphic trance,
And lifted her thin fingers, that were thrilled
With tremulous motion, like the slender spray
On which a throbbing song-bird clings, and pours
His sweet incontinence of ecstasy,
And then in broken whispers said to me:
'Do you not hear them? They have caught the news;
And all the sky is ringing with their song
Of gladness and of welcome. '*Paul is saved!*

Paul is redeemed and saved!' I hear them cry :
And myriad voices catch the new delight,
And carry the acclaim, till heaven itself
Sends back the happy echo : '*Paul is saved!*' "

She stretched her hands, and took me to her breast.
I kissed her, blessed her, spoke my last adieu,
And yielded place to her whom God had given
To be our child. After a long embrace,
She whispered : "I am weary ; let me sleep !"

She passed to peaceful slumber like a child,
The while attendant angels built the dream
On which she rode to heaven. Not once again
She spoke to mortal ears, but slept and smiled,
And slept and smiled again, till daylight passed.
The night came down ; the long hours lapsed away;
The city sounds grew fainter, till at last
We sat alone with silence and with death.
At the first blush of morning she looked up,
And spoke, but not to us : "I'm coming now !"

I sought the window to relieve the pain
Of long suppressed emotion. In the East,
Tinged with the golden dawn, the morning star
Was blazing in its glory, while beneath,
The slender moon, at its last rising, hung,
Paling and dying in the growing light,
And passing with that leading up to heaven.
My daughter stood beside her mother's bed,
But I had better vision of the scene
In the sweet symbol God had hung for me
Upon the sky.

Swiftly the dawn advanced,
And higher rose, and still more faintly shone,
The star-led moon. Then, as it faded out,
Quenched by prevailing day, I heard one sigh—
A sigh so charged with pathos of deep joy,
And peace ineffable, that memory
Can never lose the sound : and all was past !

The peaceful summer-day that rose upon
This night of trial and this morn of grief,

Rose not with calmer light than that which dawned
Upon my spirit. Chastened, bowed, subdued,
I kissed the rod that smote me, and exclaimed :
" The Lord hath given ; the Lord hath taken away
And blessed be His name !"

Rebellion slept.
I grieve, and still I grieve ; but with a heart
At peace with God, and soft with sympathy
Toward all my sorrowing, struggling, sinful race.
My hope, that clung so fondly to the world
And the rewards of fame, an anchor sure,
Now grasps the Eternal Rock within the veil
Of troubled waters. Storms may wrench and toss,
And tides may swing me, in their ebb and flow,
But I shall not be moved.

Once more ! once more !
I shall behold her face, and clasp her hand !
Once more—forevermore !

So here I give

The gospel of her precious Christian life.
I owe it to herself, and to the world.
Grateful for all her tender ministry
In life and death, I bring these leaves, entwined
With her own roses, dewy with my tears,
And lay them as the tribute of my love
Upon the grave that holds her sacred dust.

END OF KATHRINA

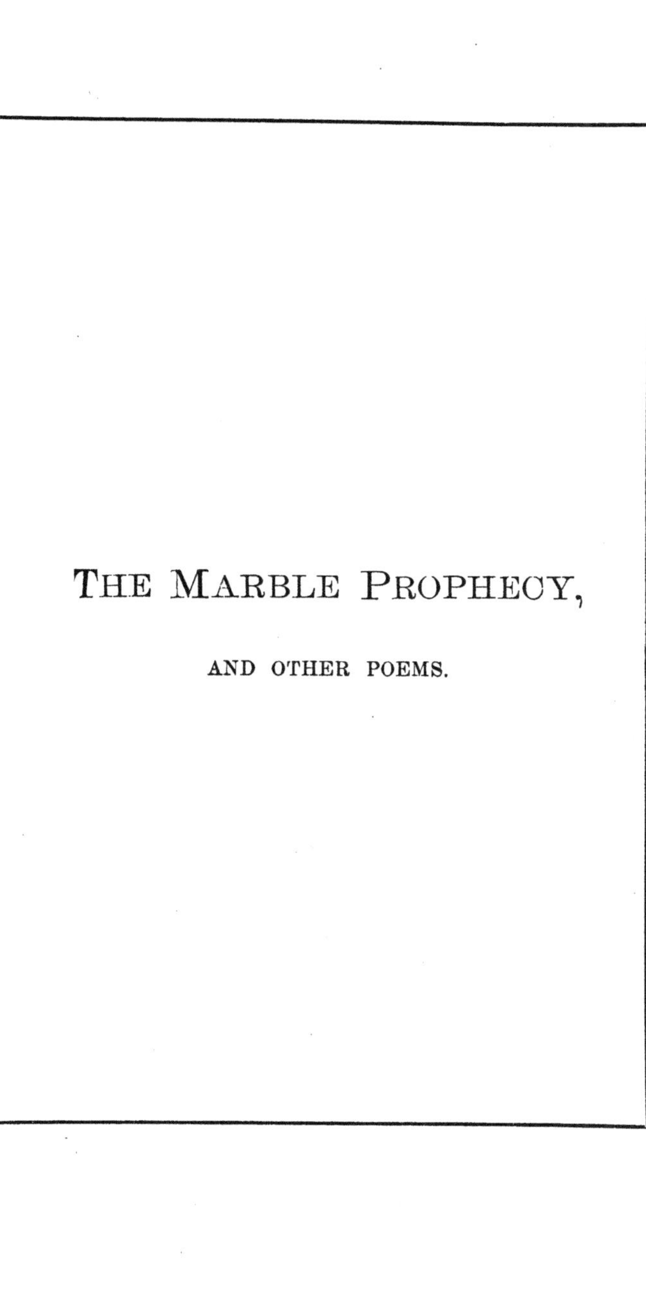

THE MARBLE PROPHECY,

AND OTHER POEMS.

THE MARBLE PROPHECY,

THE harlequins are out in force to-day—
The piebald Swiss—and in the vestibule
Of great St. Peter's rings the rhythmic tread
Of Roman nobles, uniformed and armed
As the Pope's Guard ; and while their double line
With faultless curve enters the open door,
And sways and sparkles up the splendid nave,
Between the walls of humbler soldiery,
And parts to pass the altar—keeping step
To the proud beating of their Roman hearts—
A breeze of whispered admiration sweeps
The crowds that gaze, and dies within the dome.
St. Peter's toe (the stump of it) was cold

An hour ago, but waxes warm apace
With rub of handkerchiefs, and dainty touch
Of lips and foreheads.

Smug behind their screen
Sit the Pope's Choir. No woman enters there ;
For woman is impure, and makes impure
By voice and presence ! Mary, mother of God !
Not thy own sex may sing thee in the courts
Of The All-Holy ! Only man, pure man !
Doubt not the purity of some of these—
Angels before their time—no doubt
That they will sing like angels, when Papa,
Borne on the shoulders of his stalwart men
(The master rode an ass), and canopied
By golden tapestries—the triple crown
Upon his brow, the nodding peacock plumes
Far heralding his way—shall come to take
His incense and his homage.

I will go.
Tis a brave pageant, to be seen just once.

'Tis a brave pageant, but one does not like
To smutch his trousers kneeling to a man,
Or bide the stare that follows if he fail :
So, having seen it once, one needs not wait.

What is the feast ? Let's see : ah ! I recall :
St. Peter's chair was brought from Antioch
So many years ago ;—the worse for wear
No doubt, and never quite luxurious,
But valued as a piece of furniture
By Rome above all price ; and so they give
High honor to the anniversary.
'Tis well ; in Rome they make account of chairs.
If less in heaven, it possibly may be
Because they're greatly occupied by joy
Over bad men made penitent and pure
By this same chair ! Who knows ?

I'll to the door !
The sun seems kind and simple in the sky
After such pomp. I thank thee, Sun ! Thou hast
A smile like God, that reaches to the heart

Direct and sweet, without the ministries
Of scene and ceremonial! Thy rays
Fall not in benediction at the ends
Of two pale fingers; but thy warmth and light
Wrap well the cold dark world. I need no prism
To teach my soul that thou art beautiful:
It would divide thee, and confuse my sight.
Shine freely, sun! No mighty mother church
Stands mediator between thee and me!
Ay, shine on these—all these in shivering need—
To whom God's precious love is doled or sold
By sacerdotal hucksters! Shine on these,
And teach them that the God of Life and Light
Dwells not alone in temples made by hands;
And that the path to Him, from every soul,
In every farthest corner of the earth,
Is as direct as are thy rays to thee!
Ha! Pardon! Have I hurt you? Welladay!
I was not looking for a beggar here:—
Indeed, was looking upward! But I see
You're here by royal license—with a badge
Made of good brass. Come nearer to me! there:

Take double alms, and give me chance to read
The number on your breast. So: "Seventy-
seven!"
'Tis a good number, man, and quite at home
About the temple. Well, you have hard fare,
But many brothers and no end of shows!
Think it not ill that they will spend to-day,
Touching this chair, enough of time and gold
To gorge the poor of Rome. The men who hold
The church in charge—who are, indeed, the
Church—
Have little time to give to starving men.
Be thankful for your label! Only one
Can be the beggar "Number seventy-seven!"
They are distinguished persons: so are you!
You must be patient, though it seems, I grant,
A trifle odd that when a miracle
Is wrought before you, it will never take
A useful turn, as in the olden time,
And give you loaves and fishes, or increase
Your little dinners!

Still the expectant crowds
Press up the street from round St. Angelo,
And thread the circling colonnade, or cross
With hurried steps the broad piazza—crowds
That pass the portal, and at once are lost
Within the vaulted glooms, as morning mist
Is quenched by morning air.

It is God's house—
The noblest temple ever reared to Him
By hands of men—the culminating deed
Of a great church—the topmost reach of art
For the enshrinement of the Christian faith
In sign and symbol. Holiness becomes
The temple of the Holy!

And these crowds?
Come they to pour the worship of their hearts
Like wine upon the altar? Who are they?
Last night, we hear, the theatre was full.
It was a spectacle: they went to see.
All yesterday they thronged the galleries,

Or roved among the ruins, or drove out
Upon the broad campagna—just to see.
This afternoon, with gaudy equipage,
(Their Bædeker and Murray left at home,)
They'll be upon the Pincio—to see.
And so this morning, learning of the chair
And the Pope's coming, they are here to see
(The men in swallow-tails, their wives in black,)
The grandest spectacle of all the week.
Make way ye men of poverty and dirt
Who fringe the outer lines! Make open-way
And let them pass! This is the House of God,
And swallow-tails are of fine moment here!

The ceremony has begun within.
I hear the far, faint voices of the choir,
As if a door in heaven were left ajar,
And cherubim were singing....Now I hear
The sharp, metallic chink of grounded arms
Upon the marble, as His Holiness
Moves up the lines of bristling bayonets
That guard his progress....But I stay alone.

Nay, I will to the Vatican, and there,
In converse with the thoughts of manlier men,
Pass the great morning ! I shall be alone—
Ay, all alone with thee, Laocoon !

"A feast day and no entrance ?" Can one's gold
Unloose a soul from purgatorial bonds
And ope the gates of heaven, without the power
To draw a bolt at the Museum ? Wait !
Laocoon ! thou great embodiment
Of human life and human history !
Thou record of the past, thou prophecy
Of the sad future, thou majestic voice,
Pealing along the ages from old time !
Thou wail of agonized humanity !
There lives no thought in marble like to thee !
Thou hast no kindred in the Vatican,
But standest separate among the dreams
Of old mythologies—alone—alone !
The beautiful Apollo at thy side
Is but a marble dream, and dreams are all
The gods and goddesses and fauns and fates

That populate these wondrous halls ; but thou,
Standing among them, liftest up thyself
In majesty of meaning, till they sink
Far from the sight, no more significant
Than the poor toys of children. For thou art
A voice from out the world's experience,
Speaking of all the generations past
To all the generations yet to come
Of the long struggle, the sublime despair,
The wild and weary agony of man !

Ay, Adam and his offspring, in the toils
Of the twin serpents Sin and Suffering,
Thou dost impersonate ; and as I gaze
Upon the twining monsters that enfold
In unrelaxing, unrelenting coils,
Thy awful energies, and plant their fangs
Deep in thy quivering flesh, while still thy might
In fierce convulsion foils the fateful wrench
That would destroy thee, I am overwhelmed
With a strange sympathy of kindred pain,
And see through gathering tears the tragedy,

The curse and conflict of a ruined race!
Those Rhodian sculptors were gigantic men,
Whose inspirations came from other source
Than their religion, though they chose to speak
Through its familiar language,—men who saw,
And, seeing quite divinely, felt how weak
To cure the world's great woe were all the powers
Whose reign their age acknowledged. So they sat—
The immortal three—and pondered long and well
What one great work should speak the truth for them,—
What one great work should rise and testify
That they had found the topmost fact of life,
Above the reach of all philosophies
And all religions—every scheme of man
To placate or dethrone. That fact they found,
And moulded into form. The silly priest
Whose desecrations of the altar stirred
The vengeance of his God, and summoned forth
The wreathed gorgons of the slimy deep
To crush him and his children, was the word

By which they spoke to their own age and race,
That listened and applauded, knowing not
That high above the small significance
They apprehended, rose the grand intent
That mourned their doom and breathed a world's
despair!

Be sure it was no fable that inspired
So grand an utterance. Perchance some leaf
From an old Hebrew record had conveyed
A knowledge of the genesis of man.
Perchance some fine conception rose in them
Of unity of nature and of race,
Springing from one beginning. Nay, perchance
Some vision flashed before their thoughtful eyes
Inspired by God, which showed the mighty man,
Who, unbegotten, had begot a race
That to his lot was linked through countless time
By living chains, from which in vain it strove
To wrest its tortured limbs and leap amain
To freedom and to rest! It matters not:
The double word—the fable and the fact,

The childish figment and the mighty truth,
Are blent in one. The first was for a day
And dying Rome; the last for later time
And all mankind.

These sculptors spoke their word
And then they died; and Rome—imperial Rome—
The mistress of the world—debauched by blood
And foul with harlotries—fell prone at length
Among the trophies of her crimes and slept.
Down toppling one by one her helpless gods
Fell to the earth, and hid their shattered forms
Within the dust that bore them, and among
The ruined shrines and crumbling masonry
Of their old temples. Still this wondrous group,
From its long home upon the Esquiline,
Beheld the centuries of change, and stood,
Impersonating in its conscious stone
The unavailing struggle to crowd back
The closing folds of doom. It paused to hear
A strange New Name proclaimed among the streets,
And catch the dying shrieks of martyred men,

And see the light of hope and heroism
Kindling in many eyes ; and then it fell ;
And in the ashes of an empire swathed
Its aching sense, and hid its tortured forms.

The old life went, the new life came ; and Rome
That slew the prophets built their sepulchres,
And filled her heathen temples with the shrines
Of Christian saints whom she had tossed to beasts,
Or crucified, or left to die in chains
Within her dungeons. Ay, the old life went
But came again. The primitive, true age—
The simple, earnest age—when Jesus Christ
The Crucified was only known and preached,
Struck hands with paganism and passed away.
Rome built new temples and installed new names ;
Set up her graven images, and gave
To Pope and priests the keeping of her gods.
Again she grasped at power no longer hers
By right of Roman prowess, and stretched out
Her hand upon the consciences of men.
The godlike liberty with which the Christ

Had made his people free she stole from them,
And bound them slaves to new observances.
Her times, her days, her ceremonials
Imposed a burden grievous to be borne,
And millions groaned beneath it. Nay, she grew
The vengeful persecutor of the free
Who would not bear her yoke, and bathed her hands
In blood as sweet as ever burst from hearts
Torn from the bosoms of the early saints
Within her Coliseum. She assumed
To be the arbiter of destiny.
Those whom she bound or loosed upon the earth,
Were bound or loosed in heaven ! In God's own place,
She sat as God—supreme, infallible !
She shut the door of knowledge to mankind,
And bound the Word Divine. She sucked the juice
Of all prosperities within her realms,
Until her gaudy temples blazed with gold,
And from a thousand altars flashed the fire

Of priceless gems. To win her countless wealth
She sold as merchandise the gift of God.
She took the burden which the cross had borne,
And bound it fast to scourged and writhing loins
In thriftless Penance, till her devotees
Fled from their kind to find the boon of peace,
And died in banishment. Beneath her sway,
The proud old Roman blood grew thin and mean
Till virtue was the name it gave to fear,
Till heroism and brigandage were one,
And neither slaves nor beggars knew their shame!

What marvel that a shadow fell, world-wide,
And brooded o'er the ages? Was it strange
That in those dim and drowsy centuries,
When the dumb earth had ceased to quake beneath
The sounding wheels of progress, and the life
That erst had flamed so high had sunk so low
In cold monastic glooms and forms as cold,
The buried gods should listen in their sleep
And dream of resurrection? Was it strange
That listening well they should at length awake,

And struggle from their pillows? Was it strange
That men whose vision grovelled should perceive
The dust in motion, and with rapture greet
Each ancient deity with loud acclaim,
As if he brought with him the good old days
Of manly art and poetry and power?
Nay, was it strange that as they raised themselves,
And cleaned their drowsy eyelids of the dust,
And took their godlike attitudes again,
The grand old forms should feel themselves at home—
Saving perhaps a painful sense that men
Had dwindled somewhat? Was it strange, at last,
That all these gods should be installed anew,
And share the palace with His Holiness,
And that the Pope and Christian Rome can show
No art that equals that which had its birth
In pagan inspiration? Ah, what shame!
That after two millenniums of Christ,
Rome calls to her the thirsty tribes of earth,
And smites the heathen marble with her rod,
And bids them drink the best she has to give!

And when the gods were on their feet again
It was thy time to rise, Laocoon!
Those Rhodian sculptors had forseen it all.
Their word was true: thou hadst the right to live

In the quick sunlight on the Esquiline,
Where thou didst sleep, De Fredis kept his vines;
And long above thee grew the grapes whose blood
Ran wild in Christian arteries, and fed
The fire of Christian revels. Ah what fruit
Sucked up the marrow of thy marble there!
What fierce, mad dreams were those that scared the souls
O men who drank, nor guessed what ichor stung
Their crimson lips, and tingled in their veins!
Strange growths were those that sprang above thy sleep:
Vines that were serpents; huge and ugly trunks
That took the forms of human agony—
Contorted, gnarled and grim—and leaves that bore
The semblance of a thousand tortured hands,
And snaky tendrils that entwined themselves

Around all forms of life within their reach,
And crushed or blighted them !

At last the spade
Slid down to find the secret of the vines,
And touched thee with a thrill that startled Rome,
And swiftly called a shouting multitude
To witness thy unveiling.

Ah what joy
Greeted the rising from thy long repose !
And one, the mighty master of his time,
The King of Christian art, with strong sad face
Looked on, and wondered with the giddy crowd,—
Looked on and learned (too late, alas, ! for him),
That his humanity and God's own truth,
Were more than Christian Rome, and spoke in
words
Of larger import. Humbled Angelo
Bowed to the masters of the early days,
Grasped their strong hands across the centuries,
And went his way despairing !

Thou, meantime,
Did'st find thyself installed among the gods
Here in the Vatican ; and thou, to-day,
Hast the same word for those who read thee well
As when thou wast created. Rome has failed :
Humanity is writhing in the toils
Of the old monsters as it writhed of old,
And there is neither help nor hope in her.
Her priests, her shrines, her rites, her mummeries,
Her pictures and her pageants, are as weak
To break the hold of Sin and Suffering
As those her reign displaced. Her iron hand
Shrivels the manhood it presumes to bless,
Drives to disgust or infidelity
The strong and free who dare to think and judge,
And wins a kiss from coward lips alone.
She does not preach the Gospel to the poor,
But takes it from their hands. The men who tread
The footsteps of the Master, and bow down
Alone to Him, she brands as heretics
Or hunts as fiends. She drives beyond her gates

The Christian worshippers of other climes,
And other folds and faiths, as if their brows
Were white with leprosy, and grants them there
With haughty scorn the priviledge to kneel
In humble worship of the common Lord !

Is this the Christ, or look we still for him ?
Is the old problem solved, or lingers yet
The grant solution ? Ay Laocoon !
Thy word is true, for Christian Rome has failed ;
And I behold humanity in thee
As those who shaped thee saw it, when old Rome
In that far pagan evening fell asleep.

MISCELLANEOUS PIECES.

THE WINGS.

A FEEBLE wail was heard at night,
  And a stifled cry of joy ;
And when the morn broke cool and light,
They bore to the mother's tearful sight
  A fair and lovely boy.

Months passed away ;
And day by day
  The mother hung about her child
As in his little cot he lay,
  And watched him as he smiled,
And threw his hands into the air,
  And turned above his large, bright eyes,
With an expression half of prayer
And half of strange surprise ;

For hovering o'er his downy head
A dainty vision hung.
Fluttering, swaying,
Unsteadily it swung,
As if suspended by a thread,
His own sweet breath obeying.

Sometimes with look of wild beseeching
He marked it as it dropped
Almost within his awkward reaching,
And as the vision stopped
Beyond his anxious grasp,
And cheated the quick clasp
Of dimpled hands, and quite
Smothered his chirrup of delight,
And he saw his effort vain
And the bright vision there again
Dancing before his sight,
His eyes grew dim with tears,
Till o'er the flooded spheres
The soothing eyelids crept,
And the tired infant slept.

He saw—his mother could not see—
A presence and a mystery :
Two waving wings,
Spangled with silver, starlike things :
No form of light was borne between ;
Only the wings were seen !

Years steal away with silent feet,
And he, the little one,
With brow more fair and voice more sweet
Is playing in the sun.
Flowers are around him and the songs
Of bounding streams and happy birds,
But sweeter than their sweetest tongues
Break forth his own glad words.
And as he sings
The wings, the wings !
Before him still they fly !
And nothing that the summer brings
Can so entice his eye.
Hovering here, hovering there,
Hovering everywhere,

They flash and shine among the flowers,
While dripping sheen in golden showers
Falls through the air where'er they hover
Upon the radiant things they cover.
Hurrying here, hurrying there,
Hurrying everywhere,
He plucks the flowers they shine upon,
But while he plucks their light is gone!
And casting down the faded things,
Onward he springs
To follow the wings!

Years run away with silent feet;
The boy, to manhood grown,
Within a shadowy retreat
Stands anxious and alone.
His bosom heaves with heavy sighs,
His hair hangs damp and long,
But fiery purpose fills his eyes,
And his limbs are large and strong:
And there above a gentle hill,
The wings are hovering still,

While their soft radiance, rich and warm,
Falls on a maiden's form.

And see! again he starts,
And onward darts,
Then pauses with a fierce and sudden pain,
Then presses on again,
Till with mixed thoughts of rapture and de-
spair,
He kneels before her there :—
With hands together prest,
He prays to her with low and passionate calls,
And, like a snow-flake pure, she flutters, falls,
And melts upon his breast.

Long in that dearest trance he hung—
Then raised his eyes; the wings that swung
In glancing circles round his head
Afar had fled,
And wheeled, with calm and graceful flight,
Over a scene

That glowed with glories beauteously bright
Beneath their sheen.

High in the midst a monument arose,
Of pale enduring marble : calm and still,
It seemed a statue of sublime repose,
The silent speaker of a mighty will.

Its sides were hung around
With boughs of evergreen ; and its long shaft was crowned
With a bright laurel wreath,
And glittering beneath
Were piled great heaps of gold upon the ground.
Children were playing near—fair boys and girls,
Who shook their sunny curls,
And laughed and sang in mirthfulness of spirit,
And in their childish pleasures

Danced around the treasures
Of gold and honor they were to inherit.

The sight has fired his brain ;
Onward he springs again.
O'er ruined blocks
Of wild and perilous rocks,
Through long damp caves, o'er pitfalls dire,
And maddening scenes of blood and fire,
Fainting with heat,
Benumbed with cold,
With weary, aching feet,
He sternly toils, and presses on to greet
The monument, the laurels and the gold.

Years have passed by ; a shattered form
Leans faintly on a monument ;
His glazing eyes are bent
In sadness down : a tear falls to the ground
That through the furrows of his cheek hath
wound.

The children beautiful have ceased to play,
Tarnished the marble stands with dark decay,
The laurels all are dead, and flown the gold away.

Once more he raised his eyes; before him lay
A dim and lonely vale,
And feebly tottering in the downward way
Walked spectres cold and pale.
And darkling groves of shadowy cypress sprung
Among the damp clouds that around them hung.
One vision only cheers his aching sight;
Those wings of light
Have lost their varied hues and changed to white,
And, with a gentle motion, slowly wave
Over a new-made grave.
He casts one faltering, farewell look behind,

Around, above, one mournful glance he throws,
Then with a cheerful smile, and trusting
mind,
Moves feebly toward the valley of repose.
He stands above the grave; dull shudders
creep
Along his limbs, cold drops are on his brow;
One sigh he heaves, and sinking into sleep
He drops and disappears;—and dropping now,
The wings have followed too.
But, lo! new visions burst upon the view!
They reappear in glory bright and new!
And to their sweet embrace a soul is given,
And on the wings of HOPE an angel flies to
HEAVEN.

INTIMATIONS.

WHAT glory then! What darkness now!
 A glimpse, a thrill, and it is flown!
 I reach, I grasp, but stand alone,
With empty arms and upward brow!

Ye may not see, O weary eyes!
 The band of angels, swift and bright,
 That pass, but cannot wake your sight,
Down trooping from the crowded skies.

O heavy ears! Ye may not hear
 The strains that pass my conscious soul,
 And seek, but find no earthly goal,
Far falling from another sphere.

Ah! soul of mine! Ah! soul of mine!
 Thy sluggish senses are but bars

That stand between thee and the stars,
And shut thee from the world divine.

For something sweeter far than sound,
And something finer than the light
Comes through the discord and the night
And penetrates, or wraps thee round.

Nay, God is here, couldst thou but see;
All things of beauty are of Him;
And heaven that holds the cherubim,
As lovingly embraces thee!

If thou hast apprehended well
The tender glory of a flower,
Which moved thee by some subtle power
Whose source and sway thou couldst not tell;

If thou hast kindled to the sweep
Of stormy clouds across the sky,
Or gazed with tranced and tearful eye,
And swelling breast upon the deep;

If thou hast felt the throb and thrill
Of early day and happy birds,
While peace, that drowned thy chosen words
Has flowed from thee in glad good-will,

Then hast thou drunk the heavenly dew;
Then have thy feet in rapture trod
The pathway of a thought of God;
And death can show thee nothing new.

For heaven and beauty are the same,—
Of God the all-informing thought,
To sweet, supreme expression wrought,
And syllabled by sound and flame.

The light that beams from childhood's eyes,
The charm that dwells in summer woods,
The holy influence that broods
O'er all things under twilight skies,—

The music of the simple notes
That rise from happy human homes,

The joy in life of all that roams
Upon the earth, and all that floats,

Proclaim that heaven's sweet providence
Enwraps the homely earth in whole,
And finds the secret of the soul
Through channels subtler than the sense.

O soul of mine! Throw wide thy door,
And cleanse thy paths from doubt and sin;
And the bright flood shall enter in
And give thee heaven forevermore!

WORDS.

The robin repeats his two musical words,
The meadow-lark whistles his one refrain;
And steadily, over and over again,
The same song swells from a hundred birds.

Bobolink, chickadee, blackbird, and jay,
Thrasher and woodpecker, cuckoo and wren,
Each sings its word, or its phrase, and then
It has nothing further to sing or to say.

Into that word, or that sweet little phrase,
All there may be of its life must crowd;
And lulling and liquid, or hoarse and loud,
It breathes out its burden of joy and praise.

A little child sits in his father's door,
Chatting and singing with careless tongue;

A thousand beautiful words are sung,
And he holds unuttered a thousand more.

Words measure power; and they measure thine;
Greater art thou in thy prattling moods
Than all the singers of all the woods;
They are brutes only, but thou art divine.

Words measure destiny. Power to declare
Infinite ranges of passion and thought
Holds with the infinite only its lot,—
Is of eternity only the heir.

Words measure life, and they measure its joy!
Thou hast more joy in thy childish years
Than the birds of a hundred tuneful spheres,
So—sing with the beautiful birds, my boy!

SLEEPING AND DREAMING.

I SOFTLY sink into the bath of sleep :
   With eyelids shut, I see around me close
The mottled, violet vapors of the deep,
   That wraps me in repose.

I float all night in the ethereal sea
   That drowns my pain and weariness in balm,
Careless of where its currents carry me,
   Or settle into calm.

That which the ear can hear is silent all ;
   But, in the lower stillness which I reach,
Soft whispers call me, like the distant fall
   Of waves upon the beach.

For the earth that had sickened with thirst so
      long,

My spirit leaves the couch, and seeks the air
For freedom and for joy.

Drunk up like vapors by the morning sun
The past and future rise and disappear ;
And times and spaces gather home, and run
Into a common sphere.

My youth is round me, and the silent tomb
Has burst to set its fairest prisoner free,
And I await her in the dewy gloom
Of the old trysting tree.

I mark the flutter of her snowy dress,
I hear the tripping of her fairy feet,
And now, pressed closely in a pure caress,
With ardent joy we meet.

I tell again the story of my love,
I drink again her lip's delicious wine,
And, while the same old stars look down above,
Her eyes look up to mine.

I dream that I am dreaming, and I start;
Then dream that nought so real comes in dreams;
Then kiss again to reassure my heart
That she is what she seems.

Our steps tend homeward. Lingering at the gate,
I breathe, and breathe again, my fond good night.
She shuts the cruel door, and still I wait
To watch her window-light.

I see the shadow of her dainty head,
On curtains that I pray her hand may stir,
Till all is dark; and then I seek my bed
To dream I dream of her.

Like the swift moon that slides from cloud to cloud,
With only hurried space to smile between,
I pierce the phantoms that around me crowd,
And glide from scene to scene.

I clasp warm hands that long have lain in dust,
  I hear sweet voices that have long been still,
And earth and sea give up their hallowed trust
  In answer to my will.

And now, high-gazing toward the starry dome,
  I see three airy forms come floating down—
The long-lost angels of my early home—
  My night of joy to crown.

They pause above, beyond my eager reach,
  With arms enwreathed and forms of heavenly
      grace;
  And smiling back the love that smiles from each,
  I see them, face to face.

They breathe no language, but their holy eyes
  Beam an embodied blessing on my heart,
That warm within my trustful bosom lies,
  And never will depart.

I drink the effluence, till through all my soul
  I feel a flood of peaceful rapture flow,
That swells to joy at last, and bursts control,
  And I awake ; but lo !

With eyelids shut, I hold the vision fast,
  And still detain it by my ardent prayer,
Till faint and fainter grown, it fades at last
  Into the silent air.

My God ! I thank Thee for the bath of sleep,
  That wraps in balm my weary heart and brain,
And drowns within its waters still and deep
  My sorrow and my pain.

I thank Thee for my dreams, which loose the bond
  That binds my spirit to its daily load,
And give it angel wings, to fly beyond
  Its slumber-bound abode.

I thank Thee for these glimpses of the clime
  That lies beyond the boundaries of sense,

Where I shall wash away the stains of time
  In floods of recompense :—

Where, when this body sleeps to wake no more,
  My soul shall rise to everlasting dreams,
And find unreal all it saw before
  And real all that seems.

ON THE RIGHI.

On the Righi Kulm we stood,
  Lovely Floribel and I,
While the morning's crimson flood
  Streamed along the eastern sky.
Reddened every mountain peak
  Into rose, from twilight dun;
But the blush upon her cheek
  Was not lighted by the sun!

On the Righi Kulm we sat,
  Lovely Floribel and I,
Plucking blue-bells for her hat
  From a mound that blossomed nigh,
"We are near to heaven," she sighed,
  While her raven lashes fell.
"Nearer," softly I replied,
  "Than the mountain's height may tell."

Down the Righi's side we sped,
  Lovely Floribel and I,
But her morning blush had fled,
  And the blue-bells all were dry.
Of the height the dream was born ;
  Of the lower air it died ;
And the passicn of the morn
  Flagged and fell at eventide.

From the breast of blue Lucerne,
  Lovely Floribel and I
Saw the hand of sunset burn
  On the Righi Kulm, and die.
And we wondered, gazing thus,
  If our dream would still remain
On the height, and wait for us
  Till we climb to heaven again !

GRADATIM.

HEAVEN is not reached at a single bound ;
  But we build the ladder by which we rise ;
  From the lowly earth to the vaulted skies,
And we mount to its summit round by round.

I count this thing to be grandly true :
  That a noble deed is a step toward God,—
  Lifting the soul from the common clod
To a purer air and a broader view.

We rise by the things that are under feet ;
  By what we have mastered of good and gain ;
  By the pride deposed and the passion slain,
And the vanquished ills that we hourly meet.

We hope, we aspire, we resolve, we trust,
  When the morning calls us to life and light,

But our hearts grow weary, and, ere the night,
Our lives are trailing the sordid dust.

We hope, we resolve, we aspire, we pray,
And we think that we mount the air on wings
Beyond the recall of sensual things,
While our feet still cling to the heavy clay.

Wings for the angels, but feet for men!
We may borrow the wings to find the way—
We may hope, and resolve, and aspire, and pray;
But our feet must rise, or we fall again.

Only in dreams is a ladder thrown
From the weary earth to the sapphire walls;
But the dreams depart and the vision falls,
And the sleeper wakes on his pillow of stone.

Heaven is not reached at a single bound;
But we build the ladder by which we rise
From the lowly earth to the vaulted skies,
And we mount to its summit, round by round.

RETURNING CLOUDS.

THE clouds are returning after the rain.
  All the long morning they steadily sweep
From the blue Northwest, o'er the upper main,
  In a peaceful flight to their Eastern sleep.

With sails that the cool wind fills or furls,
  And shadows that darken the billowy grass,
Freighted with amber or piled with pearls,
  Fleets of fair argosies rise and pass.

The earth smiles back to the smiling throng
  From greening pasture and blooming field,
For the earth that had sickened with thirst so long,
  Has been touched by the hand of The Rain, and healed.

The old man sits 'neath the tall elm trees,
And watches the pageant with dreamy eyes,
While his white locks stir to the same cool breeze
That scatters the silver along the skies.

The old man's eyelids are wet with tears—
Tears of sweet pleasure and sweeter pain—
For his thoughts are driving back over the years
In beautiful clouds after life's long rain.

Sorrows that drowned all the springs of his life,
Trials that crushed him with pitiless beat,
Storms of temptation and tempests of strife,
Float o'er his memory tranquil and sweet.

And the old man's spirit, made soft and bright
By the long, long rain that had bent him low,
Sees a vision of angels on wings of white,
In the trooping clouds as they come and go.

EUREKA.

Whom I crown with love is royal;
Matters not her blood or birth;
She is queen, and I am loyal
To the noblest of the earth.

Neither place, nor wealth, nor title.
Lacks the man my friendship owns;
His distinction, true and vital,
Shines supreme o'er crowns and thrones.

Where true love bestows its sweetness,
Where true friendship lays its hand,
Dwells all greatness. all completeness,
All the wealth of every land.

Man is greater than condition,
And where man himself bestows,

He begets, and gives position
  To the gentlest that he knows.

Neither miracle nor fable
  Is the water changed to wine ;
Lords and ladies at my table
  Prove Love's simplest fare divine.

And if these accept my duty,
  If the loved my homage own,
I have won all worth and beauty ;
  I have found the magic stone.

WHERE SHALL THE BABY'S DIMPLE BE?

OVER the cradle the mother hung,
  Softly crooning a slumber-song;
And these were the simple words she sung
  All the evening long:

  "Cheek or chin, or knuckle or knee,
  Where shall the baby's dimple be?
  Where shall the angel's finger rest
  When he comes down to the baby's nest?
  Where shall the angel's touch remain
  When he awakens my babe again?"

Still as she bent and sang so low,
  A murmur into her music broke;
And she paused to hear, for she could but know
  The baby's angel spoke.

"Cheek or chin, or knuckle or knee,
Where shall the baby's dimple be?
Where shall my finger fall and rest
When I come down to the baby's nest?
Where shall my finger's touch remain
When I awaken your babe again?"

Silent the mother sat, and dwelt
Long in the sweet delay of choice;
And then by her baby's side she knelt,
And sang with pleasant voice:

"Not on the limb, O angel dear!
For the charm with its youth will disappear;
Not on the cheek shall the dimple be,
For the harboring smile will fade and flee;
But touch thou the chin with an impress deep,
And my baby the angel's seal shall keep."

THE HEART OF THE WAR.

(1864.)

PEACE in the clover-scented air,
  And stars within the dome;
And underneath, in dim repose,
  A plain, New England home.
Within, a murmur of low tones
  And sighs from hearts oppressed,
Merging in prayer, at last, that brings
  The balm of silent rest.

I've closed a hard day's work, Marty, —
  The evening chores are done;
And you are weary with the house,
  And with the little one.
But he is sleeping sweetly now,
  With all our pretty brood;

So come and sit upon my knee,
  And it will do me good.

Oh, Marty! I must tell you all
  The trouble in my heart,
And you must do the best you can
  To take and bear your part.
You've seen the shadow on my face;
  You've felt it day and night;
For it has filled our little home,
  And banished all its light.

I did not mean it should be so,
  And yet I might have known
That hearts which live as close as ours
  Can never keep their own.
But we are fallen on evil times,
  And do whate'er I may,
My heart grows sad about the war,
  And sadder every day.

I think about it when I work,
And when I try to rest,
And never more than when your head
Is pillowed on my breast;
For then I see the camp-fires blaze,
And sleeping men around,
Who turn their faces toward their homes,
And dream upon the ground.

I think about the dear, brave boys,
My mates in other years,
Who pine for home and those they love,
Till I am choked with tears.
With shouts and cheers they marched away
On glory's shining track,
But, ah! how long, how long they stay!
How few of them come back!

One sleeps beside the Tennessee,
And one beside the James,
And one fought on a gallant ship

And perished in its flames.
And some, struck down by fell disease,
Are breathing out their life ;
And others, maimed by cruel wounds,
Have left the deadly strife.

Ah, Marty ! Marty, only think
Of all the boys have done
And suffered in this weary war !
Brave heroes, every one !
Oh ! often, often in the night,
I hear their voices call :
" *Come on and help us. Is it right*
That we should bear it all?"

And when I kneel and try to pray,
My thoughts are never free,
But cling to those who toil and fight
And die for you and me.
And when I pray for victory,
It seems almost a sin

To fold my hands and ask for what
 I will not help to win.

Oh! do not cling to me and cry,
 For it will break my heart;
I'm sure you'd rather have me die
 Than not to bear my part.
You think that some should stay at home
 To care for those away;
But still I'm helpless to decide
 If I should go or stay.

For, Marty, all the soldiers love,
 And all are loved again;
And I am loved, and love, perhaps,
 No more than other men.
I cannot tell—I do not know—
 Which way my duty lies,
Or where the Lord would have me build
 My fire of sacrifice.

I feel—I know—I am not mean;
  And, though I seem to boast,
I'm sure that I would give my life
  To those who need it most.
Perhaps the Spirit will reveal
  That which is fair and right;
So, Marty, let us humbly kneel
  And pray to Heaven for light.

Peace in the clover-scented air,
  And stars within the dome;
And underneath, in dim repose,
  A plain, New England home.
Within, a widow in her weeds,
  From whom all joy is flown,
Who kneels among her sleeping babes,
  And weeps and prays alone!

TO A SLEEPING SINGER.

LOVE in her heart, and song upon her lip—
A daughter, friend, and wife—
She lived a beauteous life,
And love and song shall bless her in her sleep.
The flowers whose language she interpreted,
The delicate airs, calm eves, and starry skies
That touched so sweetly her chaste sympathies,
And all the grieving souls she comforted,
Will bathe in separate sorrows the dear mound,
Where heart and harp lie silent and profound.
Oh, Woman! all the songs thou left to us
We will preserve for thee, in grateful love;
Give thou return of our affection thus,
And keep for us the songs thou singst above!

SONG AND SILENCE.

"My Mabel, you once had a bird
In your throat; and it sang all the day!
But now it sings never a word:
Has the bird flown away?

"Oh sing to me, Mabel, again!
Strike the chords! Let the old fountain flow
With its balm for my fever and pain,
As it did years ago!"

Mabel sighed (while a tear filled and fell,)
"I have bade all my singing adieu;
But I've a true story to tell,
And I'll tell it to you.

"There's a bird's nest up there in the oak,
On the bough that hangs over the stream,

And last night the mother-bird broke
Into song in her dream.

"This morning she woke, and was still;
For she thought of the frail little things
That needed her motherly bill,
Waiting under her wings.

"And busily, all the day long,
She hunted and carried their food,
And forgot both herself and her song
In her care for her brood.

"I sang in my dream, and you heard;
I woke, and you wonder I'm still;
But a mother is always a bird
With a fly in its bill!"

ALONE!

ALL alone in the world! all alone!
With a child on my knee, or a wife on my breast,
Or, sitting beside me, the beautiful guest
Whom my heart leaps to greet as its sweetest and best,
Still alone in the world! all alone!

With my visions of beauty, alone!
Too fair to be painted, too fleet to be scanned,
Too regal to stay at my feeble command,
They pass from the grasp of my impotent hand:
Still alone in the world! all alone!

Alone with my conscience, alone!
Not an eye that can see when its finger of flame

Points my soul to its sin, or consumes it with
shame!
Not an ear that can hear its low whisper of blame!
Still alone in the world! all alone!

In my visions of self, all alone!
The weakness, the meanness, the guilt that I see,
The fool or the fiend I am tempted to be,
Can only be seen and repented by me:
Still alone in the world! all alone!

Alone in my worship, alone!
No hand in the universe joining with mine,
Can lift what it lays on the altar divine,
Or bear what it offers aloft to its shrine:
Still alone in the world! all alone!

In the valley of death all alone!
The sighs and the tears of my friends are in vain,
For mine is the passage, and mine is the pain,
And mine the sad sinking of bosom and brain:
Still alone in the world! all alone!

Not alone! never, never alone!
There is one who is with me by day and by night,
Who sees and inspires all my visions of light,
And teaches my conscience its office aright:
Not alone in the world! not alone!

Not alone! never, never alone!
He sees all my weakness with pitying eyes,
He helps me to lift my faint heart to the skies,
And in my last passion he suffers and dies:
Not alone! never, never alone!

ALBERT DURER'S STUDIO.

In the house of Albert Durer
  Still is seen the studio
Where the pretty Nurembergers
  (Cheeks of rose and necks of snow)
Sat to have their portraits painted,
  Thrice a hundred years ago.

Still is seen the little loop-hole
  Where Frau Durer's jealous care
Watched the artist at his labor,
  And the sitter in her chair,
To observe each word and motion
  That should pass between the pair,

Handsome, hapless Albert Durer
  Was as circumspect and true

As the most correct of husbands,
  When the dear delightful shrew
Has him, and his sweet companions,
  Every moment under view.

But I trow that Albert Durer
  Had within his heart a spot
Where he sat, and painted pictures
  That gave beauty to his lot,
And the sharp, intrusive vision
  Of Frau Durer entered not.

Ah! if brains and hearts had loop-holes,
  And Frau Durer could have seen
All the pictures that his fancy
  Hung upon their walls within,
How minute had been her watching,
  And how good he would have been!

THE OLD CLOCK OF PRAGUE.

THERE'S a curious clock in the city of Prague—
A remarkable old astronomical clock—
With a dial whose outline is that of an egg,
And with figures and fingers a wonderful stock.

It announces the dawn and the death of the day,
Shows the phases of moons and the changes of tides,
Counts the months and the years as they vanish away,
And performs quite a number of marvels besides.

At the left of the dial a skeleton stands;
And aloft hangs a musical bell in the tower,

Which he rings, by a rope that he holds in his
hands,
In his punctual function of striking the hour.

And the skeleton nods, as he tugs at the rope,
At an odd little figure that eyes him aghast,
As a hint that the bell rings the knell of his hope,
And the hour that is solemnly tolled is his last.

And the effigy turns its queer features away
(Much as if for a snickering fit or a sneeze,)
With a shrug and a shudder, that struggle to say :
"Pray excuse me, but—just an hour more, if
you please !"

But the funniest sight, of the numerous sights
Which the clock has to show to the people be-
low,
Is the Holy Apostles in tunics and tights,
Who revolve in a ring, or proceed in a row.

Their appearance can hardly be counted sublime ;
And their movements are formal, it must be allowed ;
But they're prompt, for they always appear upon time,
And polite, for they bow very low to the crowd.

This machine (so reliable papers record)
Was the work, from his own very clever design,
Of one Hanusch, who died in the year of our Lord
One thousand four hundred and ninety and nine.

Did the people receive it with honor ? you ask ;
Did it bring a reward to the builder ? Ah, well !
was proper that they should have paid for the task !
And they did, in a way that it shocks me to tell.

For suspecting that Hanusch might grow to be vain,

Or that cities around them might covet their
prize,
They invented a story that he was insane,
And, to stop him from labor, extinguished his
eyes!

But the cunning old artist, though dying in
shame,
May be sure that he labored and lived not amiss;
For his clock has outlasted the foes of his fame,
And the world owes him much for a lesson like
this:

That a private success is a public offence,
That a citizen's fame is a city's disgrace,
And that both should be shunned by a person of
sense,
Who would live with a whole pair of eyes in his
face.

A CHRISTMAS CAROL.

THERE'S a song in the air!
There's a star in the sky!
There's a mother's deep prayer
And a baby's low cry!
And the star rains its fire while the beautiful sing,
For the manger of Bethlehem cradles a king.

There's a tumult of joy
O'er the wonderful birth,
For the virgin's sweet boy
Is the Lord of the earth,
Ay! the star rains its fire and the Beautiful sing,
For the manger of Bethlehem cradles a king!

In the light of that star
Lie the ages impearled;

And that song from afar
Has swept over the world.
Every hearth is aflame, and the Beautiful sing
In the homes of the nations that Jesus is King.

We rejoice in the light,
And we echo the song
That comes down through the night
From the heavenly throng.
Ay! we shout to the lovely evangel they bring,
And we greet in his cradle our Saviour and King!

VERSES READ AT THE HADLEY CENTENNIAL.

(*June 9th,* 1859.)

HEART of Hadley, slowly beating
Under midnight's azure breast,
Silence thy strong pulse repeating
Wakes me—shakes me—from my rest.*

Hark ! a beggar at the basement !
Listen ! friends are at the door !
There's a lover at the casement !
There are feet upon the floor !

---

* The pulsations of Hadley Falls, on the Connecticut, are felt for many miles around, in favorable conditions of the atmosphere.

But they knock with muffled hammers,
They step softly like the rain,
And repeat their gentle clamors
Till I sleep and dream again.

Still the knocking at the basement;
Still the rapping at the door;
Tireless lover at the casement;
Ceaseless feet upon the floor.

Bolts are loosed by spectral fingers,
Windows open through the gloom,
And the lilacs and syringas
Breathe their perfume through the room.

'Mid the odorous pulsations
Of the air around my bed,
Throng the ghostly generations
Of the long forgotten dead

"Rise and write!" with gentle pleading
They command and I obey;
And I give to you the reading
Of their tender words to-day.

"Children of the old plantation,
Heirs of all we won and held,
Greet us in your celebration—
Us—the nameless ones of Eld!

"We were never squires or teachers,
We were neither wise nor great,
But we listened to our preachers,
Worshipped God and loved the State.

"Blood of ours is on the meadow,
Dust of ours is in the soil,
But no marble casts a shadow
Where we slumber from our toil.

"Unremembered, unrecorded,
  We are sleeping side by side,
And to names is now awarded
  That for which the nameless died.

"We were men of humble station;
  We were women pure and true;
And we served our generation,—
  Lived and worked and fought for you.

"We were maidens, we were lovers,
  We were husbands, we were wives;
But oblivion's mantle covers
  All the sweetness of our lives."

"Praise the men who ruled and led us;
  Carry garlands to their graves;
But remember that your meadows
  Were not planted by their slaves.

"Children of the old plantation,
Heirs of all we won and held,
Greet us in your celebration,—
Us, the nameless ones of Eld."

This their message, and I send it,
Faithful to their sweet behest,
And my toast shall e'en attend it,
To be read among the rest.

Fill to all the brave and blameless
Who, forgotten, passed away!
Drink the memory of the nameless,—
Only named in heaven to-day!

WANTED.

God give us men! A time like this demands
Strong minds, great hearts, true faith, and ready hands;
Men whom the lust of office does not kill;
  Men whom the spoils of office cannot buy;
Men who possess opinions and a will;
  Men who have honor,—men who will not lie;
Men who can stand before a demagogue,
  And damn his treacherous flatteries without winking!
Tall men, sun-crowned, who live above the fog
  In public duty, and in private thinking;
For while the rabble, with their thumb-worn creeds,
Their large professions and their little deeds,—
Mingle in selfish strife, lo! Freedom weeps,
Wrong rules the land, and waiting Justice sleeps!

MERLE, THE COUNSELLOR.

Old Merle, the counsellor and guide,
And tall young Rolfe walked side by side
At the sweet hour of eventide.

The yellow light of parting day
Upon the peaceful landscape lay,
And touched the mountain far away.

The tinkling of the distant herds,
And the low twitter of the birds
Mingled with childhood's happy words.

The old man raised his trembling palm,
And bared his brow to meet the balm
That fell with twilight's dewy calm ;

And one could see that to his thought,
The scenes and sounds around him brought
Suggestions of the heaven he sought.

But Rolfe, his young companion, bent
His moody brow in discontent,
And sadly murmured as he went.

For vagrant passions, fierce and grim,
And fearful memories haunted him,
That made the evening glory dim.

Then spoke the cheerful voice of Merle :
"Where yonder clouds their gold unfurl,
One almost sees the gates of pearl.

"Nay, one can hardly look amiss
For heaven, in such a scene as this,
Or fail to feel its present bliss.

"So near we stand to holy things,
And all our high imaginings,
That faith forgets to lift her wings!"

Then answered Rolfe, with bitter tone:
"If thou hast visions of the throne,
Enjoy them; they are all thy own.

"For me there lives no God of love;
For me there bends no heaven above;
And Peace, the gently brooding dove,

"Has flown afar, and in her stead
Fierce vultures wheel above my head,
And hope is sick and faith is dead.

"Death can but loose a loathsome bond,
And from the depths of my despond,
I see no ray of light beyond."

It was a sad, discordant strain,
That brought old Merle to earth again,
And filled his soul with solemn pain.

At length they reached a leafy wood,
And walked in silence, till they stood
Within the fragrant solitude.

Then spake old Merle, with gentle art:
"I know the secret of thy heart,
And will, if thou desire, impart."

Rolfe answered with a hopeless sigh,
But from the tear that brimmed his eye,
The old man gladly caught reply,

And spoke: "Beyond these forest trees
A city stands; and sparkling seas
Waft up to it the evening breeze.

"Thou canst not see its gilded domes,
Its plume of smoke, its pleasant homes,
Or catch the gleam of surf that foams

"And dies upon its verdant shore,
But there it stands; and there the roar
Of life shall swell for evermore!

"The path we walk is fair and wide,
But still our vision is denied
The city and its nursing tide.

"The path we walk is wide and fair,
But curves and wanders here and there,
And builds the wall of our despair.

"Make straight the path, and then shall shine
Through trembling walls of tree and vine
The vision fair for which we pine.

"And thou, my son, so long hast been
Along the crooked ways of sin,
That they have closed, and shut thee in.

"Make straight the path before thy feet.
And walk within it firm and fleet,
And thou shalt see, in vision sweet

"And constant as the love supreme,
With closer gaze and brighter beam,
The peaceful heaven that fills my dream."

He paused: no more his lips could say;
And then, beneath the twilight gray,
The silent pair retraced their way.

But in the young man's eyes a light
Shone strong and resolute and bright,
For which Merle thanked his God that night.

DANIEL GRAY.

If I shall ever win the home in heaven
For whose sweet rest I humbly hope and pray,
In the great company of the forgiven
I shall be sure to find old Daniel Gray.

I knew him well; in truth, few knew him better;
For my young eyes oft read for him the Word,
And saw how meekly from the crystal letter
He drank the life of his beloved Lord.

Old Daniel Gray was not a man who lifted
On ready words his freight of gratitude,
Nor was he called among the gifted,
In the prayer-meetings of his neighborhood.

He had a few old-fashioned words and phrases,
Linked in with sacred texts and Sunday rhymes ;
And I suppose that in his prayers and graces,
I've heard them all at least a thousand times.

I see him now—his form, his face, his motions,
His homespun habit, and his silver hair,—
And hear the language of his trite devotions,
Rising behind the straight-backed kitchen chair.

I can remember how the sentence sounded—
" Help us, O Lord, to pray and not to faint !"
And how the " conquering-and-to conquer " round-
ed
The loftier aspirations of the saint.

He had some notions that did not improve him,
He never kissed his children—so they say :
And finest scenes and fairest flowers would move
him
Less than a horse-shoe picked up in the way.

He had a hearty hatred of oppression,
And righteous words for sin of every kind;
Alas, that the transgressor and transgression
Were linked so closely in his honest mimd!

He could see nought but vanity in beauty,
And nought but weakness in a fond caress,
And pitied men whose views of Christian duty
Allowed indulgence in such foolishness.

Yet there were love and tenderness within him;
And I am told that when his Charley died,
Nor nature's need nor gentle words could win him
From his fond vigils at the sleeper's side.

And when they came to bury little Charley,
They found fresh dew-drops sprinkled in his hair,
And on his breast a rose-bud gathered early,
And guessed, but did not know who placed it
there.

Honest and faithful, constant in his calling,
Strictly attendant on the means of grace,
Instant in prayer, and fearful most of falling,
Old Daniel Gray was always in his place.

A practical old man, and yet a dreamer,
He thought that in some strange, unlooked-for way
His mighty Friend in Heaven, the great Redeemer,
Would honor him with wealth some golden day,

This dream he carried in a hopeful spirit
Until in death his patient eye grew dim,
And his Redeemer called him to inherit
The heaven of wealth long garnered up for him.

So, if I ever win the home in heaven
For whose sweet rest I humbly hope and pray,
In the great company of the forgiven
I shall be sure to find old Daniel Gray.

THE MOUNTAIN CHRISTENING.

(A Legend of the Connecticut.)

How did they manage to busy themselves—
  Our sires, in the early plantation days ?
Grinding their axes and whittling their helves ?
  Fishing for salmon and planting maize?

How when the chopping and splitting were done?
  How when the corn-fields were planted and hoed?
How when the salmon had ceased to run,
  And the bushes were cleared from the old Bay
    Road ?

They were not men who stood still in their shoes,
  Or who clung to their cabins when forests were
    damp ;

So, when labor was finished, they cut the blues
  And their sticks for a lively exploring tramp.

'Twas a beautiful morning in June, they say—
  Two hundred and twenty years ago,
When armed and equipped for a holiday,
  They stood where Connecticut's waters flow,

With five upon this side and five upon that,—
  Agawam's bravest and hardiest men,
Hailing each other with lusty chat,
  That the tall woods caught and tossed over again.

Holyoke, the gentle and daring, stood
  On the Eastern bank with his trusty four,
And Rowland Thomas, the gallant and good,
  Headed the band on the other shore.

"Due North!" shouted Holyoke and all his men.
  "Due North!" answered they on the opposite beach;

And northward they started, the sturdy ten,
With their haversacks filled and a musket each.

The women ran panting to bid them good-bye,
And sweet Mary Pynchon was there (I guess),
With a sigh in her throat and a tear in her eye
As Holyoke marched into the wilderness,

And the boys were all wondering where they would go,
And what they would meet in the dangerous way;
And the good wives were gossiping to and fro,
And prating and shaking their heads all day.

Up the bright river they travelled abreast,
Calling each other from bank to bank,
Till the hot sun slowly rolled into the West,
And gilded the mountain-tops where it sank.

They lighted their camp-fires, and ate of their
fare,
And drank of the water that ran at their feet,
And wrapped in the balm of the cool evening air,
Sank down to a sleep that was dreamless and
sweet.

The great falls roared in their ears all night,
And the sturgeon splashed and the wild-cat
screamed,
But they did not wake till the morning light
Red through the willowy branches beamed.

Brief was the toilet and short the grace,
And strong were the viands that broke their
fast;
Then onward they pressed till they reached the
place
Where the river between two mountains passed.

Up the rough ledges they clambered amain,
Holyoke and Thomas on either hand,

Till high in mid-passage they paused, and then
They tearfully gazed on a lovely land.

Down by the Ox-Bow's southerly shore
Licking the wave bowed an antlered buck :
And Northward and Westward a league or more
Stretched the broad meadows of Nonotuck.

Straight up the river an Indian town
Filled the soft air with its musical hum,
And children's voices were wafted down
From the peaceful shadows of Hockanum.

Rude little patches of greening maize
Dappled the landscape far and wide,
And away in the North in the sunset's blaze,
Sugar-loaf stood and was glorified !

The morning dawned on the double group
Facing each other on opposite shores,

Where ages ago with a mighty swoop
  The waters parted the mountain doors.

"Let us christen the mountains," said Holyoke in glee;
  "Let us christen the mountains," said Thomas again;
"That mountain for you, and this mountain for me!"
  And their trusty fellows responded: "Amen!"

Then Holyoke buried his palm in the stream,
  And tossed the pure spray toward the mountain's brow,
And said, while it shone in the sun's first beam,
  "Fair mountain, thou art Mount Holyoke now!"

The sun shone full on the Western height,
  When Thomas came up from the crystal tide:

"I name thee Thomas by Christian rite!"
"Thou art Mount Thomas!" they all replied.

They paused but a moment when rounding a bluff
Shot an Indian's boat with its stealthy oar,
And with strings of wampum and gaudy stuff
They beckoned it in to the Western shore.

Gracious and brief was the bargain made
By the white man's potent pantomime;
And the delicate boat with its dainty blade
Bore them over the river one man at a time.

There were greetings and jests in every mouth,
And hearty farewells to "Holyoke" and "Tom:"
Then the gleeful men turned their steps due South,
And took a bee-line for Agawam.

They passed Willimansett at noon that day,
And Chicopee just as the sun went down,

And when the last daylight had faded away,
All hungry and weary they entered the town.

Mr. Pynchon demanded a full report,
Which Holyoke wrote for the two commands ;
And when he went down to the General Court
He placed it in Governor Winthrop's hands.

A GOLDEN WEDDING SONG.

THE links of fifty golden years
  Reach to the golden ring
Which now, with glad and grateful tears,
  We celebrate and sing.
O chain of love ! O ring of gold !
  That have the years defied ;
And still in happy bondage hold
  The old man and his bride !

The locks are white that once were black,
  The sight is feebler grown ;
But through the long and weary track
  The heart has held its own !
O chain of love ! O ring of gold !
  That time could not divide ;
That kept through changes manifold
  The old man and his bride !

The little ones have come and gone ;
  The old have passed away ;
But love—immortal love—lives on,
  And blossoms 'mid decay.
O chain of love ! O ring of gold !
  That have the years defied ;
And still with growing strength infold
  The old man and his bride !

The golden bridal ! ah, how sweet
  The music of its bell,
To those whose hearts the vows repeat
  Their lives have kept so well !
O chain of love ! O ring of gold !
  O marriage true and tried !
That bind with tenderness untold
The old man and his bride !

www.ingramcontent.com/pod-product-compliance
Lightning Source LLC
LaVergne TN
LVHW021058110826
845150LV00001B/108

* 9 7 8 1 4 2 5 5 6 6 2 2 7 *